Battling Jack

I would like the book to be dedicated to my wife, Betty.
I loved her when she was here but I'm crazy about her now.

BATTLING JACK

JACK

YOU GOTTA FIGHT BACK

JACKIE TURPIN
AND W. TERRY FOX

MAINSTREAM
PUBLISHING
EDINBURGH AND LONDON

First published in Great Britain in 2005 by
MAINSTREAM PUBLISHING COMPANY
(EDINBURGH) LTD
7 Albany Street
Edinburgh EH1 3UG

ISBN 1 84596 064 5

A catalogue record for this book is available
from the British Library

Typeset in Galliard, Stone and Triplelex

Printed in Great Britain by
William Clowes Ltd, Beccles, Suffolk

Contents

Preliminaries

i

The Poet and the Pugilist

I first met John Matthew Turpin senior on 6 December 1998, in a Burger King restaurant halfway between Warwick and Stoke-on-Trent. 'Jackie' greeted me like an old friend – partly because that's the kind of man he is and partly because of my apparently remarkable similarity to his window cleaner. 'What are you doing here?' he asked me.

I was holding part-time lectureships in Writing and English Literature at the Manchester Metropolitan and Keele universities in Stoke-on-Trent. My specialism is poetry but I had agreed to help a family friend, sculptor Carl Payne, by researching the subject of his first big commission: Jackie Turpin's younger brother, the legendary boxer, Randolph Adolphus Turpin.

My own boxing career had ended two seconds after it had begun, with a punch delivered some 50 years earlier in a youth club in Watford, Hertfordshire, by a smaller boy, thin as a ration book, wearing 16 oz gloves on the ends of his pipe-cleaner arms and a matching 16 oz grin on his upturned face, who reduced me to tears of pain and ignominy with a single triumphant haymaker. I groped my way back through the ropes nursing a bloodied nose and a newly found wisdom, believing I was leaving the sporting world for good.

The purpose of the meeting at the Burger King was for Carl to discuss the proposed statue of Randolph Turpin with Adrian Bush, Chairperson of the Randolph Turpin Memorial Fund. This, fortuitously, left Jackie and I talking to each other.

Jackie Turpin is an ex-professional featherweight boxer, 5 ft 7 in. tall, whose years of retirement from the ring have seen him go up a weight division or two. He dresses comfortably, keeps his white hair cropped short and shaves to leave himself with a neat goatee beard. He is an animated conversationalist: irreverent, informal and funny. His Warwick accent is characteristically laced with echoes of nearby Birmingham and he possesses a thousand anecdotes which he delivers at speed in a mid-pitch voice: of ring wars and street fights; horses and dancers and nights in New York; fairgrounds and hop fields; a count in a castle; tin fish in the Arctic sea; the pride of grandfatherhood; and the pleasure of cream cakes. His eyes sparkle behind his glasses. He has led an extraordinary life.

'Nobody's ever written the truth about me and me brothers,' he told me with a shrug. The movement of his shoulders revealed a strength which belied his 74 years.

'Why not write the truth yourself?' I asked him.

He laughed. 'We've been trained to use our hands in a different way. We done our talking with our fists. I couldn't write a book.'

'We could write a book together,' I heard myself say.

Thrust back into the red-in-tooth-and-claw end of the sporting world, I am grateful to Jackie Turpin for the fascinating years I have spent as his audience, confidante, friend and scribe – and all on the safe side of the ropes.

W. Terry Fox
Stoke-on-Trent

ii

By the Book

There was a time when nobody would cross the road to speak to the Turpins. We was just little black kids as used to run around Wathen Road and Parkes Street. Then, all of a sudden, one of us becomes world famous and everybody's crossing the road to talk to us.

I meet people up the town who've heard I'm writing a book and they say, 'You couldn't write a book, Jack.' I tell them, 'I've got this university bloke, a Professor of Advanced Writing, as comes down from Staffordshire. I done the fighting, he does the writing.' That shuts them up.

When the book comes out, all these people who've written, 'The Turpins done this', 'The Turpins done that', they'll all be proved bloody liars, cuz I'm the only Turpin left as can talk about it, and they know nothing.

John Matthew Turpin senior,
Warwick

Main Event

1

Hold Out Your Hand, John Turpin

I'm standing on the corner of Willes Road, Leamington Spa, 20 or 30 yards from where we live at No. 6. Me mum's warned me, 'Keep on the footpath, right against the wall.' I've obeyed her exactly and rubbed along the wall away from the bicycles and carthorses in the road; away from the feet of the people walking home from work. I seem to have been waiting for ever. Suddenly, I see him coming slowly towards me from the foundry where he works as an iron moulder. He's wearing his tweed jacket and the billy-cock hat he sometimes folds up and puts in his pocket. I'm jumping up and down with excitement. He's holding up his hand like a policeman to say, 'STOP! DON'T RUN TO ME.' I'm a bit bumble-footed and inclined to fall over a lot. He's about eight foot tall. He's smiling a big warm safe smile as he's reaching down to swing me onto his shoulders. From high up in the air I can hear him talking to me as he carries me to the door of our basement flat. His voice is as soft as velvet. I can feel it on the outside of my ears like somebody stroking them. He's asking me how I've been today.

*

He's playing the violin and making me laugh by lying on the floor and lifting his back off the lino so's only his feet and his head are touching the ground. The violin is singing a hymn.

*

Me aunt Gert is picking me up and pretty near putting me in the coffin with him: 'Kiss him ta-ra.'

15

I'm kissing him. 'He's cold,' I'm saying. 'Put his coat on.'

'We can't. He's asleep. He's got to go somewhere in that box but he'll be coming back.'

*

I was only a kid of three years old when my father died. I used to sit thinking about it at school: 'He's got to go somewhere in that box but he'll be coming back . . .' The teacher would be talking and I'd be thinking, 'What shall I say to him when he comes back?' She'd ask me a question and I'd answer something like, 'I haven't seen him yet.'

'You haven't seen who, Turpin?'

'Oh . . . I was thinking of summat else, miss.'

'Come here, John Turpin. Hold out your hand.' – WHACK! 'Now *listen*.'

I used to hear other kids boasting about their dads, so I used to invent what my dad had done. I'd brag about him helping to win the war out in France by shooting entire German patrols to pieces on his own and filing notches in his gun to keep count. I never actually thought of it as being a war between Britain and Germany; I thought of it as my dad fighting to save me from the Germans. Anyhow, the teacher heard me one day and had me out in front of the class: 'You are a nasty little liar, John Turpin. Your father died when you were young. You have no idea what he did or didn't do.'

She was right. Until this book was started, all I had was those little fragments of memories and a few odd things me mum and other people had said about him. One bloke over in Leamington told me, 'They used to call your dad Sam.' Short for 'Sambo', see?

'All right,' I says, 'they called him Sam. So what?' I suppose if he was close when they called him that, they'd have got a punch in the face. That's p'raps where the stories about him boxing come from.

It prompted another memory of him, though, one that I think of as my first nobbins. We've gone to see me dad in hospital over at Coventry somewhere. He's in a big room, in his pyjamas in bed. All round him there are other beds with other men in pyjamas. They're calling him 'Sam', like he's their best friend. I can tell that my dad likes them too. A nurse takes me by the hand and leads me to each of them in turn. They feel my hair and call me 'Little Sam' and push money in my hands. Soon, I've got more money than I can hold and the nurse fetches a towel. She takes one end and I'm gripping on to the other. We carry the money over to me mum.

It's a tradition in boxing: if you've put up a good show, people throw money into the ring. It's called nobbins and it's to be shared between the two boxers. Sometimes it's collected in a towel.

Over the years, I'd meet people who knew me dad, or said they knew him, and they'd tell me stories. I'd listen, cuz I didn't want to be rude, but I used to think, 'They're just telling me a load of crap here.' Any number of them would go on about what a good boxer me dad was and that's how it was in our blood, but my mum never ever told me my dad was a boxer. Well, you just think to yourself, how could he box with his lungs half burnt away and a wound in his back that'd send him near to tears at times?

Learning the truth about my father is like being born again. I'm on a high. I couldn't be higher if I was on cocaine or summat. I just wish the others was still here to know about it.

My mother's father was called Tom Salmon Whitehouse. It's an unusual name, innit? I don't know where the 'Salmon' come from. When I was a kid, I thought, 'Why has he named hisself after a fish?' I used to make out he was Irish. When visitors come, I'd say, 'This is Tamus Salmon Whoithouse, be Jaysus.' I used to catch no end for it. I'd tell him, 'Only an Irishman would give hisself a fish's name.'

Granddad was born on 24 February 1860 in Banbury, Oxfordshire – the son of an earthenware dealer. He was 5 ft 11 in. tall with close-cropped hair, a big moustache, a chest like an oak beer barrel, and he always wore hobnailed boots. There wasn't a man on earth Tom Whitehouse feared, only God. He was solid muscle from top to toe and looked exactly the prizefighter he was. He wouldn't have had to do much training to keep himself fit in his fighting days cuz he worked as a blacksmith's striker and swung a sledgehammer all day long, year in, year out. Even when he was an old man we was careful not to get on the wrong side of him.

People have always fought with their fists and I think they always will. Boxing, our family sport, is just that, only with rules. My granddad fought all round the Midlands. He was of the very old school and never done the gloved stuff, even though knuckle fighting had been banned and the Marquis of Queensberry's rules had come out while he was still doing it. It's always been ordinary

17

blokes fighting and the posh suits organising it and taking most of the money – just giving the fighters some sort of prize, or 'purse', for taking part.

Knuckle fighters used leather gloves lined with horsehair, like our old contest gloves, but only in training, or 'sparring' as it's called. It used to puzzle me, that word, when I was little. I used to think, 'Spar? It's a lump of wood, innit? What's that got to do with boxing?' It's a word taken from cock fighting. A lot of boxing words are. The padded gloves, or 'mufflers', were used for sparring to save the fighters' hands for the prize bouts, cuz when you punch somebody in the head with your bare hands, your hands are likely to suffer more than the head you hit. The bones in your hand are still vulnerable even with bandages and gloves on, as I was to find out for myself on the head of Ben Duffy. The bare-handed fighters used to punch their hands to pulp sometimes. He'd long stopped doing it by the time I was born, me grandfather Whitehouse. Well, for money, anyway.

Bare knuckling had never been properly legal but the authorities mostly turned a blind eye to it. Every now and then they'd crack down if someone had got badly hurt or there was a riot over the betting. Once, my granddad was in a knuckle fight in the stables at the back of the Woolpack hotel in Warwick. It was a coaching house then. The police raided it, stopped the contest and tried to arrest the fighters. Granddad ran out into the yard but the coppers got him cornered and he lashed out at them with his feet. One of his boots shot off and landed on the roof of the Corn Exchange. While the police stood watching his boot sailing through the air, he nipped off home and they didn't catch him.

Next to the Corn Exchange was Whittaker's fish and chip shop. Jack Whittaker used to box a bit as a bantam but he was nothing spectacular, so he turned his hand to promoting. He used to hire the Corn Exchange to put on boxing shows. Kaiser Bates from Dudley and all the Black Country crowd used to box on them. Local lads as fought there would get paid out in chips: a bag of chips if you lost and a full fish supper if you won. When Dick, me older brother, turned pro getting on for half a century after me granddad's near-arrest at the Woolpack, Granddad asked him, 'If you get booked at the Corn Exchange, have a look on the roof an' see if me boot's still there.'

You'd hardly recognise Warwick from when we was kids. The Corn Exchange is Woolworth's and Smith's – a lot of the old buildings have been demolished and replaced. Little roads have been filled in and big roads laid over the top of them, but you can still see it's ancient. In between the modern buildings are little old Elizabethan timber-framed cottages and ruler-square Georgian stone houses. It's popular with tourists who come to see the castle and dungeon. Another attraction for visitors to Warwick is the racecourse. It was a big attraction to us kids an' all. We thought of it as one big adventure playground.

Warwick must have been even more different in me granddad's day, when it consisted of more or less one big main street with a gate at each end and a few small streets going off it. The military barracks would've been going strong as the home of the Royal Warwickshire Regiment and there would have been more common land. When I was a kid, I used to wait for hours to see a car, but for Granddad it would have been all horses and stables and blacksmiths' forges. Halfway down Parkes Street was Bromage's stables and then the Eagle Engineering works where he worked after he left the forge. The whole pace of life would have been slower. The world's gone crazy now. I mean, me great-grandfather, Thomas Whitehouse senior, used to go from Banbury up to Birmingham in a horse and buggy to buy china to sell on the local markets. It'd take a while to do that. Granddad said his dad made more money than the other dealers because he never used to pay for a pitch. He'd just set up alongside another stall and when the rent man come round, he'd pick up his baskets of ware, sling them on his buggy and bugger off.

Granddad Whitehouse fell under the spell of a gypsy girl, Miss Lydia Taplin Giles, who he met when she took horses to be shod at the forge where he worked. They got married in 1883 in Saint Mary's Parish Church, Warwick. He was 23 and she was 18.

They rented a house at Barracks Street, Warwick, and that's where, on 28 March 1904, my mum, Beatrice Elizabeth, was born, the youngest of seven – my two uncles, Jim and Tom; and my four aunties, Ethel, May, Maude and Gertrude.

Granny Whitehouse, with her being a gypsy, she probably never ever went to school. Years later, when me mum and dad got married, she signed their marriage certificate with a cross. But she was sharp as a razor and wouldn't let nobody get one across her. She was as handy with her fists as any of us. Oh ar! She could use herself all right. Her hands were like knots out of a tree and she always hit where she aimed.

Battling Jack

When me mum was ten and a quarter years old, a fight broke out that was to cause the way of life of the British people to be changed for ever and, in a roundabout way, it was the cause of me.

2

Thriller in France, August 1914

In the main arena of north-west Europe, a super-heavyweight contest is about to take place. Training camps have been busy for months, building muscle, fine-tuning bodies for battle. Contracts have been signed, the pre-fight talking done. Two cousins, packing the biggest punches of all time, are squaring up for the fray. A grudge match.

In the blue corner:

> The Sovereign of the British Empire, 'Son of the Peacemaker'
> King George V, representing the House of Saxe-Coburg-Gotha
> – fighting out of Britain and her Dominions; out of Belgium,
> Russia, France, Serbia, Montenegro and Japan.

In the red corner:

> The Emperor of Germany, 'The Beast of the Apocalypse'
> Prince Wilhelm II, representing the House of Hohenzollern
> – fighting out of Germany and the Austro-Hungarian Empire.

A world title is at stake. The giants eyeball each other across the neutral territory of Belgium, their faces catching the dying rays of the summer sun. A roll of drums like a slow intake of breath and the strains of a hundred national anthems are sent flailing upwards over the heads of the cheering crowd. Europe is ready to rumble.

3

In the Arms of Mother

He felt British, my dad did. He was descended from slaves taken from West Africa and he lived in a tropical paradise but British English was his first language. His schoolbooks were written by British people; he lived under British law; he was brought up to admire British poets and British musicians and British scientists and British politicians and British nobility. His allegiance was to King George V, to his Mother Country and to British people all over the world. When Britain declared war on Germany in August 1914, he felt included.

His full name was Lionel Fitzherbert Turpin and he was born in February 1896, on the north-east coast of South America, in Georgetown, the capital of what's now the Co-operative Republic of Guyana but was then known as British Guiana – the only colony in the continent of South America owned by the British crown. If you look on the map, you'll find it sandwiched between Venezuela on the left and Surinam on the right. It was such a wild place, a lot of it wasn't explored until recently. All I know about it is bits and pieces I've been told or I've picked up from encyclopaedias, and I couldn't sleep one night and a film come on the television. It's mostly rainforests with some grasslands. It'd be too hot to live there if it wasn't for the trade winds and the rain, and it rains more than my height every year.

Before the foreigners come floating in on the tide – Columbus, Raleigh, all them – it was a peaceful place called the Land of

Glistening Waters cuz of its four big rivers and it bordering the Atlantic Ocean.

The Europeans planted sugar, coffee, rice, cotton and tobacco, and they kidnapped people from Africa to do the work. Slaves. 'Black Ivory.' They auctioned them off and frequently worked them to death.

Under the earth, there's iron ore, copper, diamonds and gold. My dad's brothers had a small goldmine. They never struck enough to make them millionaires but it was enough to make them better off than a lot of people.

Georgetown's a port on the mouth of the Demerara river and my dad would've woke every day to the sound of ships coming in and out of the harbour, and he'd have gone to sleep at night to the thump and wash of the sea. He'd have heard parrots and toucans squawking, monkeys chattering, hummingbirds whirring, the whine of mosquitoes and the scream of logging saws. He would've seen pelicans fishing from the harbour walls, flamingos feeding on the mud flats and vultures circling over the rice fields and sugar plantations.

At certain times of the year, hurricanes would come and rip up trees and tear down the tin-roofed, stilt-legged shacks on the outskirts of town. When there was an earthquake over in the Caribbean, he would have felt it, and there would've been times when Georgetown was plunged into darkness by black volcano dust brought in on the wind.

When it was just sunshine, the sky would've been a pure blue glass bowl; iguanas and lizards and snakes would've been sunning theirselves on the rocks; alligators sunbathing on the banks of the swamps; and chameleons lying around flicking out their tongues, reeling in insects. There'd have been mangoes, melons, pineapples, guavas, oranges, bananas, lemons and limes for my dad to pick whenever he wanted. Giant butterflies, in more colours than a rainbow, would've flapped from flower to flower – flowers like you'd think only grew in dreams.

When I was little, I used to look at photographs of him and wonder where he come from. There was nobody else like him round here. 'He looks like a loaf that's been in the oven too long. He must have come from somewhere by the seaside cuz he's so sunburnt.'

How did my dad get hisself over here to fight in the First World War? That's a good question. Mum said he come over as a merchant seaman. It's likely he worked his passage as a stoker or summat, because he couldn't afford to pay for his ticket. There's a rumour that he left home at 16 cuz of a fall-out with his father. If that's true, he might have come straight to England then, or he might have tasted the world a little bit as a sailor beforehand.

War Office Records, dated 5th & 6th August, 1915:
(The War Office suffered incendiary bomb damage during World War Two and records were lost. Many of those which survived are damaged.)

What is your name?
– Lionel Turpin.
What is your full address?
– Collingwood, (scorch mark), North Shields.
Are you a British subject?
– Yes.
What is your age?
– 19 years 5 months.
What is your trade or calling?
– Labourer.
Are you married?
– No.

It's a fantastic feeling touching the papers my father would've touched. He's signed up at the York Depot of the York and Lancaster Regiment for the duration of hostilities.

Height?
– 5 ft 5 in.
Chest measurement when fully expanded?
– 33¾ in.

He was only a little fella, wasn't he! I used to think of him as being really big and tall but I'm two inches taller than him and bigger round the chest.

Name and address of next of kin?
– John Turpin, 291 Thomas Street, Georgetown, British Guinea.
Relationship?
– Father.

I was named after my dad's dad in South America – a master carpenter with the city works. They've put Guinea instead of Guiana. P'raps the enlistment officer was a bit deaf or summat.

> I, Lionel Turpin, swear by Almighty God, that I will be faithful and bear true allegiance to His Majesty King George the Fifth, His Heirs and Successors, and that I will, as in duty bound, honestly and faithfully defend His Majesty, His Heirs and Successors, in Person, Crown and dignity against all enemies, and will observe and obey all orders of His Majesty, His Heirs and Successors, and of the Generals and Officers set over me. So help me God.

The King's Royal Rifle Corps – the 60th of Foot. Legendary, they are! Everybody used to tell me my dad must've been put in the West Indian Rifle Corps because he was black. I *knew* he wasn't put in them. It was the Americans that had segregated troops, not us.

Rifleman Turpin A202638.

You don't know how all this makes me feel, finding out about my dad. Thank you ever-so. I anna kidding, it's like I'm walking on air!

> MESSAGE FROM KING GEORGE THE FIFTH TO ALL HIS TROOPS:
>
> You are leaving home to fight for the safety and honour of my Empire.
>
> Belgium, whose country we are pledged to defend, has been attacked, and France is about to be invaded by the same powerful foe.
>
> I have implicit confidence in you, my soldiers. Duty is your watchword, and I know your duty will be nobly done . . .

Nobody thought the war was gonna last very long, did they? We thought we'd knock out the Germans easy. 'Over by Christmas,' was what everyone said.

Me dad was sent out in February 1916 with the No. 32 British Expeditionary Force to the Western Front in Europe. He participated in the BEF campaigns of 1916, 1917 and 1918. My dad *was* in the battles of the Somme, then. People have said that from time to time. Trench warfare. Hell on earth. It was a miracle anyone come through that. The Great War lasted for four years and two months and was a bloody free-for-all. They was only lads in soldier coats.

ACTIVE SERVICE PAY BOOK. INSTRUCTIONS ISSUED BY FIELD MARSHAL LORD KITCHENER TO EVERY SOLDIER:

You are ordered abroad as a soldier of the King to help our French comrades against the invasion of a common enemy. You will have to perform a task which will need your courage, your energy, your patience. Remember that the honour of the British Army depends on your individual conduct . . . Be invariably courteous, considerate and kind. Never do anything likely to injure or destroy property, and always look upon looting as a disgraceful act. You are sure to meet with a welcome and to be trusted; your conduct must justify that welcome and that trust.

Your duty cannot be done unless your health is sound. So keep constantly on your guard against any excesses. In this new experience you may find temptations both in wine and women. You must entirely resist both temptations, and, while treating all women with perfect courtesy, you should avoid any intimacy.

It sounds more like an invitation to a night out in a shady part of town than a war, doesn't it? My dad got gassed and wounded.

I know we didn't exactly beat the Germans in the Great War. It was a sort of no-decision contest. The Allies and Central powers had virtually run out of men and ammunition, and with the Americans vaulting over the top rope to fight with us in 1917, with fresh troops and all the firepower money could buy, Kaiser Bill weighed up his chances and threw in the towel. In retrospect, it looks like he was just thinking about getting back into training and building up for a rematch.

My dad had survived the worst battles the world had ever seen but a gas shell caught up with him in the last weeks of the war when he was fighting with the 2nd Battalion of the King's Royal Rifle Corps near Arras in northern France.

'No longer physically fit for War Service.'
Gassed. Shell wound.
3rd February, 1919

That'll be his official discharge date when they were repatriating the wounded. He would have been posted to a field hospital before that.

> Turpin, Lionel Rifleman K.R.R.C. A/202638 3.2.19
> War Badge No.B164952
> British War Medal 4955 I.V. No.112/1

Two medals, two gas-burnt lungs and a shell wound in his back. They brought him over to England, to a hospital in Coventry.

When the hospital had done all they could, he was sent to Hill House in Warwick to convalesce – a nice quiet place along the Birmingham Road by the Lodge and the railway bridge. There were so many casualties coming back, they had to get all these extra places for them to go to be treated.

It gets me because people nowadays think having black people in this country is new. My dad was the first black man in Warwick and Leamington Spa but hundreds of black people have been living in Britain, and been born in Britain, for hundreds of years. And hundreds of people from British colonies settled up and down the country after fighting in the First World War or the Second World War. They didn't teach me that at school, and there's nothing about it in the history books, but they were British people and it's proper British history.

One of the blokes that worked at Hill House become good friends with my dad. He was a survivor off the *Titanic* and the son of a terrific lady called Mrs Rose. Mrs Rose was so overweight, she was housebound. She sat propped up in a chair in a corner of the front room. She never moved out of that room, I don't think. Me mum, while she was still living with me granny and granddad and they'd all moved to Parkes Street in Warwick, used to help Mrs Rose – doing her cleaning and all that. One day, me dad's mate took me dad home to Mrs Rose's house and that's when Lionel Fitzherbert Turpin met Beatrice Elizabeth Whitehouse.

When we was kids, Mrs Rose would be wedged in the corner in her padded chair telling us stories. Winter nights, her room used to be absolutely bulging with neighbourhood kids listening to her. She told me about a fight me dad had once with a bloke he thought was paying too much attention to me mum. The fight took place outside the bus station and they ended up rolling under a stationary bus, still fighting. The bus was late going out because they had to jack it up to pull them out. Me dad spent that night in the nick. He was only 5 ft 5 in. tall, with a bad back and lungs. The name Lionel means 'Little Lion'. He'd certainly got the heart of one. Mrs Rose said he was always immaculately dressed. A perfect gentleman.

It was love at first sight for me mum and dad, and, early in 1920, me mum found herself pregnant. On 26 November that year, she gave birth to her first child, a boy. I don't know anything of what was said but I do know having a baby 'out of wedlock' was considered a very shameful thing then and I suppose a white girl having a baby by a black man was thought of as being even more terrible. The spaces for filling the name and occupation of the father on me brother's birth certificate are left blank. His names are given as Lionel Cecil Turpin. Technically he was L.C.T. Whitehouse but he always used Turpin as his surname. I've only just seen his certificate but me brother must've known all along, cuz he was always sensitive to being called a certain word, if you know what I mean.

It's obvious that a boy with the surname Turpin is gonna be nicknamed 'Dick' after the famous highwayman. In fact, all us brothers were at one time or another but with Lionel Cecil it stuck and he was known as 'Dick' to everybody.

Dick wasn't brought up with us. He was virtually given to me grandparents and brought up in Warwick with me cousins Jim and Bill Farnell. Don't forget we're talking about the 1920s here, before the Welfare State, and not working meant not eating. Him being looked after by me grandparents allowed me mum to go to work. When we was young, we always sailed close to the wind, money-wise, and me mum worked all the hours God sent.

When convalescence had done all it could for me dad, he got hisself a job. Me mum got pregnant again and, with me dad now working, they were in a position to get married, which they did on Christmas Eve 1921, at Warwick Register Office. My sister, Joan Victoria, was born on 19 June 1922.

Just before my mum and dad had got married, my dad was awarded the Victory medal for 'Service in a Theatre of War Overseas – The Great War for Civilisation – Between 5th August 1914 and 11th November 1918'.

Most people in those days wouldn't have rented a flat to a black man but an old lady offered me mum and dad a basement flat in Willes Road, Royal Leamington Spa, a couple of miles from Warwick. It's a posh ol' town with neat rows of Victorian and Regency terraced houses full of pound-notish people, nice public gardens, a lake and health springs with Royal Pump Rooms. It's still there, the house is. It was a basement flat, admitted, but it was all right. We were allowed to sit in the garden but we weren't allowed to play on the grass, because the lawn was reserved for the people of the house. The old lady said my dad was a good patriot. He had come over from one of our colonies to fight for Britain in the war and had got badly wounded doing it, and it was only right that he should have somewhere here to live.

Me dad's job was master moulder at Bissel's Foundry. Working at a foundry couldn't have done him any good but you had to take work wherever you could get it and there was no medicals for jobs then. His doctor had recommended he went back to Guiana cuz of the better weather but me mum couldn't face the idea of going out there and me dad couldn't face the idea of leaving me mum.

A year or so after our Joan was born, my mum had another baby but it was born dead. Another brother. How me mum kept working I'll never know. She was a real fighter. I was born on 13 June 1925, while they were living there in Willes Road, the place of my earliest memories. I was two shades darker than the others – more like me dad, who was very dark.

Another baby boy arrived in our family on 7 June 1928 – Randolph Adolphus – and I know exactly how heavy he was when he was born. I suppose me mum must have told me and it stuck in my mind – 9 lb 7 oz – and he was the lightest of us, evidently. We was all heavyweights when we first weighed in.

My father put up with his war wounds best as he could but his health deteriorated fast. He was going backwards and forwards to the Coventry hospital more and more often. They took half his lung away. It reached a point where he needed round-the-clock nursing and he was taken to the Ministry of Pensions Hospital in Highbury, Kings Heath, Birmingham.

On the morning of 6 March 1929, 11 years after it had struck him down, the German gas shell took the last breath from what was left of my poor dad's lungs. He was 33 years of age.

Lionel Fitzherbert Turpin, male, 33 years, of 6 Willes Road, Leamington, an iron moulder. Cause of death:
  (a) Capillary Bronchitis
  (b) Chronic Bronchitis
Emphysema.
No P.M.
Widow of deceased: Mrs B. Turpin

I think they should put my dad's name, and millions of others like him, on the Roll of Honour with those as lost their lives on the battlefields. All over the world, people died slow unofficial deaths in peacetime beds but it was the war that'd killed them.

My dad is buried in Brunswick Street Cemetery, Leamington Spa. He had a glass hearse drawn by four black horses and an escort of six soldiers. The Leamington branch of the British Legion paid his funeral expenses.

My mum was a widow at 25, left to bring us up on a widow's pension of less than 30 shillings a week, and whatever else she could earn cooking and cleaning for people.

4

Low Shoes and Gingold Ankles

All the big houses along Willes Road was ex-army officers, colonels or rear-admirals from the navy, retired, and they all had maids and servants. One of the lady wives come round to me mum and asked if she could adopt me. 'Why?' me mum asked.

'I want to dress him up like a little Indian, in silk pantaloons and a turban, and train him to answer the door when people come to the house.'

Joan told me, 'I thought Mum was gonna smack her in the mouth.' That would've put us right in trouble, cuz you ain't allowed to hit anybody higher class than you, sort of thing, but mum controlled herself enough to say, 'My son's no slave, and you aren't gonna dress him like a slave. Now sod off!'

With me dad gone, we couldn't afford to stay at Willes Road and we moved into a top-floor flat of a five-storey house in Church Street at the bottom end of town.

When I started at the Milverton School in Rugby Road back in 1930, school uniform was unheard of – no bugger could afford it – but I wanted low shoes. All the other kids had got low shoes and I wanted low shoes. I'd got grey flannel shorts – the sort that come just below your knees – and a jersey to go with them, and I was happy with them but I wanted low shoes. I'd been born with Gingold ankles and I used to have to wear boots to support them. Anyway, I went on and on about it, so me mum got me some sandals. I could out-run most of the kids round here but all of a

31

sudden me ankles would give way and I'd go flat on me face, and then I couldn't walk for two days. I had to go back to the boots.

The headmistress, Miss Jacobs, I anna kidding, she only had to look at me and I almost could've filled me pants. She had one blue eye and one brown eye, and when she lost her temper her hair stood on end. I swear she could see straight through into what I was thinking. I was convinced she was a witch.

The witch never used to cane you on your hands. She used to pull you across the desk and go BANG!BANG!BANG!BANG! like a machine gun across your backside. She was a savage old git. My class teacher would shout, 'TURPIN! GO AND SEE THE HEADMISTRESS!' and my heart would sink into me stomach.

Mrs Constable, another teacher, liked to humiliate you. This crippled kidda, called White, come to the school and every time he did something wrong she'd hang a poster on him saying, I AM AN IDIOT or I CANNOT SPELL MY OWN NAME and make him walk round the playground wearing it. It had a reverse effect on us, though, cuz all the kids felt sorry for him and hated her bleeding guts.

One day, I fell all the way down three flights at our flat and mum decided the place was too dangerous to have kids in. Besides that, she needed to work more hours to keep us and couldn't look after us at the same time. We was farmed out to relations. I went to me granny and granddad in Warwick, Randolph went to me aunty Ethel, who lived opposite them in Parkes Street, and Joan went to stay in the Rhondda Valley with a Mrs Davies me mum had met. That meant a change of school for me and I was taken to Westgate in Bowling Green Street, the same school Dick was at.

Of all the things to send me to school in: blue velvet trousers with pearl buttons on the legs. Me mum had got them at a jumble sale and I was chuffed to death with them but this kid, Pettifer, pulled one of the buttons off and tore the material. I told him, 'Do that again and I'll smash your head in!'

'Come on then!' he said. He was much bigger than me, so I tried to back down, but he started giving me 'cowardy' punches on my shoulder and it hurt so much I took a swing at his face with me fist and knocked him over. Then I was scared of what he would do when he got up so I took a run and jump, CRUNCH! – right in his guts. I was still wearing those big boots to support me ankles and Pettifer was sick all over the place. Next thing I knew I was flying through the air. Our Dick had seen what'd happened and thumped me. I thought, 'How can he be my brother when he hits me because I hit some other kid?'

Dick said, 'You jumped on him with your boots. You've got to fight fair.'

I was always copping it from the headmaster at Westgate. I'd make a joke and the class would start laughing. 'Out you come for the cane, Turpin,' he'd say. One time after he'd caned me he said, 'Perhaps, now, you won't be so smart, Turpin.'

'I'm already smarting, sir,' I told him. I got another one then.

We were all sat around me granny's table one night, about to have tea, when me mum shows up with this strange little girl. She was five or six years old and had her legs in irons. Me mum sits her at the table, points to Randolph and says to the girl, 'Do you know who this is?'

'Yes,' she says, 'Marmadukes.' Immediately, a piece of tea-soaked cake comes flying across the table – SPLAT! – straight in her face.

'My name's Randolph, not Marmadukes.'

Granddad Whitehouse leans over and clonks Randolph on the head with his knuckles. Randolph goes away from the table crying his eyes out. Me mum says, 'Do you know who it is, Jack?'

'Ain't got a clue.'

'This is your sister.'

'Joan's me sister.'

'This is your other sister.'

'I on'y got one sister,' I said, and it was my turn for a smack across the head from Granddad Whitehouse.

'This is your sister Kathleen. Say hello.'

Kathleen Priscilla was born with her feet the wrong way round, so she was in an orthopaedic hospital from birth, over in Coventry. Me mum couldn't afford the bus fares backwards and forwards, so a cousin, 'Aunty' Ada Greaves, who lived just along from the hospital, looked after Kath when she was allowed out between operations. Kath grew up to feel that Aunty Ada was more related to her than our mum was.

I'm not kidding you, Kathleen could out-run and out-climb any kid round here. She had massive muscles in her shoulders cuz of the leg irons. You'd see her go up a tree just with her arms. By God she could motor. And fight. There should've been four Turpin brothers! She was only in the callipers as a child. Then she had them off and that was it.

Randolph and meself, we was always very, very close. He also got very matey with our sister Kath. They used to go anywhere and everywhere together, and if anybody argued with him they had her to settle – and, I'm not akidding, she could hit. When she was grown up, I saw her punch a 15-st. man – knocked him straight over the bonnet of a car. Laid him out.

Our mum met a bloke called Ernest Frank Manley from down where our Warwick Racing Amateur Boxing Club is now. He got us a place back in Leamington – the ground-floor flat of No. 14 Portland Street. Portland Street was a pretty posh ol' street but our flat was an awful place. It wasn't rat-infested like I read in a stupid book about Randolph – some people are never satisfied with the truth, are they? – but it was cold and dark and a bit damp. There's me and Kath lived there at first, cuz Aunty Ethel still had Randolph, and Joan was still away.

Although it was described as a ground-floor flat, it was only the living room that was on the ground floor. Our bedroom was right at the top of the building and there was no electricity up there. It put the fear of God up us. My bed was on one side of the room and Kath's was on the other. We had a little Kelly lamp on the table between the two beds – one of those little paraffin lamps that's got sand inside the base of it so's it can't be knocked over – and we were rationed half a cupful of oil for the week. We'd snuggle down and I'd say, 'Who's gonna blow the lamp out?' Kath would say, 'It's your turn tonight.' I'd blow it out – Phfffffff! – and dash back into bed, nearly breaking my leg trying to be that quick. The darkness was like a big block. You'd think if you put your hands up, you'd push on something.

When Randolph came to stop for the weekend, he used to sleep in with me. I'd get out of bed, Phffffff the lamp out and a great wail would go up from Randolph – 'WHOAH! OI! WHOAH!' – till me mum would come up looking. 'What's he shouting for?'

'Cuz we've put the light out.'

'Well,' she'd say, 'we'll put it back on for him.'

'But we'll use all the paraffin up and we shan't have no light for the rest of the week.' She always put it back on for him, though. Oh ar, he was petrified of the dark. He'd never stop indoors on his own either.

On 22 October 1932, me mum and Ernie Manley got married. He was a good old stick, Ernie. He took care of us but we didn't get on with him when he first came into the family. We asked him, 'What do we call yer?'

'Anything you like,' he says.

'How about "Big Ears"?' I suggested. I got a back-hander off him for that. He wanted us to call him 'Dad' but we wouldn't. He wasn't our real dad, so we stayed Turpin and our mum became Mrs Manley.

He'd been a regular soldier, Ernie. After he'd served his time out, they stuck him on the reserve list and sent him back to civvy street and he got hisself a job on the canals. He'd be up to his waist in mud and water all the time. He was paid a bit better than most people but with a wife and us kids to pay for, it wasn't enough for me mum to stop working.

He'd actually known my real dad, Ernie had. My proper dad was swimming in the canal one day when Ernie was up at Budbrooke Barracks with the Royal Engineers. Ernie comes walking past with his army mates and sees me dad in the water. 'Get out of there, Sambo,' he shouts. 'You're making the water dirty.' My dad got out and two seconds later Ernie was in the canal hisself with me dad sitting on his back. If it wasn't for Ernie's mates pulling me dad off him, Ernie would have been drownded and me mum couldn't have married him. Anytime Ernie walloped me for anything, I used to think, 'You're only doing this cuz me dad chucked you in the canal.' I resented Ernie at first. It was nothing against *him*, I just wanted my real dad.

We moved out of Portland Street to a flat over Dillow's chip shop in Warwick Market Place so's we could have Randolph with us permanently. After that, me and Randolph used to moan and moan that Joan should come back from Wales. She'd been away three or four years. We thought we wouldn't get in so much trouble with her around. We were always copping it for summat. She eventually come back speaking better Welsh than the Welsh could. She told us her name wasn't Turpin, it was Davies. I said to her, 'If your name ain't Turpin, let's see you wash the black off of you then.' She admitted she couldn't. 'Then you must be Turpin,' I told her.

With Joan back, the flat above the chip shop wasn't big enough, so Ernie rented a house off the council: 19 Wathen Road on the Packmore's Estate in Warwick. The houses there are terraces, really nice and nearly new at the time, and the very best thing we'd ever had.

I don't think there was a kid on Packmore's that wasn't on probation and it wasn't long before I was in trouble. Not for real crimes – mostly scrumping and things like that. I mean, when you go and nick apples and things in orchards, that's fair game, innit? Most of the dads on that estate were only on a couple of quid a week and the kids weren't given nothing for sweets, so when we saw lovely sweet, juicy apples hanging on the trees, it was too big a temptation.

When you got caught, they'd really lay into you. Old 'Swan Neck', the bloke as had these onions on the allotment, I see him give one kid a right hammering with his walking stick. Tanned the arse off him. I used to sneak into his allotment and pinch his onions, and when I see him in the street he'd say, 'Hello, young Turpin.'

I'd say, 'Hello, Mister.' When he'd gone along a bit, I'd cup me hands round me mouth and shout, 'OI, SWAN NECK, I 'AD SOME OF YOUR ONIONS LAST NIGHT!' and run like hell.

There was a probation officer as used to come round and check up on me: 'What have you been doing lately, John? Are you behaving yourself?'

'Yes, Mrs Tempest.' I always told her that. She knew I wasn't really bad.

The first friend I had when I was very little, I can't remember his name. He was the nephew of Drummer Harting, a heavyweight boxer in the army who'd served out in India. I went up to play one day and the kid said, 'My aunty told me I can't play with you any more.'

'Why not?'

'Because you're black.'

'Oh,' I said, 'but it don't come off.' I lost a friend but it prepared me for later on in life.

One of my best mates was Arthur Taylor. We called him 'Banjo', cuz he was so bow-legged he looked like a bloody banjo. His mum was a little fat lady who had a soft spot for my dad. Banjo's dad got wounded the same time as my dad and had been in the same hospital as him. The army sent him home with a brace down one leg so he couldn't walk properly. Banjo's parents doted on Banjo and give him everything he wanted.

All boys at that time wanted lead soldiers and Banjo's dad bought him stacks and stacks of them. I used to go to his house to play. He'd do something and I'd give him a smack across the head or summat. He'd yell at me and then we'd have a fight. His mum used to come running out, telling him, 'Get to bed, Arthur.' She'd put him to bed and let me stay in the back yard playing with his soldiers.

Even up to when he was about 14 or 15, our Dick still used to join in. His army never used to get beat, though. If we captured any of his soldiers, he used to give us a thump. One day he bought a massive great cannon. He'd fire these shells out of it and when it exploded amongst our soldiers they used to go in all directions and we'd spend the rest of the day putting legs back on and sticking packs back on the ones that was marching.

Poor old Banjo, he got sent to bed regular. He'd complain to his mum that I'd taken some of his soldiers. 'I don't believe you, Arthur,' his mum would say. 'Gosher wouldn't take them.' But I had.

She always called me Gosher. Most people did at one time. It was a nickname I got cuz of me granddad. Me mum's dad and all that side of the family were very strict Methodists. I used to be always saying 'God!' or 'God strike me!' – stuff like that, and, BANG!, me granddad Whitehouse would crack me one across the head. 'That's for taking God's name in vain.' I learned to duck just before he hit me and change it to 'Gosh!' I said it that often, me cousins started calling me 'Gosher' and it caught on. One day, a kid asked me, 'Is Gosher your tribal name?' Granddad Whitehouse was a very religious bloke.

Religion used to puzzle me. I think it was because I always wanted to know where me dad was. I asked the Sunday School teacher, 'You keep saying, "We'll meet again." When will it be?'

'One day in the Hereafter.'

'What's the Hereafter?'

'It's a wonderful place you go to when you are dead.'

'What's the point of going there when you're dead?' She knew it was bothering me, so she used to keep me behind after the class and talk to me for hours but I never could get it straight in me mind.

*

'Don't keep going on about it,' me aunt Gert said, but I did and one day she'd had enough. She took me to the Brunswick Street Cemetery and stood me in front of a grave. 'That's where your dad is,' she said, 'and the next time you see him is when you go in there.'

*

Every Armistice Day, either my mum or Banjo's mum or one of me aunties would take me and him to the parade. We'd meet it coming down the Saltisford at the bottom of Parkes Street and as the Royal Warwickshire regiment come marching past we'd fall in at the back of it and march with them to the Market Place. We'd march past the Union Jack and salute it, and when they sang the patriotic songs, I'd holler them out as loud as I could. I did it to honour my dad. I thought it was a part of life and we'd all do it for as long as we lived. Nowadays, they hold it outside the church at the cenotaph and hardly anybody goes. Me and Banjo still go though.

5

A Hoomey Shmooley

My very best mate was Dougie Kensit. He went to a different school to me – the National school. Every Saturday morning either I'd call for him or he'd call for me. We'd fill two bottles with cold tea and go down to the shop to buy two packets of the old penny biscuits and go off across the fields.

We knew every bird's nest there was around Budbrooke Barracks and the fields there. During the summer holidays, it was nothing for us to come home at one o'clock in the morning. All we got was a smack round the head cuz it was gone eleven and asked where the bloody hell we'd been. We used to say, 'Well, we went up there . . . round here . . . over there . . . across that field . . .' We never used to remember the names of the places we visited. We'd go for miles and miles and miles.

Once, we saw a yellowhammer making a nest out of roots and grass in some bushes. It was beautiful. Perfect. Me and Dougie made a pact we wouldn't let anybody else know where it was. We looked after it right through the spring, when it laid four eggs and hatched them, and into the summer when the young birds flew. The next year it came back to the same place again.

I called for Dougie one day and his mum said, 'He's not very well, Gosher. We've got to fetch the doctor to him.' I sat on the top of the three steps up to our granny's front door to watch the doctor going to his house. I ran to me granny, saying, 'He's dead.'

'Who's dead?'

'Dougie. A car come and took him away. A big white un.'

'He's not dead. That'll be the ambulance taking him to the hospital to make him better.' We wasn't allowed to see him in the hospital. His parents was allowed but his brother and sisters couldn't go. I remember asking his mum how he was. 'We don't know' – that's all she would tell me. That hurt my feelings, with me and Dougie going everywhere together. I mean, Saturdays we used to go up to the market when it was closing and buy six or eight of these wooden crates off the fruit stall for sixpence. We chopped them up in my granny's back yard and sold them around the street as firewood for tuppence a bundle. We made our picture money that way.

The old County Theatre in Warwick ain't there any more but we used to see all the films they showed. *Robin Hood*, *The Three Stooges*, *The Scarlet Pimpernel* – all sorts of things. We liked *The Scarlet Pimpernel* best. We'd come out and, next thing, you'd see us over the racecourse playing it out. We used to argue who was going to be the Scarlet Pimpernel. 'You *can't* be him,' Dougie'd say. 'You're too dark.'

Dougie was 11 when he died. Meningitis. I asked his mum, 'Can I go and see him?' She said, 'No. They've cut his head open and everything.' What they'd done, I suppose, him being like with meningitis and them still trying to find a cure for it, they'd opened his head up to see if there was anything they could do.

When Mrs Kensit told me Dougie was dead, I went home and cried me eyes out. I had two days off school cuz I'd made meself that ill. After that, I'd go to school, come straight home and go to bed. Other than school, I never went out of the house for three months. Then Granddad give me a good hiding and told me, 'Get out and play.' I think if it hadn't have been that me Granddad Whitehouse was like he was, I would have very likely laid down and died. I missed Dougie that much. He was a smashing kid. I saw him when he went into hospital and that was it. Not long. A week. Ten days at the outside.

Three years running we nearly lost Randolph with bronchitis and pneumonia. The third time, me mum sent for the doctor in the evening cuz Randolph was so bad and Dr Tibbets took a long look at him and said, 'You should prepare yourself for the end, Beattie. If this young man is still alive in the morning, we'll be very lucky.' Mum sat up all through the night and persevered and persevered with Randolph, sponging him down and feeding him little bits of soup. When the doctor come in the morning, there was Randolph sitting up in bed playing cards. It was like me mum had brought him into the world all over again.

When Randolph was little and ill, we did anything and everything for him. We got that used to doing it we carried on when he was grown up and people used to say we was afraid of him. We wasn't afraid of him. We was just afraid he might die.

One thing people always get wrong is how Randolph acquired the nickname 'Licker'. It was nothing to do with boxing or fighting – he was only three or four years old for a start. Randolph, me and Joan were all born in June – Randolph on the 7th, me on the 13th and our Joan on the 19th. When our birthdays come round, because his birthday come first, Randolph thought that made him the eldest. Joan would shake her head, 'No, you're the littlest.' He used to scream and swear at her, and he couldn't half cuss for a littl'un, 'I'M NOT THE LICKEREST,' he'd shout. 'I'M THE BLOODY OLDEST!' Joan would mimic his pronunciation, 'You're just a *licker* boy, and if you don't behave, *licker* boy, I shall spank your bottom!' – teasing and taunting him till he rushed at her with his little fists flying. 'Licker' become our pet name for him. Somewhere down the line it got used when he was boxing: 'The Leamington Licker'. It's a real good name for a boxer, innit?

We were still like two separate families: Joan, me, Kath and Randolph with me mum and Ernie; Dick with me granny and granddad. It got so's we hardly ever used to see Dick. I swear he used to think of himself as being white. He used to refer to me and Joan as his 'black brother and sister'. I asked him, 'What colour do you think you are then?' And then I told him the same as I'd told Joan, 'Have a wash and see if the colour comes off.'

'Get out of here,' he said, 'before I give you a smack in the ear.'

You wouldn't have thought Dick was our big brother if you'd seen the way he treated us. He'd make us play 'Schools'. He was the teacher, of course. The steps at our granny's were our desks. He'd stand in front and this is the sort of question he'd ask, 'How many foolygoos in a hoomey shmooley?' I'd make a wild guess, 'Er . . . a hundred-hundred?'

'WRONG!' he'd shout, and I'd get the cane.

My sister, Joan, would say, 'Well, it must be nearly right,' and then he'd lay into *her*. I've seen him bat her over the head with a rolled-up newspaper till her nose bled. Me, the little hero, used to go steaming in punching his kneecaps trying to fight him off her but I'd come out with a thump on the nose and that was it. Dick was a bully but, at a very early age, he learned to fear Randolph.

People always go on about how poor we was. It's true we didn't have hardly any money in spite of me mum working her fingers to the bone but times was hard for a lot of people then. There'd been the General Strike the year after I was born and there was still an economic depression over the whole country, and I suppose we was at the bottom end of it.

Our Joan used to laugh about her and Randolph fighting over some orange peel. It would have been quite a battle, I tell you, but Randolph won, of course, and he grabbed the peel and run into the street to eat it. One of his mates saw him and asks, 'What you eating that for?' Lick was too embarrassed to say 'Cuz I'm hungry'. So he told him, 'It's very good for your teeth,' and showed him a big smile. But we used to have some wonderful meals me grandma used to do. Chittlins, for instance. I used to sit and watch Granny Whitehouse washing them, squeezing them out, then plaiting them. And you've never tasted meat more tender than what that is. It melts in your mouth. It's got a taste on its own. Wonderful! Some people used to think, 'Urrrgh! Fancy eating pig's innards!' But it's the best meat you could ever eat.

When me granny still lived in Parkes Street – before she moved into the alms houses – starting in the late summer, we all used to get sent up the Butts. The Butts is a rifle range the soldiers from Budbrooke used. There was three fields there absolutely covered in blackberry bushes and around the edges was crab-apple trees. We used to bring baskets and bagfuls of crab apples and blackberries from there, and Granny Whitehouse used to make sufficient jam, not just for us but for half of Parkes Street. 'Bring all yer old jars,' she'd say. 'You can't have no jam if you don't bring yer own jars.' We lived on jam all through the winter. Nobody ever suffered from constipation in our house. I'm not akidding; we was really healthy, cuz we never used to have all this fancy stuff like people eat today.

Me and Randolph, as kids and living at our granny's, we really looked forward to Christmas. It gave us a chance to give our mum a good time. Christmas Day was her day. She wouldn't have to go to work.

A while before, we'd be up the market doing little odd jobs – stacking boxes, loading and unloading fruit and veg – and any money we got for it we'd save it up and give it to our mum so's she'd have something in her purse.

She'd come back from having a Christmas drink with our aunties and uncles and cousins, and we'd get her to sing for us. She'd sit me and Randolph on the table and sing 'Pal Of My Cradle Days'. She could take Gracie Fields off to a T. We'd gaze at her with tears rolling down our faces. When it come to the chorus, we'd all join in.

My mum worked at all sorts of jobs. She was even a midwife sometimes. Nurse Mills, whenever she wanted help, she'd give me a note to ask me mum to go to a certain house the next night.

We liked it best when Mum worked in the kitchen at the Shire Hall, because there was always food left over from the big dinners the circuit judges give theirselves. Whenever we had potatoes with butter on them, we knew she'd been working there.

Our life wasn't easy when we was kids but it was fun. In spite of how hard our mum had to work she *always* tried to make things fun for us. We couldn't afford to have holidays, so she did the next best thing. The lady who lived on the Rock used to organise it.

6

Like in the Beginning of the World

The farmer, Mr Steadman, was in touch with the lady on the Rock and he'd tell her to get so many people, according to what he wanted. You'd knock on her door and ask, 'Are you looking for hop pickers?' She'd take your name and address, write down how many was in the family and how many would be working, and then you'd wait until she give you the date, and you'd all come up on Warwick station for the train to the hop gardens of Hereford. They paid all your fares.

Mum used to go and get us off classes from the end of August through September. I tell you, if I could've bunked off school and gone down there all the time, I would've done. We used to have to work, but the great thing was we was with our mum.

She'd scrape together to buy tins of beans, tins of corned beef, tea and sugar, and save it all in these big tin trunks. I used to think, 'Where are we gonna put our clothes?' Well, you'd put your clothes in a sack, or summat, but you always had one good suit put into a suitcase, so's on Sundays, when you went to church, you looked smart. I never used to sleep much the night before we left. I couldn't wait to be on that train chuffing down to Stoke Edith.

Mr Steadman used to allot us all these barns around the place. They was always clean and well scoured. Some people was put in cleaned-up pig sties but we lived in a barn with big ol' bales of hay and everything. You'd take your own blankets and sheets with you. They sectioned the barns off so's you'd got your own private rooms. If you was single, it was blokes one side, women the other.

To the left of the barns was the hop yards and on the other side was the apple orchards. I think the apples were used for making cider. You'd help yourself to fruit and every Sunday you had apple tart or summat for dinner. The food was terrific. Most of the stuff was out of our tins, then, at night, we'd have potatoes roasted over the brazier fires outside the barns.

Your first job in the morning was to get the fire going and get the kettle on. After you'd had a cup of tea, you went off to work. The hop bines grow ten or fifteen feet high and you walked along the aisles pulling 'em down and stripping them off. If it was before the sun had been up long, you got yourself soaked in dew. If the bines got stuck, a bloke would come round with a big long stick with, like, a pair of scissors on the end and snip them down for you. If they couldn't do it, a bloke on stilts would come.

The hops are like a green pine cone, only soft. You get rid of all the leaves, then run the bine through your thumb and forefinger held in a circle: BRRRM-B-B-B-BRRRM! and skin it into the crib – like a canvas trough on a frame about six-foot long.

You'd fill your crib and then they'd come along with a basket and collect what you'd picked. The collectors would yell out, 'CLEAN 'EM UP. CLEAN 'EM UP. WE AIN'T WEIGHING IN LEAVES!' You got paid by how many bushels you'd done, at a shilling a bushel.

A lot of people who used to come down regular was gypsies. Me mum told me they'd run off with me if I was bad, so I used to make sure there was plenty of people around me when I was with them.

The main gypsy family was the Brazils. Danny Brazil was a terrific singer and dancer, and all the girls used to tap dance. They'd dress up in the proper costumes: Spanish dresses in bright shiny materials; they'd have the old guitars, a barrel organ – everything. They put on plays in the field across from where we was staying. It was like going to a big show in London.

When we'd finished work, we'd come back and have a wash. If you'd got muddy gear on, you'd get rid of that and put summat else on. You never changed into posh clothes; you'd just put on clothes that was cleaner than the ones you'd taken off. You'd have something to eat and you'd sit there and wait to see what was happening. There'd be a bloke, like, from the gypsy camp come round and he'd start hollering from the square at the top,

'THERE'S A SHOW ON AT THE GYPSY CAMP TONIGHT! EVERYBODY WELCOME!'

They used to have two flat wagons that they'd lock up together and make into a stage. I'm not akidding, the way they improvised with stuff, some of these big theatres could have took lessons from them. They only used what was knocking around. They'd find some ivy growing, follow it right to the root and cut it so that there was yards of it in a string, then they'd drape it over where they put the curtains and weave wild flowers into it. The curtains was two big tarpaulins which they worked on wires.

They used to have massive fires that lit up the whole field and us kids would be sat around there close to the fire, watching all what was going on. Listening to the music, an' all that, you know, I used to fall asleep some nights. I was often sleeping so deep and peaceful they couldn't wake me and they used to have to carry me back to the barn.

There was always something going on at night time. The Welsh girls used to make their own little choirs up and sing for everybody. Some nights somebody would shout, 'FOLEY NIGHT TONIGHT!' Us kids would get all excited at the thought of going to the pub and then they'd turn round and say, 'You buggers better be in bed when we get back.'

'Oh, can't we come down?'

'You can come down on Saturday night, cuz you don't work Sundays.' We used to go down on Saturday nights but we still had to get up early on Sunday to go to church.

It was at the church that me mum had got to know the Mrs Davies that Joan went to stay with. Mrs Davies took a liking to our Joan and asked me mum if she could adopt her. Mum said, 'You can't adopt her but I'll let her come and stop with you for a holiday sometime.'

There was no buses or anything and nobody had cars. One or two people had pushbikes but mostly everybody walked everywhere. It was a two-mile hike to the Foley and we all used to go together. Coming back along the road there, the grown-ups would be singing all the songs – drunk out their bleeding minds! Occasionally you'd hear a yell and that would mean somebody had fallen through a hedge, or fallen in a ditch, or summat. It used to be great. My mum never used to get drunk, though.

If it was a warm enough day, me mum would say, 'You had a bath?'

'No.'

'Get your towel and go off down the river.' There was a river coming past – not dangerous or anything, you could walk across it. You'd sit in there and it was great, especially if it was a really hot day. You used to see blokes and girls stripped naked, washing down, with their clothes hanging on a tree. Nothing ever went wrong amongst it. You never found that some bloke had assaulted a girl because these girls were standing in the water in the nude – none of that. I should imagine it was like in the beginning of the world when people walked around in the nude and nobody noticed.

When Dick come with us, he never helped out much. He was always chasing these Welsh biddies round the haystacks. I got some smacks in the ear from him over that. We used to climb up on top of the hayricks and spy on him. Once, him and a mate of his and these two Welsh girls were down below performing and I give this kid I was with a shove and he crashed down on top of them. All bloody hell let loose! We used to have some fun. I learnt more about life down there than I ever did at school.

I used to go and watch them put the hops in the big kilns to dry them out. The bags of hops would be stacked ten-foot high and a big stamper would push them down and shove them in the kiln. They was used to flavour beer and to make the khaki for army uniforms. It was an essential job. What they do now, they've modernised everything and the hops are picked by machines.

A lot of local people looked down on the hop picking but no end of them there had good numbers and didn't need to come. One woman, her old man was a Midland Red bus inspector. There was another bloke who was a train driver. What it was, was a paid holiday. You'd be surprised, come the end of the season, how much me mum had saved out of what we'd earned as well as feeding us.

7

A Storm Brewing

They was having the annual carnival in Warwick. All proceeds to
Warwick Hospital. There was a fair down on the park and the
Avon Street Boxing Club had got a big tent rigged up and the fella
on the front was asking kids to challenge his young boxers. I was
stood watching. Cocoa Harris tapped me on the shoulder. They
called him Cocoa because he was so dark from being out in all
weathers with his dogs. I think he was a gypsy. He was white, like.
Anyway, 'You can 'ave a go,' he says, picks me up and stands me on
the front.

Dick and Randolph were always interested in fighting but I
couldn't bear it. If people threatened me, I was away on me toes if
I could. But there was kids from Westgate watching and I thought,
'I can't get down now, cuz they'll take the mickey in school.'

Cocoa drags me across to another kid, Mickey Lawton, who's
about my size, and announces to the crowd, 'He'll fight this one.'
I'd had a couple of arguments with Mickey but it'd never come to
fighting. I was all of a tremble and he's there beside me shadow
boxing like a professional. I thought, 'Hello, I'm gonna get a
battering here.' I reckoned the only way I could stop Mickey hitting
me was if I kept hitting him.

We had a right old battle – hands going like windmills. First it
went one way, then the other – backwards and forwards. I was glad
there was only three one-minute rounds. At the end of it, Mickey
Lawton had a beautiful black eye and Cocoa Harris give us

sixpence each. I thought, 'Oooh, boxing ain't so bad!' I went back the next day but Mickey wouldn't fight me a second time.

It's funny, money always learned me. I didn't want a pat on the head, or one of them trophies, or a cup, or a shield, or a medal. It was money I wanted. I could give some to me mum then.

That fight with Mickey Lawton is why I count myself as the first of the Turpin brothers to have a professional fight – even if it was only for sixpence.

There was another kid, Frankie Walker, whose dad was the Metropolitan Police heavyweight champion. Frankie was a heavyweight an' all. He was two or three years younger than me but whereas he was really tall, I was really short. I used to have to go round and spar with him. Well, I thought I had to. Mr Walker told me one day, 'I want you to help train our Frankie.'

'I don't box, Mr Walker.'

'Oh yes you do,' he said. 'I saw you at the Warwick carnival.'

I thought, 'He's a policeman. If I don't do what he wants, he'll pinch me for summat.' I used to have to go to the Bear and Bacculas, I think, on the corner of Brook Street near the West Gate. I got some horrible hidings off Frankie.

Halfway up the walls in the room we sparred in was panelled with wood and he used to smash me against that – no ropes or anything. He'd come tearing in BANG! BANG! BANG! I used to think to myself, 'You're a bloody fool doing this for a bag of toffees.' So this night, we're down there and his dad ain't come and I got lucky and hit Frankie with a cracking left hook. His legs went funny and I thought, 'Hey, you can hurt him!' He comes steaming in and lets go with a big right-hand. I turned to the side and it whistled past, SMACK! I looked round and Frankie's fist's stuck in the wooden panelling. The wood's splintered inwards and he can't pull his fist out. While he was fastened in there, I had a birthday. I punched him up the trousers and he went down on his knees. I blacked his eye and knocked seven bells out of him. I took me gloves off and went home. I thought, 'The times old man Walker's smacked me round the face for chasing cows on the racecourse, at least I've got my own back on his kid.'

By the time his dad come to collect him, Frankie'd got free. Mr Walker asked, 'Where's Jack?' Frankie could have got me into trouble but he didn't. He just said, 'He's gone home.' The next time I saw Mr Walker he asks me, 'When are you coming down to spar with Frankie?'

'I ain't gonna come down no more, Mr Walker,' I told him. 'He's too big, I can't get near him.'

'All right, Jack,' he said. 'Just come and train with him then.' So I just used to train with him. No sparring.

Frankie was boxing on a show once at Upton House and his dad took me with them. Orme Tyler, from Kineton, was organising it. He used to have eight lads dressed all in white. They toured round the country as 'The Kineton Sparring Eight'. He put blacking on their gloves and they'd spar with each other.

The target area in boxing is the front of the body above the waist and the front and sides of the head. Punches that land behind an imaginary line down the middle of the sides of your head and body or below your belt are fouls. The blacking left marks on their opponent's white boxing gear so's you could see who was landing the vital shots. It looked fantastic. They'd got other boxers on besides this team and one of them was left without an opponent. Tyler come across to Frankie's dad. 'Do you think he'll box him?' he said, nodding towards me. I was about 11 then but I was stodgy, so I looked a bit older.

Mr Walker said, 'Yeah, Jack can box him.' I took a look at my proposed opponent, Titch Kellow – a stable lad, bigger than me. 'I don't wanna box 'im, Mr Walker,' I said.

'It'll be easy for you, Jack,' he assured me. I took another look at the kid. He seemed even bigger than he had the minute before.

'I *really* don't wanna box him,' I said. 'Look at him, Mr Walker, he's got long trousers.'

Mr Walker seemed upset. 'See that little man there?' he said, pointing to Orme Tyler, who was walking back over to the ring. 'He's told everybody you're going to box and you'll make him look stupid if you don't.'

'I don't care.'

'You'll have everyone round here saying you're chicken.'

'I'll say it then. I'm chicken.'

'Dear me,' he sneered, 'I thought you Turpins were supposed to be tough.'

They eventually talked me into it. I sat in the corner shivering from head to foot. The bell went and I shot off the stool, ran to the centre of the ring and threw a wild right-hand at the kid. It missed by miles but on the follow through our heads collided – CLUNK! – and Titch Kellow's eye was split wide open. I leapt back out of the way, blood splattered all over the place and the referee

50

stopped the fight. I thought I was in trouble till somebody shouts, 'Bloody hell! What a punch!' and suddenly they're clapping me on the back. 'What a punch, kid. What a punch!' They presented me with a yellow medal on a red ribbon. I thought, 'It must be gold.'

I see Titch Kellow in the street a few days later with his eye all stitched up. I stopped to talk to him. 'What school do you go to?' I asked.

'I don't go to school,' he said. 'I'm 16.'

'You sneaky git!' I said. 'I'm only 11.'

'Well,' he said, pointing to his eye, 'you can't half punch.' I felt about 20 ft tall.

'You're very lucky I didn't lose my temper,' I told him.

I took my medal to the jewellers. 'I've just won this. How much is it worth please, Mister?'

The jeweller smiled. 'It's worth as much as you put on it, son.'

'Five pounds! Would you give me five pounds for it?'

He laughed. 'I wouldn't give you tuppence for it,' he said.

I thought, 'That's it. They've screwed me.' And that's why my whole amateur career lasted for only one punch and that wasn't really a punch at all.

While our Joan was away on the farm in Wales with Mrs Davies, it left me, Randolph and Kath with nobody looking after us. We'd go scrumping; we'd go and fight the kids along the bottom of Parkes Street; we'd go round all the other streets on Packmore's and fight the kids there. If we weren't doing that, we'd be knocking doors and running away. There'd be people in the street shouting, 'I'll knock their sodding 'eads off!' and we'd run down the Wallace and dodge round the back of Eagle Engineering where they'd got these piles of planks that they used to make trailer bodies with – just sliced rashers of trees. Cuz of their funny shapes and the way they were stacked, they made little rooms we could hide in. We used to have gang meetings and all sorts of games in those planks.

We took the front forks and wheel off of somebody's bike and rammed it into the planks to make a ship's wheel. The *Queen Mary*. When any new kids come to play, we'd let them steer the ship. They thought it was a real honour. They'd stand there turning the wheel, ploughing the imaginary waves, not noticing that the rest of us had crept off to hide round the sides with buckets of water. Somebody would shout out, 'OH NO, THERE'S

A STORM BREWING!' and WHOOOSH! WHOOOSH! some poor little bugger would go home drownded.

My mum was as bad as any of us. If she come down there and we was playing *Queen Mary*, she'd get a bucket of water and chuck it over *us*. 'Well,' she'd say, 'you was in the storm an' all!' She was a great lady, she was. We regretted how much work she did but there was nothing we could do. When she did have a couple of days' break, instead of being in bed resting, she was with us for the whole two days, playing games and running about.

Warwick has an annual fair called the Mop and our mum used to love riding the painted wooden horses on the merry-go-round. She was a big kid at heart. I think that's what affected us so much. I mean, we didn't see her very often but when we did see her she'd play for hours with us.

As soon as Joan come back, me and Randolph were her charges. We played her up something rotten. Randolph was on the go the whole time and I wasn't much better. She pulled us out of the canal once. It was the middle of winter and the canal had a thick layer of ice on it, so, instead of using the bridge, I decided to walk across. I was doing all right, then: CRACK! I dropped straight through into the water. The water was deep near the bridge. At the same time, Randolph tried to jump from one bank to the other and crashed through the ice as well. I was close to the side, so Joan hauled me up on the towpath by my hair. Randolph was further out, thrashing his arms trying to stay afloat. Joan couldn't swim but she never thought twice about it, she leapt in the freezing water and dragged him out.

'Keep it up,' me mum would say, 'and I'll have you put in a home.' We tried not to upset her but we just couldn't help it sometimes. I think it was with there being a lot of us. You had to shout before anybody would take any notice of you, and we'd all got tempers.

After he'd got over his illnesses, Randolph was a bleeding demon. I remember him chasing our Dick from Wathen Road, along here, up what we call The Park, under the railway bridge, through Warwick Market Place, down the main street, right the way round, up through the station and back here, waving an axe. Dick had upset him over summat or other and, all the time he's being chased, Randolph's yelling and swearing at him. Dick run in the house and got behind our mum. Randolph comes in waving the axe and shouting, 'I'LL CHOP HIS BLEEDING HEAD OFF!'

and I think he would have done if it hadn't been for me mum stopping him.

I hit Randolph with a cricket bat once and jumped over a fence to get away. As I was running off, I felt something hit my arm. When I got in the house, a knife was stuck in it. I'm not akidding you, Randolph didn't have to be a boxer, he could have gone in the circus throwing knives. He had three of them and when he was older, he used to get Dick's son, Howard, to stand against a wooden fence and throw these knives round him. Plus he'd got an old cut-down bayonet. He used to throw this bayonet right down the middle above Howard's head. Howard used to stand there and not blink an eyelid. Me mum used to have pink fits. 'You'll kill somebody!' she'd say.

Randolph had a terrible temper but he never ever lost it in the ring and he never ever used it against kids or women; but if we upset him and didn't put plenty of space between us, we was in trouble.

I'd had a row with our Kath one day. She said summat nasty and walked off, so I punched her in the back. She whirled round and threw a hairbrush at me. It hit me in the eye and me eye come out like a nut – almost popped out of its socket. That's when I decided I was gonna leave home and join the navy. I think I was thirteen then and Randolph was ten.

I put some clothes in a carrier bag, and said goodbye to Randolph. 'I'm going in the navy,' I told him.

'If you're going, I'm going,' he said. So he packs a bag an' all and we set off. I'd heard you joined the navy in Coventry.

We're hiking up the road and it's starting to rain and it's getting darker and darker. We get to the other side of Kenilworth and the road there is as straight as a die to Coventry. It's the middle of the night now and it's bucketing down. We're trudging along and I kep' looking behind me, seeing all sorts of ghosts and ghouls coming out of the trees. I put my arm around Randolph's shoulders and the water squelched out of his jersey. I took my jacket off and wrapped it round him. It's black dark and the more we walked, the further the road seemed to be stretching. I stopped. 'Come on, kid,' I said. 'We're going home.'

When we got back to Wathen Road, I stood Randolph at the front door and nipped round the back to let us in. The kitchen door was locked, so I thought, 'We'll have to try a window.' I went to fetch Randolph but he's gone and the front door's wide open. I walks in: CRACK-BANG-WALLOP! 'I'LL GIVE YOU TAKING HIM OUT IN THIS WEATHER!' Mum stripped Randolph's wet clothes off him, towelled him down, put him in some clean dry clothes and shoved him off to bed with hot water bottles. I sat on the floor cuddled up to the fire with the steam clouding off me. I thought if I kept quiet she'd forget I was there. 'As for you,' she said, BANG! 'get them wet clothes off and get to bed. And don't sleep in his bed, sleep in the other one.'

'The other one?'

'The one on the floor by the wall.' So that's where I had to sleep – on the floor by the wall. I was lying there in the black dark and I heard Randolph say, 'Pssst! Jack.'

'Go to sleep,' I whispered, 'You'll wake mum up an' I'll get another walloping.'

'I on'y wanted to know you was all right.'

'Yes, ta. Go to sleep.'

'Are we joining the navy tomorrow?'

'Shhhh! Lick, *please*!'

Granddad Whitehouse was sensitive to the fact that we'd have to stick up for ourselves more than other people, with our mum marrying a black man, and he was an absolute stickler about defending yourself.

I come in to him one day in tears. Me nose is split, me eye's closed and me lip's gone. 'Look what Jack Parsons done, Granddad.'

Granddad says, 'Get back out and fight him again.' I was scared but if Granddad told you to do summat, you did it. But Jack Parsons was three or four years older than me and I couldn't reach no higher than his chest. I got another pasting and went back to Granddad. 'Get back out an' fight him again,' he said. I trundled off to have another go and got hurt even more. I went back really wailing this time. Granddad stabbed his finger in the direction of the door and shouted, 'GET BACK OUT THERE AN' FIGHT HIM AGAIN!' The fourth time I come back crying, Granddad raised his eyebrows. 'How big is this kid?' he asked. I held me hand in the air a few inches above my head. 'Well then,' he says, 'you've got a good pair of boots on you, son. Use 'em.'

'Thank you, Granddad!' I said, and ran down Parkes Street to Jack Parsons, grabbed him round the waist and clung on for dear life, paddling away with me boots as hard as I could. I was knocking chunks out of his shins and he fell to the ground hollering and clutching his legs. I caught holt of his hair and whacked his head up and down on the pavement until there was no fight left in him, and walked home chuffed to death.

Dick used to talk me and Randolph into sparring with him in Granddad's back yard. 'I won't hit you,' he'd say, but we always ended up going in the house crying. He was sparring with me cousin Bill one day and Granddad says to Bill, 'I'll fight you for a pint.'

'OK,' me cousin says. Granddad held his fists turned forwards up by his eyes in the ol' bare-knuckle style. Bill squared up orthodox. Granddad twisted his left hand in the air. Bill looked up at it and Granddad's right hand shot out and knocked Bill flat on his back, out cold. Granddad bent down, took the price of a pint out of Bill's trouser pocket and went off down the pub.

He made sure we all stuck up for ourselves, Granddad did, but he never showed Dick any proper boxing. That was Mr O'Leary.

8

You Gotta Fight Back

He had four or five daughters, Mr O'Leary, and the eldest one took a shine to us and used to take us to their house. Their dad had done a bit of boxing and after he saw Dick and his mates messing about with some boxing gloves in the street, he started showing Dick the fundamentals of boxing.

Three lads used to come to Westgate school on pushbikes from the village of Long Bridge. The eldest, Tommy Trustlove, was a big lad with a taste for a battle. Kids are always on about who's the best fighter in the school and Dick and Tommy had risen up the playground ranks until it could only be those two it was out of. At dinner times, the three lads used to sit in the playground and eat their sandwiches. Dick suggested they went with us to our granny's house. They started coming there regular every dinner time, bringing a packet of cocoa powder that me granny would make up into hot drinks for them. Tommy and Dick still argued over who was the best fighter and after Dick started learning off Mr O'Leary, him and Tommy decided to join the Catholic amateur boxing club held in the school down the road from us in Warwick.

There are some things in boxing, you've either got it or you haven't. It's to do with your hand-and-eye coordination and your balance. Dick turned out to be a natural. By the time he left Westgate in 1934, he was recognised as without doubt the best fighter there and he'd also become undisputed best boxer at the Catholic place. He got bored of the lack of opposition and joined the boxing team at the Liberal Amateur Boxing Club in Leamington. They had some real good fighters but it wasn't long before Dick was the best there an' all, winning seven out of his nine contests.

Before my set-to with Jack Parsons, I'd had another fight. I used to walk to school with a girl named Rene Cox who lived in Parkes Street. I was usually ever so careful: DON'T HOLD HANDS NEAR THE SCHOOL OR THE OTHER KIDS'LL TAKE THE MICKEY but this day I forgot. We come out of Theatre Street still holding hands and a big cheer went up from all the kids. Rene went off to the girls' school and I went down to the boys' playground.

This kidda, Percy Jones, starts saying things about me and Rene. It worried me but I pretended to ignore it and I walked away. A little later on, I went to the toilet and Jones sends this little kid in, Dickie Savage, to start on me. He'd got a posse of his mates with him. 'You're shagging her, aren't yer?' he said. I didn't know what it meant at the time but all the other kids sniggered, so I knew it was summat dirty. I thought, 'Keep on and I'll give you such a smack in a minute.' The kid kep' on and kep' on, so, BANG! he went arse-over-tip out of the toilet into the playground. Before I had a chance to do anything else the kids were crowding round me shouting, 'HE'S HIT DICKIE SAVAGE!'

'I didn't! I didn't!' I said, trying to get out of it.

A muffled voice come from the back, 'Yeah, yer did. You smacked me in the mouf.'

'But you was saying filthy things,' I pleaded.

'That's besides the point,' some other kid chirps up. 'You've got to fight now, after school.'

'I'll fight him anytime,' I said.

'Not him,' they told me, 'his mate' – and Percy Jones steps forward. My heart sank. Since Dick'd left, Percy Jones had the reputation of being the best fighter in the school.

Johnny Turpin's fighting Percy Jones! It spread like scarlet fever.

I'd got it all planned: as soon as the bell went for going home I was gonna be up out of me seat and away. If I could just get through the main gate onto the street, I'd break all records back to Wathen Road where I'd be safe.

The bell rang and I raced out the classroom, across the playground, whizzed through the gate and run SMACK! into a solid pack of them. They'd read my mind. They bunched round me chanting, 'Fight! Fight! Fight!' and marched me up to the racecourse. Percy Jones elbowed his way through the crowd and stood in front of me. I nearly passed out.

Jones looked me up and down, clenched his fists and started. Everything sort of clicked into slow motion. He hammered his fist into me mouth and stepped back. I was glued to the spot. Jones waited a few seconds and when he got no reply, he slammed his fist into me face again. A voice in my head shouted, 'DO SUMMAT! DO SUMMAT!' I made a weak gesture of a punch but Percy Jones brushed it aside and socked me in the eye. He followed it up with a bang on the mouth that left me drinking blood. I felt like I wanted to die.

He started pounding away at me with both fists. I thought, 'Sit down on the floor, then it'll be over.' I was dying to sit down so's he'd have to stop hitting me but the voice inside me was shouting, 'YOU GOTTA FIGHT BACK!' I swung my fist with all my might full in his face: ZZZZONK! He went down flat on his back and a fountain of blood come spouting up from his nose: CHOOCH . . . CHOOCH . . . CHOOCH . . . CHOOCH . . . Most of the kids ran off. A few of them hung around in the background watching Percy Jones's blood rising and falling.

My hand was all bust up, my right eye was completely closed, my left eye was severely bruised, my mouth was swollen over to one side where he'd cut me lips on me teeth and me ears were swelled. I looked at Percy Jones lying there. I didn't know what I was supposed to do, so I started walking slowly home.

My clothes were covered in blood and I knew how hard me mum had worked to buy them and how hard she'd worked washing and ironing them. I was dreading getting in and copping another hiding. I wished I was dead.

I got in the house and me mum started. A kid from down the street had followed along behind me and he come in. 'It wasn't his fault, Mrs Manley. The kids made 'im fight. That Percy Jones didn't harf wallop 'im. He looks like a train's 'it 'im, don't 'e?'

'Who's this Percy Jones?' me mum asked, looking like she wanted to kill somebody.

The next day at school, word had got round about what I'd done to Percy Jones: 'HEADMASTER'S STUDY!' I anna kidding, my knees was knocking like castanets. I used to get the feeling I could never do anything right. My face was still a mess but the headmaster don't even bother looking at me: WHACK! WHACK! WHACK! WHACK! WHACK! WHACK!

The next day, me mum paid him a visit. She left me stood in the corridor outside his office, strode in and slammed the door behind her. I didn't hear any yells or raised voices and she never told me what she said or did to him. All I know is that for the six months I'd got left at Westgate, the headmaster was very, very careful with me. It was the longest period of my life I'd ever gone without the cane.

When Percy Jones come out of hospital, he shook my hand and said, 'You've got my title now, John. You're the best fighter at Westgate.'

I was 12 years old when Dick made his debut as a professional boxer. It all hinged on a fella from Brunswick Street, Leamington Spa: Mr Middleton. George Middleton was a smartly dressed bloke with a pencil-line moustache and heavy-framed round glasses, and he invariably had a fountain pen in his top pocket. He was my mum's age and the eldest of six kids. Same as us, as a kid George'd had to earn as much money as he could, as soon as he could. He got paid to hold horses for people on the Parade in Leamington when they come to town in their pony and traps; he got hisself a pitch selling newspapers and learned to use his fists fighting off yobs who regularly tried to take his pitch off of him. He went to the National school at Bath Place, in Leamington, where Dougie Kensit was at later on. George's first proper job was as a baker's boy. He met Lily Sweet and got married and had a daughter, Josie, younger than us. A really lovely girl.

George had got a business brain. During the recession in the 1930s, he become a bookie's runner – collecting bets on the horses from people. I don't think you were supposed to do it, really, but he saved up enough from that and his other jobs to buy a newsagent's. There wasn't hardly any money around but George reckoned people always found a little bit for cigarettes and newspapers. He put Mrs Middleton in charge of the shop and got hisself another job as a tool setter for Lockheed. His spare time was devoted to sport. He was a bit of a snooker addict and one of the blokes he used to see down the snooker hall was a bookie, Clem Wharrad.

They were having a game one night and Clem said, 'I've seen this darkie kid boxing at the Liberal Club. He's a brilliant little fighter and I'm thinking of talking to him about turning pro under my management. Fancy coming along?' George went along but

Dick must have been having an off night. He won but he had to work hard to get the decision. Clem turned to George and said, 'He ain't ready yet.'

It'd got George thinking, though, and he followed Dick's path after that. When he thought Dick was ready to go, he approached him about it. 'Well, OK, Mr Middleton,' Dick said. 'But you'll have to see my granddad first.'

A real shrewd old fella was Granddad. He'd lost an eye when he was working at Eagle Engineering after he'd left the smithy – I think it was there. Summat blew up and a piece of metal blinded him on one side. His artificial eye was a bit smaller than his good eye. When I was little, I asked him, 'How did you get that marble in your eye?' I got a crack on the ear for that but, I anna kidding, that one good eye of his could see everything.

'Well, then,' Granddad says, after he'd heard George Middleton's proposition, 'let's have it in writing.' George didn't have any pre-printed contracts in those days, so they hunted around for some paper. All they found was this old envelope. They opened it out and George wrote down all what Granddad told him to. They both signed it and got me uncle Bill to sign it as a witness, and that was it. George showed it me not long before he passed on – the Turpin's first professional management contract handwritten on an old torn-open envelope. And that was how Dick got to take off his amateur vest and climb in the professional ring as a £2-a-time fighter. And that was the start of George Middleton becoming one of the most important people in our lives and one of the most important people in British boxing.

Like I say, George had got a business mind but mostly all he knew about boxing was from outside of the ring. What he needed was someone who knew the game from the inside, and knew it inside out.

9

Alexander and Moses

Mick Gavin was an Irishman from Manchester with a squint where he'd lost an eye. His real name was Michael O'Gara but he'd boxed under 'Gavin' back in 1929 before the rules come in and knew the fight game inside out, upside down and round the bends. George Middleton enlisted his help.

To us, Mick Gavin was 'Mr Boxing'. He was our trainer, second and everything. Your trainer is absolutely *all* to you. He should know when you're tired, when you're worried or upset, when you're hurt, when you've had enough and when you can do a little bit more. Mick only had to watch one round of a fight and he knew how it was gonna go. If Mick told you something and you acted on what he told you, you'd win.

Boxing people were forever asking him different things: 'How do you stop cuts?', 'How do you toughen up your skin?' an' all that. If he'd have been working out of London, he'd have been known all over the world. It was just he was in a little cow town like this.

The methods Mick used was really simple. Other corner men went up the hospital and got full-strength adrenalin to stop cuts. The first cut I got over my eye, Mick put his tongue into it, run it along the cut, closed it shut with his fingers and dabbed it with some clean cotton wool. After that, it got hit a couple of times in the fight but it never bled again.

When we was being driven back from fights in later years, we used to get Mick to tell us stories from his pro days. People like us, and even more so people like Mick from the generation before, didn't box carefully controlled careers, being babied through a series of buttered-up fights against safe opponents and earning fame and glory and millions of pounds in the process. We boxed for pennies and ha'pennies compared with what they get today. Even though boxing was *the* sport, there wasn't any thought of stardom involved. Of course, the better you got, the more money you'd earn and your pride made you want a good reputation in the boxing world – and that was a bigger world than it is today. I mean, the armed forces, schools, youth clubs, village halls, church halls, theatres, men's clubs, factories, fairgrounds and football grounds all taught boxing or put on boxing shows. The fight game in the 1930s, '40s and '50s was what football is now – the national game. There were thousands at it compared with hundreds today and you had to beat more and better people to be the best. There was fewer weight divisions and if you was champion of the world, you was just that – the best in the WHOLE WORLD, not just a section of it. If you was looking for a World title, your manager couldn't match you with the holder he'd weeded out as easiest to beat, cuz there'd only be one. Nowadays, with the WBA, WBC, IBF, WBO, WBU 'World' titles, it's like an alphabet gone mad and you'd have to win the whole alphabet before you could really consider yourself a World champion.

We trogged round the boxing halls fighting on locally advertised bills and fought countless bouts in fairground booths because we had the skill and dedication to do it, and cuz we'd earn more money than we could've otherwise. We took each fight as it come and tried to give the audience summat special. A lot of professionally licensed boxers had day jobs as well.

When he was on the circuit, Mick Gavin would take absolutely any fight offered him to earn a few bob. He even took on heavyweight champion Barney Tooley once. Mick was two divisions lighter than Tooley, so he wore a big overcoat at the weigh-in with a couple of house bricks stuffed in the pockets. Even then, he only come to 13 stone. They weren't nearly so bothered about weights in them days but it must have looked hilarious when they were stripped off in the ring – a thin un and a fat un.

Right at the start of the fight, Tooley telegraphed an almighty right-hander destined for Mick's head. Mick, thinking his hour had come, shut his eyes and ducked. Tooley's fist come roaring over his shoulder and demolished the corner post, and the whole ring collapsed. The contest was voided but both fighters were paid for turning up. They tried to stage a rematch but Mick always managed to be busy elsewhere.

Dick's professional debut was at Rugby on 27 September 1937 against a local fighter, Eric Lloyd. Scheduled for six rounds, Dick boxed real proper English defensive style with good counter-punches and he out-classed the Rugby fella. By the fourth round, the referee had seen enough and stopped the fight in Dick's favour. It was a great start to his career but his inexperience showed a week later in Coventry when he got caught with a punch that switched his engine off in the third round. You're only ever one punch away from triumph or disaster. A Welshman from Ogmore Vale done it: Trevor Burt. George told Dick, 'Don't worry, son, you'll have plenty more chances. I'll get Trevor Burt again for you.'

The trouble with getting knocked out is it makes you wary. A good gauge of your championship potential is how well you come back after a defeat; Dick won his next two fights and got his confidence back. In between those two fights, summat sad happened.

Granddad Whitehouse was 77 years old and had been ill for a while. Being like he was, he just carried on, refusing to acknowledge it. I was only a kid, so I never realised how bad he was. He'd got a duodenal ulcer and that's what he died of at home in Parkes Street. It must have burst. Me aunty Ethel who lived across the road was with him at the time.

'You little sweep!' he used to say to me. It was cuz I was always doing things I hadn't ought to do and he'd heard how mischievous chimney sweep boys were – but I didn't know that. One day I saw 'Ping' Warslow coming along the road with his bundle of sticks and his brush on his shoulder – we called him Ping cuz of the way he sounded when he walked with his artificial leg. 'What are you, Mr Warslow?' I asked him.

'What am I, son? I'm a bloody chimney sweep.'

'Oh,' I thought, 'that's what me granddad means.' I went home and tried to make my own broom out of a stick and some twigs. When Mr Warslow was doing Granny Whitehouse's chimney, I used to stop up the top of the garden by the pigeon house waiting for the brush to poke out of the chimney pot. I'd shout, 'IT'S COME OUT. IT'S COME OUT!'

'Thanks, son,' Mr Warslow would call back. There's an art to chimney sweeping.

I'm glad Granddad knew Dick was doing well at boxing before he died. He'd more or less brought Dick up, with me granny.

As promised, George fixed Dick up with a return fight with Trevor Burt. This time Dick took the Welshman for a points win. Dick finished 1937 with eight fights behind him. Seven wins, five inside the distance.

George had started Dick off with four- and six-rounders. Now 1938 had come around, Dick was fit enough and experienced enough to train for eight- and ten-rounders. He only lost three out of his fifteen fights. He was climbing the ladder.

Dick had been pro about twelve months when George Middleton come round me mum's house and me and Licker were sparring about in the back garden with an old set of gloves. If we couldn't get hold of any gloves, we'd have two handkerchiefs wrapped round our hands. Anyway, we was sparring and George was stood watching. He said, 'I'll take you two with us tomorrow night.'

'Where to?' we asked him.

'Evesham.'

'What for?'

'You can box.'

'Oh yeah!' Randolph said, grinning his head off, but I said, 'I ain't gonna box, Mr Middleton.' George looked disappointed.

'You'll get some money,' he told me.

'Eh? How much?'

'Well, it depends on how much they chuck in the ring.'

'An' we have all of it?'

'Between you, yes.' Now we both thought it was a good idea.

That day, when we'd been sparring, Randolph had knocked me into a dustbin and I'd cut me eye and had a plaster put on it. When we was fighting for the crowd in the evening, he never once hit me on that eye. He could have done but he was too honourable. I wasn't. I knocked seven bells out of him. I used to have him in tears and he HATED giving way to crying. I won easy but the boxer Larry Gains was there and he come down to the ring and says to Randolph, 'Come and see me when you're 16, son. I'll make you champion of the world.'

I thought, 'I used to think you was a good fighter, Mr Gains, but I don't like you any more. How come Randolph gets all the offers when I've just beaten him?'

I anna kidding, they took a collection and come back with two fire buckets full of money. It was sixpences and shillings, not just coppers. We'd got more from our nobbins than Dick had got for topping the bill. That was one of the reasons Dick was needled about me and Randolph, I think, cuz we got paid more than him when he was going round topping the bill at places. What made it worse for Dick that night, he lost on points.

We carried on doing the fill-ins during the intervals of boxing shows and somebody says, 'They're like Alexander and Moses, ain't they?' – two comedians that were touring the music halls. Blackface comics, I think. George liked the sound of that, so Mrs Middleton made us red velvet knicks with a mauve stripe down them and a mauve waistband with an 'A' on my leg and an 'M' on Randolph's leg.

The Alexander and Moses things were 'no-decision' exhibitions – not really contests to find a winner. Pro fights, you go all-out to win; exhibitions, you box so's to let each other go the distance – usually three or four one- or two-minute rounds – and you just try to show how good you are at boxing, but I was bigger and heavier than Randolph in those days and I used to give him some right ol' leatherings. I couldn't help it. He was to pay me back later, though, with bells on.

Quite often when we were all pro and two of us were on the same bill, the other one of us would fight an exhibition in between the official matches to earn some money. Sometimes we'd all be invited to a show and Dick and Randolph would box and I'd be the referee. It made a big attraction when all three Turpins could be seen together.

It was amazing how popular we was as Alexander and Moses and how much money we made out of it while we were still at school. It made a real big difference in our house.

When we was going to a show in Coventry, me mum told us about the orthopaedic hospital there that'd looked after our sister Kath. That night we give our nobbins to the hospital for what they'd done for her.

Randolph was coming up behind me at school by this time. He was in the Infants, where you'd got a mixture of boys and girls together. Then he moved into the big boys' school – 12 upwards. And when he moved there, one of his pastimes was fighting. He never fought anybody unless they upset him. He wouldn't pick on anybody. Most of the kids as lived down Wathen Road went to his school and that became his 'Westgate School Gang'. They was very, very much feared by the other kids. Not only the ones in his year but also the ones in the years ahead of him. He had a right mob and I'm not akidding.

The Westgate Gang had organised battles with other schools or, if they couldn't get them, with other streets. It goes without saying that Randolph left Westgate School as the third Turpin to be tagged 'playground champion'.

I had one more fight before I left Westgate. I fought and beat a kidda who was the postman's son and his dad come up the school after me and delivered me a first-class boot up the bum. As he was walking off, I shouted, 'OI, POSTMAN, I'M GONNA GET YOU FOR THAT!' cuz he'd humiliated me in front of the kids.

People write about us – particularly Randolph – having to fight colour prejudice. Randolph didn't have to fight colour prejudice. He didn't get any. As a matter of fact, we were pretty spoilt with people, as kids. With us being the only coloured kids round here, we were unique in our area. We had a great ol' life. Like, in the summer, all the tourists would come to Warwick and Granddad Whitehouse used to do the car-minding in the Market Place. We'd go wandering up there, taking him some sandwiches or something, and visitors would say, 'Let's feel your hair, son.'

I'd say, 'Get away!' Then they'd offer me money. I'd say, 'OK, you can touch it now,' and they'd feel me hair for a penny or tuppence, or even a shilling.

Our Dick, some tourist asked him, 'What tribe do you belong to?'

'The Nevawozza,' Dick says.

The tourist goes over to Granddad. 'Do you know those little darkie kids?'

'Oh yeah,' Granddad says.

'What part of Africa are the Nevawozza tribe from?'

'Say it slowly to yourself,' Granddad tells him.

'The little sod!' the bloke says, when he finally clicked on.

Our stepdad, Ernie Manley, always tried his best for us but I never got on with him. Well, not until I shot him. I did it with an air rifle in the leg. I can't remember whether it was an accident or on purpose. He sat down in the garden while I slowly dug the pellet out of his leg with a penknife. I was watching his face the whole time. He just stared straight ahead of hisself and didn't flinch once. After I'd levered the slug out, he held his hand out for it. 'Give me that,' he said, and he wiped the blood off it and put it in an envelope. 'Wherever I get sent,' he told me, 'I shall take this to remind me of the bugger as shot me first.' I didn't know what the bleeding hell he was on about.

After he'd sat there and let me dig that pellet out, I thought, 'Anyone else would have been yelling their heads off or smacking me stupid for doing that.' I told Randolph about it.

'Did he scream?' he asked me.

'No,' I said. We both thought Ernie Manley wasn't such a bad ol' sod after all.

A lot of people forget that boxing is the art of self-defence. Dick wasn't a dynamic puncher but, like I say, he was a great defensive boxer. He'd proved it by winning a lot, lot more fights than he lost, and he'd earned hisself a shot at the vacant Midland Area middleweight title.

His eliminating contest was against a fella with a perfect name for a boxer: Jack Hammer. The match, a 12-rounder cuz it was going towards a title fight, was in Northampton on 13 March 1939, with Jack Hammer fighting in his home town. You've always got an edge when you're local and Jack swung his leather hammers well, but Dick done enough to take the fight on points. He was on the championship road.

It's funny, but a lot of this stuff about Dick is what George and other people have told me over the years, cuz the rest of us never saw much of our big brother in those days. I knew he was doing well but I didn't know the details because I wasn't interested in hearing about boxing. Dick, on the other hand, was even more interested now he'd got a title shot. He kept himself busy before his looming championship contest with another five fights and he was warmed up and ready for a showdown with the other contender for the vacant area title, Jack Millburn.

On 22 May 1939, Dick out-pointed Millburn to become Midland Area middleweight champion. The Turpin family had got their very first professional boxing honours.

10

Can I Use Me Feet, Then?

A cocky little bantamweight was strutting round Germany promoting his own fights and seemingly aiming for a European title: Adolf Hitler. A veteran of my dad's war. So far, the British government had pursued a 'Policy of Appeasement', including getting the England football team to do the Nazi salute when they was over there.

Rumours were flying around about how Hitler was going to get us into a big war. I was only a kid of 14 and I thought it was all a joke, but it must have been what Ernie was thinking about when I'd shot him with the air rifle.

By 1939, Hitler had set his sights on Poland. Britain and France swore they'd come to her rescue if any jackboots goose-stepped over her border. But right now, it was ring wars not world wars that was mostly on me big brother's mind. Him and George were planning their next move. They would have to go for the British Empire middleweight championship, cuz the British Boxing Board of Control operated a colour bar stopping black boxers from fighting for English national titles. They'd let you be black in amateur boxing and other sports for national titles; but, even if you was born here black in professional boxing, you could only fight for area titles or the Empire title. Of course, if you couldn't get a national title you couldn't be lined up for a World title.

I left school that summer and went to work at Rotol's, a German-owned firm here in Warwick, for 3/6d a week as an apprentice tinsmith. I give three shillings to me mum and kept sixpence.

The top-class tinsmith at Rotol's was a cockney from Humphreys Street who'd been in the navy, so everybody called him 'Sailor'. He showed me how to make tin ashtrays and, apart from running errands for the foreman and helping to assemble the spinners, I made tin ashtrays. Hundreds and hundreds of tin ashtrays.

The spinners were aluminium nose cones for aeroplanes. I had to stand inside the cone and hold it onto the riveting dollies while Sailor pounded the ends of the rivets over with a machine to clamp the seam. To amuse hisself, Sailor used to run the machine directly onto the cone: **ZZZGONG!ZZZGONG!ZZZGONG!** . . . It was like being trapped inside a cathedral bell while a thousand heavyweights were trying to smash it to pieces with sledgehammers. I used to come out of there going round the screaming bend and Sailor would laugh his bleeding socks off. He done it three times one day and I thought it was about time I give him a bit of a shake-up. I waited till everybody had gone to dinner and I crossed the wires in his drill.

After dinner, Sailor starts drilling: D-D-D-EEEEEEEEEE . . . He's gripping the drill with the full mains voltage running through him . . . His eyes are bugging out like corks . . . EEEEEEEEEEEEE! . . . I realised what a stupid thing it was I'd done and snatched the plug out. He's on the floor: SWACK! I'd only wanted to give him a bit of a start and now I've bloody killed him. The foreman comes running over and, thank God, finds Sailor's still alive. He turns on me with a wild look, 'What a bloody good job you had the presence of mind to pull that plug out! He'd have 'lectrocuted hisself, else.' He give me a hug. 'Well done,' he said. 'You've saved his life!'

Sailor didn't come back to work for a good few weeks. He suffered from malaria and the shock brought the malaria on, and he used to go partially blind when that happened. It was quite a while before he got comfortable using the drill again.

By this time, I must have been the best tin ashtray maker in the whole of England and I was getting fed up with it. I asked George Middleton, 'Got any jobs at Lockheed?' Me and Randolph had stopped doing Alexander and Moses, cuz I was too big, but George always, always looked after us. He was in charge of his section by then and he'd already got Dick a job there.

I'd just started at Lockheed when it come in the papers that

Germany had invaded Poland. This was supposed to be the trigger point of British involvement and, sure enough, two days later, at quarter past eleven on Sunday morning, 3 September, the Prime Minister's announcement come over the wireless: **'This country is at war with Germany.'** Neville Chamberlain had sounded the timekeeper's bell for round one of Britain's inclusion in the biggest fight the world had ever known. There was no talk of this one being over by Christmas and no one was cheering.

Ernie Manley was on the reserve list of the Royal Engineers. He got his papers out:

In the event of an emergency report
immediately to Aldershot.

First thing Monday morning, Ernie packed his bags and went. He'd been in France three months before his papers come actually calling him up.

Apart from Ernie going, life here went on pretty much the same in the beginning. The Great War of 1914–18 become officially known as the 'First World War' and the government took Rotol's off its German owners. Old Sailor had some extra aeroplane nose cones to make but people still wanted tin ashtrays. Actually, life was better for me, cuz my new job, centreless grinding, was paid on piecework. My mate Harry Holland was the setter and I used to go to work in style on the back of Harry's Matchless Silver Arrow motorbike.

When you needed your grinder resetting, you clocked on a 'Waiting' card. Of course, you wasn't earning any bonus then but Harry used to come to me first, so I was really clocking up the money and able to give both me and me mum a pay rise. After a while, I learnt to do me own setting. When I retired in 1986, the foreman said I'd been one of the best-paid workers there.

Me and Harry decided to join the Home Guard together. They made him a dispatch rider cuz of his motorbike. When I asked them to make me a dispatch rider an' all, they said, 'But you haven't got a motorbike, Turpin.'

'Can't I go on the back of Harry's?' I asked them. They thought not.

Dick rounded the year off with two winning fights in the same month with the same fella: Ben Valentine. Ben was from Fiji and, I think, the first black fighter that Dick was matched with.

In early 1940, Dick drew against a South African, Eddie McGuire, which meant a re-match. I found an old boxing programme for it the other day. A Jack Incley promotion at the Tower Ballroom, Edgbaston. Monday, 20 May 1940. It's typical of the sort of tournaments they had during World War Two. Proceeds were for the Lord Mayor of Birmingham's War Relief Fund for Men and Women in HM Forces:

SMASHING TEN (3-min.) RDS. RETURN
MIDDLEWEIGHT CONTEST
DICK TURPIN
LEAMINGTON. This 19-year-old sensation is being
tipped to be our next Middleweight Champion
EDDIE MAGUIRE
SLOUGH. Middleweight Champion of South Africa.
Undoubtedly the most popular Boxer ever to appear
in Birmingham

Ticket prices were from one-and-sixpence to a guinea. Len Harvey's on the bill – British and Empire heavyweight championship – boxing three exhibition rounds. Ginger Ward, a welter, is billed as 'Chief Sparring Partner to Dick Turpin'. He was a Welsh lad with a cracking left hook: one of George's fighters, cuz George had a few more by this time. I sparred with Ginger once, before I was really boxing, and caught him a beauty on the chin with a lucky right-hander. I saw the rage flare up in his eyes, so I slipped me gloves off and said, 'Thanks, Ginge, that'll do me for today', and ducked out of the ring quick.

Dick lost on points to Maguire but only just and it was a great showing on me brother's part. Before the end of the year, he beat Jim Berry, Tommy Davies, Paddy Roche, Albert O'Brien and Pat O'Connor – all good fighters – but come unstuck with hand trouble in his second meeting with Ginger Sadd, who suddenly become Ginger Happy when me brother was forced to retire in the seventh round.

Dick told me about his win over Paddy Roche. The fight had been staged at Nuneaton in the open air and he'd given the Irishman a right old spanking. Paddy had a real broad southern Irish accent and the biggest cauliflower ears you've ever seen. He

71

was interviewed by a boxing reporter after the fight. 'What happened there tonight, Paddy?' the reporter asked him.

'The trouble was,' said Paddy, 'it was getting dark, and Turpin kept hiding in the corners and jumping out on me.'

Dick ended 1940 as reigning Midland Area middleweight champion, with 454 professional rounds behind him in 54 pro bouts against 40 different opponents: 41 wins (6 by KO), 9 losses (1 by KO), 4 draws and no disqualifications. The papers said he was THE up-and-coming British middleweight.

When you sit on the bridge up at the Cape, you can look down into the goods yard where the trains stop. In June 1940, the troops were coming home from Dunkirk. The Royal Navy had rescued thousands of soldiers from the British Expeditionary Force off of the beaches – 'Operation Dynamo' – just before the fall of France and they'd left in a hurry. Some of the lads had lost all their clothes and had to grab anything as they could find. There was lads on stretchers being put into ambulances; lads on crutches; some with bandages on, an' all that, and who should step off the train? Ernie Manley dressed in a lady's shimmy and a pair of bedroom slippers. Laugh? I was nearly bleeding sick, I tell you!

I was bored to tears with factory work. Our Dick was earning more money than me and having more fun than me, and I started thinking about doing a bit in the professional ring meself. Dick, however, decided to put his career on hold and do his bit for his country. It was a huge decision to make, cuz even if he didn't get killed or wounded, his career could be ruined simply by spending too much time out of the ring.

Dick's job was to bring all the gear round to the different sections in the factory. Not a reserved occupation as such but George offered to get him upgraded to a better job so's he could be scrubbed off the call-up list. Dick said, 'No. I wanna go,' and, in 1941, he volunteered and was sent up north for training as a signaller – a non-combatant. That's funny, innit, for a boxer? He was sent to war with the Eighth Army. Boxing matches are often described as wars but this was the real McCoy – a fight of unlimited rounds against Rommel's Afrika Korps in the desert arena of El Alamein. A fight to the death.

Like I was saying, boxing had started to seem a good proposition. George didn't know how old I was, so I put my age forward to 17, got meself in training, had the medicals and applied for a licence from the British Boxing Board of Control.

George had linked up with a bloke a little bit older than him called Jack Solomons, the son of a fishmonger – Billingsgate an' all that. His parents were Polish Jews and he'd been brought up in the East End of London, buying and selling fish. I tell you, Solomons could've sold tap dance shoes to a school of conga eels. He'd done a little bit of boxing; but, with him being a natural wheeler-dealer, he went on the promotion side. He had his own club at one time: The Devonshire.

Solomons had a gymnasium in Great Windmill Street in Soho, opposite the Windmill Theatre – the one that 'Never Closed' during the war, where they done the nude tableaux. In those days, women could be in the nude as long as they didn't move, so they used to make out they were statues and blokes would pay to have a look.

Solomons' gym, I ain't akidding, everybody congregated there – in the gym, on the stairs, on the landings and in the offices – champions; contenders; retired professionals; boxing fans hoping to see big names; managers and promoters looking for deals; gamblers sniffing around for a good bet; reporters ear-wigging for stories; gangsters and hard men like Jack Spot, Frankie Fraser, the Kray twins and Charlie and their mates; actors and comedians like Bud Flanagan out of the *Crazy Gang* – practically anybody and everybody who was interested in doing or talking about boxing. Jack Solomons lorded it over the lot of 'em, arguing and shouting, cracking jokes and telephoning, and puffing away on his king-size cigars. All day long was like Paddington Station in the rush hour. There was some right dodgy-looking bleeders there an' all, with big overcoats on and their trilbies pulled down. It'd be the middle of the summer and they'd have their hands dug in their pockets and their collars turned up. I don't think he was a vicious bloke, Solomons, but I suppose he didn't have to be with the bodyguards he had.

The papers called him the 'King Outside of the Ring'. He had it all sewn up. He became the face of boxing in Britain – a matchmaker as well as a promoter. He'd got his own fighters and he was part of the British Boxing Board. He got to promote all the big contests in London. The London fights as had another promoter's name on the bill were usually doing it on Solomons' behalf, so they reckoned.

I'm not sure how big Solomons was when George met him but that's how big he got. I'm pretty certain Dick boxed on Solomons' first promotion at the Albert Hall. If you was in boxing, you *had* to know Jack Solomons. Whenever we was in London, George was always off to see him. Anyway, Solomons and George come with me to get my licence.

When it come to the bit where you have to swear you'll never use your fists outside the ring cuz they're lethal weapons an' all that, I asked, 'Can I use me feet, then?' The bastards fined me £5 for saying that. They don't like you being cheeky. Luckily for me, they called Solomons 'Jolly Jack' sometimes, cuz he liked a joke. He thought what I'd said was that funny, he paid the fine hisself.

Now I was a professional boxer, a mercenary of the ring. Fighting Turpin No. 2. I felt 20 ft tall. I must admit I broke that rule about not fighting out of the ring a few times. I always saw it as self-defence, though.

I went over the racecourse one day, messing about with a football with some mates, and there were some strangers over there. I kicked the ball and it hit one of them. He turned round and called me a 'black bastard'. I called him over. His mates grouped round ready for a ruck but as soon as I'd given him a punch on the nose, they backed off. 'He's just bad tempered,' they told me.

'Well,' I said, 'tell him, in future, when he speaks to anybody black, to address them properly. That way he won't get a punch on the nose.'

My professional debut took place in Leamington when I was two months into my sixteenth year. There was a closed-down golf course called Gulliman's where they put on an annual fair in the grounds, and they put boxing on each time. It was a real show with bouts at all weights. George put me up against a kidda from Leamington, Sammy Stopps, a mate of Dick's from when he was at the Liberal ABC. Stopps used to call me a 'cheeky little bleeder', cuz I took the mickey all the time and my jokes got on his nerves. I thought that was funny, cuz I was taller than him. He was big-built, though, and I knew he'd done a bit of pro boxing already. I thought, 'You're gonna get your wings clipped here, Jack.'

I went down to the ring shaking from top to toe. I was desperate to hit Stoppsy before he could hit me. 'Seconds out. First Round.' I flew off the stool and banged him between the eyes. He threw a few shots at me but they were out of range. 'Hey,' I thought. 'This is easy!' BOOM-BOOM-BANG! – no proper boxing, no proper footwork, just going round and round him – BOOM-BOOM-BANG! I was tripping over me own feet half the time but Sammy couldn't catch up with me and I hammered him into retirement in the third round. I thought, 'Jackie stops Sammy Stopps. How's that for a cheeky little bleeder?'

I'd really enjoyed training for that fight and, although I'd been as nervous as a kitten at the start – and it was years before I lost those pre-fight nerves – I'd successfully got my first proper pro fight under me belt and inside the distance as well. I took the purse and went home feeling proud of meself. Boxing was looking like easy money.

Mick Gavin had me in the gym concentrating on footwork and trying to get rid of a bad habit I'd got. When I ducked to avoid a punch, I looked down at the floor. 'NEVER take your eyes off your opponent,' Mick said, but I kep' doing it. After I'd done it about 20 times, Mick aimed a shot for me to duck under and when my head went down, he brought his knee up and banged me between the eyes. It knocked me sick but it learned me.

The next fight I had was in Coventry. Most of the fights there were at the Butts Stadium, open-air fights promoted by Jimmy Gough. They used to put a ring up in the middle, with a canvas ceiling to keep the rain off the ring, and the spectators sat round it. If it was raining, the fans put their umbrellas up or got wet. I was up against an Irish kid. Well, an Irish old man, actually, cuz I found out later he was old enough to be me dad. I boxed his ears off. Everyone was so chuffed with me, saying, 'You ain't 'arf done well there, Jack!' They kep' on and kep' on. In the end I said, 'How d'yer mean? He was an old man.'

'Yeah,' Mick Gavin says, 'but he's boxed two World champions.' The bastards never told me till afterwards. I suppose they was right, looking back, cuz confidence is everything in boxing.

It's funny, but that fight doesn't show up on my record. Even Vic Hardwicke, the best record compiler in the business, can't have found it written down. Nevertheless, it took place and it was another win for me. I can't remember the name of the Irish bloke but I do remember I got two £5 notes for each of those first two fights. It sounds a joke now but in those days when the average weekly wage of a factory hand in Leamington and Warwick was a lot, lot less than I was getting for a single fight, it wasn't at all bad.

The following February I was matched with a Londoner called

Eddie Giddings at some gardens in Northampton for a six-rounder. I anna kidding, I give him a boxing lesson, too. I tanked him. I walked it. I won easy. At least, I thought I had till they announced the decision. I'd lost on points. That sometimes happens. Referees ain't perfect. They're the third man in the ring but even they don't always get it right. You can get a referee who ain't paying proper attention, or one who don't know all the rules properly, or one who's biased towards one of the fighters for some reason. It's swings and roundabouts, though, cuz sometimes I felt I'd lost a fight only to be declared the winner.

The war had been going for nearly three years and I hadn't seen Dick for ages. Most blokes who've seen action don't really say much. You get labelled 'Big Head' if you talk about your war service and, more than that, you don't want to go through it all again. Our Dick never used to talk a lot of it but I know summat about what it was like for him.

It's just dust and sand and flies, innit, the North African desert? Unbelievably hot during the day and he was only allowed a couple of pints of water for drinking and washing and cooking and everything. At night, cuz there's no clouds to hold the heat in, it's bloody freezing.

Lieutenant General Montgomery, 'Monty', was only a little fella with a pointy face and a squeaky voice. He was put in charge in 1942 after Winston Churchill, who'd took over from Chamberlain as Prime Minister, had gone out there and seen the danger the Eighth Army was in trying to protect our oil interests in the Middle East. Egypt's oil supplies kept us going. Suez: lose it and we're knocked out of the war. Hitler knew that and put his top general, Rommel, in charge of his Afrika Korps with all the troops and tanks and guns he needed. Rommel was a brilliant tactician. In war, like in boxing, having a big punch helps but it's mostly tactics.

Rommel aimed a right hook at Monty but Monty saw it coming and drove Rommel back. Then he planned to chase Rommel out of North Africa altogether.

Churchill give him more and more troops – Australians, Indians, South Africans, Greeks and New Zealanders, as well as British – and more and more weapons till we'd got twice what the Germans had. Talk about me and Banjo with lead soldiers – the desert was absolutely covered with tanks and guns and anti-tank mines. The RAF provided air support and it was the sort of battle that my dad was in: attrition.

The Eighth Army battered Rommel back and the British and Empire troops marched into Tripoli. Bells rang out all over Britain when that news was announced. They'd fought their way from El Alamein, across the Libyan desert, through Tunisia and into Italy. They become known as the 'Desert Rats' after that. Loads of our fellas had been lost but, coupled with the Americans climbing into the ring, it was a real turning point in the war.

There was nothing Randolph liked more than a good fight – in school, in the street, he didn't care where – but there was more to him than that. Larry Gains had seen it in him and so had other people.

In 1942, when he was 14, he started going to Leamington Boys' Club. The boxing section of the Boys' Club had only been going a short while. A local police inspector, Inspector John Gibbs, run it. A great ol' fella. He was Simon Pure right down the middle. Amateur boxing was his life. According to him, professional boxing was a waste of time, cuz the boxers did all sorts of dirty tricks to win and got exploited by their managers and promoters.

Inspector Gibbs teamed up with another local bloke, Ron Stefani. His dad was an Italian ice-cream man. Ron had been an amateur champion at welterweight. I've seen him fight some terrific battles. He was a real good coach, Ron was, and exactly the same as Inspector Gibbs when it come to professional boxing.

When they'd got Randolph in their club, all the crowd round here started going: Mosh Mancini; Chick Checkley; Ladda Makepeace; Dumbo Jeffrey Abercrombo . . . I can't remember them all – they'd all got nicknames. Maurice Mancini, Mosh, was Randolph's best mate in boxing.

He used to have piano lessons, Mosh did, and going to his piano teacher meant walking past our house. He'd come along carrying his music case and Randolph would snatch it off him and throw all the music in the road. It was a regular routine and gradually they got talking and become friends. Mosh started to go boxing with Randolph instead of his piano lessons. He daren't tell his mum, so he'd set off at the usual time but instead of music in his satchel he'd have a pair of football knicks to go boxing in. His mum used to wonder why he'd stopped making progress in his music. He must've caught up with his piano lessons at some point, though, cuz you should hear him now.

Randolph told me how good it was at the Boys' Club. 'You ought to come along,' he said, so I put my coat on and went with him. I was sparring with him and he hit me hard. I went raving mad. I piled on top of him and lashed him with everything. He might have been Gibbs' and Stefani's shining light but I was a stone and a half heavier than him and I could handle him, which they didn't like. If me mum had found out, I'd have been for the high jump. With her nearly losing him three times, she allowed Randolph to talk down to us. That's why he was the bossy little sod he used to be.

They had another lad there they fancied as a good prospect: a lad with a hell of a big nose. He was one of them with really posh parents. They'd be in their smart suits and I'd got a patch in the back of me pants. I thought, 'I'll smash their posh boy for 'em.' We got in the ring but he'd got long arms and I couldn't get anywhere near him, so I dropped my hands. He dropped his hands an' all. Psychology, innit? I whipped my left hand flat over his face and punched the back of it: SQUERCH! Blood was spurting all over the place. Inspector Gibbs was outraged: 'GET OUT! THIS IS A BOXING GYMNASIUM. IT'S NOT FOR HOOLIGANS LIKE YOU.' He was a miserable cow sometimes.

I never told me mum what happened 'cept I'd been banned. Some time later, she asked Gibby why I couldn't go down any more. 'He's a bully with Randolph,' he told her. That made my mum roar with laughter, cuz Randolph was much bigger than me by then. I stayed little, like me dad, but Randolph and Dick got to nearly 6 ft, after Granddad Whitehouse.

Stefani and Gibbs was all over Randolph. He was the best thing they'd had there. Randolph would talk ever so nice to people he respected but if he didn't think much of them, he'd walk away when they spoke to him. With those two, it was, 'Yes, Mr Gibbs. No, Mr Stefani,' an' all that but when they wasn't around, he'd say, 'I don't know who they think they are. I do the bloody boxing, not them.'

He did respect Inspector Gibbs but not to the extent he'd grovel to him. He wouldn't grovel to no one. Ron was a weepy sort of fella. What he couldn't get by shouting he'd get by making you feel sorry for him. Some people get the impression Gibbs and Stefani taught Randolph how to box. Of course they didn't but they did show him how to build on what he'd got. We was still doing Alexander and Moses when Randolph started there and they used to get really shirty over it. Not long after he'd started at the Boys' Club, Randolph left school and worked for Bill Tarver, a builder and contractor here in Warwick, labouring for him.

It's hard to believe Randolph lost his first amateur fight, but he did. They'd put him up against a more experienced kid from the West Ham Boxing Club and he lost on points. But, as an amateur, in getting on for a hundred contests, including getting his own back on the kidda from West Ham, he only ever lost two other fights. People were saying he was the most naturally talented boxer they'd ever seen.

It wasn't the case in those days that a prospect would get sponsored by big-money people and do nothing but boxing. You'd have your day job but most bosses would give you time off for your fights, cuz they'd be proud of you. I'd have the afternoon off, have a bit of a sleep, then go out to my fight. You'd hope to get a few titles until eventually you was doing nothing but boxing and I felt I was on my way with one fight inside the distance, one easy points win and one dodgy decision loss but it was getting obvious that I was gonna get called up for war.

My heart was still set on going in the navy. When I told George I was going to volunteer, he kept saying, 'You don't have to go right now, Jack.' He was thinking of me being only a few fights into my boxing career and it being hard on me mum cuz she'd already got one son away at war. P'raps he didn't want nothing to happen to me neither. 'It'll come round quick enough when you've got to go,' he told me.

'That's just it, George,' I said. 'I want to volunteer straight away so's I can pick which one I'm going in to.' I wanted to make absolutely sure I got in the navy. If I was conscripted, I wouldn't get a choice.

I'd got a mate, Jackie Lewis, and we went over to Sibley Hall in Coventry. He went in as an artificer and I went in as an ordinary seaman. We come home and, after a short while, Jackie went off but I'm waiting and waiting.

After six weeks, there's a BOOM-BOOM-BOOM! on the front door. Two policemen are standing there. 'John Matthew Turpin?'

'Yes. What's up?'

'I'm arresting you for desertion from His Majesty's Forces . . .'

'Desertion? I'm still waiting for me bleeding papers to come!' The coppers laughed and said they'd look into it.

A few days later, a special envelope arrived with a pass to travel down to HMS Collingwood in Fareham, Hampshire, to report to this rear admiral. I was about to have the biggest fight I'd ever have: World War Two. This was one contest I was particularly anxious to go the distance in.

11

Lead With Your Left

HMS Collingwood is what the matelots call a 'stone frigate' – not a ship but a training camp – just inland from Portsmouth Harbour. When I arrived, there was a P.O. – a petty officer – standing in the doorway of the hut next to the gate. I held my letter out. 'I've got to see this bloke,' I said, pointing to the rear admiral's name on the bottom of the page. 'Where is he?' The petty officer waved towards some buildings in the distance and I set off, carefully stepping over a newly painted white line that was glistening on the road. On my way over, I heard someone shout, 'THAT RATING!' I carried on walking. The voice went up an octave, 'HEY YOU! THAT RATING!'

'Oh,' I thought, 'they must mean me.' I shouted back, 'What you want, mate?' The voice went ballistic. **'I AM NOT YOUR MATE! GET BACK HERE AT THE DOUBLE!'** I wandered over. The voice belonged to the petty officer. His face was crimson. 'What's up?' I asked him.

'YOU do NOT cross that white line.'

'I've got to see that rear admiral bloke,' I reminded him.

'NO, YOU HAVEN'T.'

'This letter says I have.'

'DON'T GET BLOODY CLEVER WITH ME!' I'm standing right next to the bloke and he's yelling like we're at opposite ends of Warwick racecourse. 'I'm beginning to wish I anna come,' I said, putting me bag down.

He rushed me and me bag over to this other hut, which was evidently where I should have reported to in the first place, and told me to wait there. Inside, there's a bloke lying on a bench behind some chicken wire. He's in civvies same as me. I give him a nod and he nods back. 'What you waiting for?' I asked him.

'Court martial. What you waiting for?'

'I'm six weeks overdue.'

'Hmm,' he said. 'Desertion.'

'There was a mix-up with the paperwork,' I explained.

'Well,' he said, giving me a funny look, 'you might get away with it.'

Just then, the officer from the front gate comes back and shouts, 'FALL IN.'

'What do you want me to fall in to?' I asked him.

'If you're always this witty, Sunshine,' he said, 'you're going to get into a lot of trouble here. ATTENTION!' I picked up my bag and sprang to attention in my best Home Guard manner, carefully stamping my feet as hard as he'd stamped his.

He marches me, at the double, across the parade ground to some huts and knocks on one of the doors. It's opened by this old doctor and I'm escorted inside. The quack says, 'Shirt off, undo your trousers.' He plonks a stethoscope on my chest, asks me for a few deep breaths, then shoves his hand under my privates: 'Cough.'

'ERHEM.'

'Get dressed.'

Next, I was marched over to Hut No.7 where I was kitted out with a sailor suit.

I'm sitting on me bunk when all the other lads started rushing out. I said, 'Where you going?'

'Fall in outside or you won't get no tea.' I fell in and off we go to the mess. No matter how much you had to eat, you was always hungry down there at Fareham. It was good food and everything but you'd lick the plate near enough and you were still hungry.

When the others had finished eating, they all got up and disappeared in a big rush. I goes tearing along after them and they zip into the canteen and queue up to buy cheese rolls. When I'd seen what they were doing, I got ahead of most of them. Fourth in the queue. 'Let me get there, Darkie,' this fella says.

'You don't think I've run over here like a bloody idiot just to let you get in front of me, do you?' I asked him.

'You either let me get there or you get a punch in the mouth,' he said.

'Listen, Sonny . . .' I began, POW! he punched me on the chin. I went down but I come off the deck like a ricocheting bullet and before he knew what was happening I'd hit him four times on the jaw. He dropped to his knees but his hands ain't on the floor, so I hit him again and stretched him out. Then the patrol come galloping in and I copped it on the back of the head with a rubber stick. A voice boomed, 'THERE'LL BE NO CANTEEN TODAY FOR ANY OF YOU!' The kid who'd started the fight had been helped up and as I was being marched past him he whispered, 'I'll see you later, you black-faced bastard.'

He'd sealed his fate by calling me that. He was a brave kid, though, cuz he did come after me, but I'd got round the back of the hut first. It was nearly evening and as he come out of the light into the dark, I hit him. Not just once – I fully sorted him out. Anyway, three days later he became one of my best mates.

I was always fighting in the navy and yet I was petrified. My mates used to say to me, 'Why do you shake so much?'

'I ain't shaking,' I used to say. 'I'm warming up.' I daredn't tell them I was afraid or they wouldn't have backed me up.

The navy could be a mad place at times. Don't get me wrong, I absolutely loved it but some of the things they did was just plain crazy. The suit they'd give me fitted fine. I got a real big kick out of it; I thought I was God. Then they said, 'Hat. What size?'

'Seven.' I took the hat and put it on. I'd got really bushy hair at the time and no sooner had I pulled the hat down into position than it shot up again and floated on top of me hair. I was making the lads laugh with it and an officer screams, 'HAIR CUT!' After a brisk short back and sides, the hat fell down over me eyes. 'Can I change it, please?' I asked.

'NO. YOU'VE DRAWN THAT HAT, YOU'LL KEEP THAT HAT.' Back in Hut 7, the fellas are taking the mickey: 'How you gonna see where you're going with that on, Darkie?'

'I'll show you,' I said. I got a pair of scissors and cut two holes in it for my eyes. That got me seven days' No. 11s for 'Defacing Government Property', which meant I had to pay for another hat and, after we'd been working all day long doing our written stuff, our square-bashing and assault courses, I had to go out again and run round the parade ground until someone come and yelled 'STOP!' I got me night leave cancelled an' all.

Something I've got to tell you about being called 'Darkie' in the navy. It wasn't anything bad. If I'd have been ginger, they'd have called me 'Ginger', wouldn't they? It was Darkie, Sunburn or Sooty, but never Blackie or Nigger. If anyone had called me that, the whole ship's company would've been after them.

A couple of weeks after doing punishment for ruining my hat, I was in trouble again. Our Kath sent a telegram saying Mum had been taken to hospital very ill. I went straight in and asked for leave to go and see me mum. I was told, 'No leave of absence for any reason whatsoever during your ten-week training period.'

That night, it was my turn on Fire Watch. I was pacing up and down alongside the perimeter fence thinking about my mum lying there in hospital. 'Fuck 'em,' I thought. 'I'm going to see me mum.' And, as soon as I'd thought it, I was over the fence and legging it for Fareham railway station.

The alarm went up and they reported me Absent Without Leave. It was obvious where I'd be heading for and they immediately dispatched a three-man patrol to get to the station ahead of me.

When I come up on the platform, I could see two of them walking up and down on the lookout. I tried to sneak round them but they spotted me and approached to put me under arrest. I wasn't quite 5 ft when I went in the navy. It must have looked like I was gonna be an easy job but I was still thinking about me mum, wasn't I? I'd put them both on the deck and was looking round for the third one when a couple of porters jumped on me back. The patrol leader rushed over. He was a petty officer and physical training instructor, and he give me a right pasting. I tell you, he really set about me. I thought, 'I'll get you later, you bastard.'

My mother had been taken to hospital for a stomach operation and she was discharged earlier than she should've been because they needed the beds for the wounded coming back from France. She could hardly stand up. The operation left her with a hole in her stomach as big as a half-crown and the nurse used to have to come each day to dress it. As soon as I got leave, I went home to see her.

I could have got court-martialled for going AWOL but the padre put in a good word for me about me mum. There was no way I wanted to get chucked out of the navy, I was that proud to be in it. I had my shore leave stopped for the six weeks left of my training and they let it go at that.

The same PTI as beat me up on Fareham station took us for

boxing training. If you didn't successfully complete your training at Collingwood, you got 'back-classed', which meant doing the whole ten weeks again. This Glasgow lad, Dutchy Houston, had been back-classed three times and they was always on at him. Dutchy liked me. I don't know why, cuz I was always bawling him out about one thing or another: 'For Christ's sake, press your trousers properly'; 'Why don't you wash your fronts?' 'Get away from me,' I told him once, 'you stink.' After that, he used to have six showers a week. He said to me, 'Hey, Darkie, can I stick with you?'

'Yeah, all right.'

One day we were being given boxing instruction and the PTI picked Dutchy as a 'volunteer'. He told him, 'I want you to lead with your left hand at me.' Well, anybody as knew about boxing, as soon as someone led with the left hand would immediately go over the top of it with a right cross. Dutchy Houston didn't know. As soon as he led with his left, this PTI socked him with a right cross and sent him reeling. He did it again and again, thinking it was hilarious. Poor old Dutchy. It was making me feel sick. 'Can I have a go?' I asked the PTI.

'Of course you can, Darkie,' he says, looking pleased. 'Lead with your left.' I just showed him me left and smashed him with a right to the jaw that put him on his arse. He got up and he's really angry. 'YOU DIDN'T DO WHAT I SAID. DO IT PROPERLY. LEAD WITH YOUR LEFT.' We squared up again and the fool fell for it a second time. This time I caught him with a beauty – straight in the balls! He reported me, of course. This officer got out my papers and asked, 'How do you explain your conduct with the PTI?'

'Sir, you didn't see the way he beat the shits out of that young kid there. He must think this place is hell, sir.'

'It's our business to sort that out, Turpin, not yours.'

'Yes, sir.'

'And I warn you, Turpin, that particular PTI is the wrong man to muck around. If you're not very careful, you'll be doing jankers all the time. You'd be surprised how many kids he's broken here. Don't let one of them be you, Turpin. Kiss his arse if you have to but don't ever cross him again.'

About a month after my do with the PTI, some of the lads went ashore for a pub crawl and, lo and behold, there he was sitting in one of the pubs. Every time one of the lads come back from the bar with drinks they made sure they spilled a bit on the PTI. Eventually, he'd had enough and challenged one of them to go outside. They all piled out and give him a real kicking, and there was nothing he could do about it. Shortly afterwards, he either got moved or applied for a transfer. Either way, we never saw him again.

In spite of getting in trouble so often, I passed out of Collingwood with some good marks and they put me through for a gunnery rating on close-range weapons. I was shipped out to gunnery school on another stone frigate: HMS Excellent, on Whale Island, off the coast of Portsmouth.

I thought Collingwood was tough but it was nothing compared to Whale Island. The assault course was twice as bad. When I'd finished it one winter day, I'd taken all the skin off me hands. I'd beat the course record at Collingwood – you're timed when you do it – and I was determined to beat the record at Whale Island, which I eventually did.

I was still managing to get into trouble. This officer asked me, 'How much does this 100 lb shell weigh?' It was so obvious that I thought it must be a trick question.

'I dunno,' I said. He made me carry the shell, on the run, all round the barracks until he shouted 'STOP'. 'How much does that 100 lb shell weigh?' he asked me again.

'A hundred pounds, sir?'

'That's all I wanted to know,' he said.

Whenever I was home on leave at the same time as me stepdad, he always saved one night to come out with me and my mates. He'd say to me mum, 'I'm going out with the lads.'

She'd tell him, 'All right, but don't come home screaming they've left you drunk somewhere.' When the pubs shut, see, we used to send Ernie home and go off to a nightclub. Ernie was usually that drunk, he'd get lost or fall over or summat. Once, he toppled down this slope and there were park benches dotted all around the place, and Ernie clouted each one of them as he rolled past. The next morning, he could hardly breathe. 'I've got pneumonia, Jack,' he gasped, and he was convinced he had till he discovered all the bruises on his chest.

Another time on leave, who should I see but the postman who'd kicked me up the bum in front of the kids in the playground. I crossed the road to him and said, 'Hello, Mr Postman. How would you like to try kicking me up the arse now?' He looked round to see who else was about. Nobody. 'Ah, Jack,' he says, backing off. 'Erm . . . You're in the navy then, son.'

'No,' I says, 'I'm in the army. They've given me the wrong uniform.'

'Don't let's fall out,' he says. 'Have a cigarette.' He was shifting about, avoiding looking at me, and I started feeling sorry for him. As I was accepting a fag, he suddenly says, 'Have them all', and stuffed the packet of 20 in my hand and got out of there as fast as he could.

I passed out as an Ack-Ack Gunner – Anti-Aircraft Gunner – Third Class. One morning, a few of us were taken by lorry from Whale Island to one of the big railway stations in London. We spent the night in the station and caught the train the following morning to Walker, on Tyneside, to pick up our ship. We were part of her pre-commissioning party and they were just fitting up her guns ready for her sea trials. She was a destroyer: HMS *Myngs*.

Destroyers are not very well armoured, so's to keep their weight down, but they're very well armed. They're small enough and fast enough to get out of trouble, which makes them ideal for anti-submarine and convoy work. HMS *Myngs* was Z Class, about 400-ft long, 1,700 tons, with a top speed of 37 knots – we did that an' all, a couple of times.

They made me 'Tankey' – assistant to the supply P.O. – looking after the stores and issuing food. I was detailed off as butcher and took over from a little fat kid called Day, the son of a butcher from Nottingham. They called him 'Happy' Day, cuz he was such a miserable-looking sod. The ship's crew was a complement of a couple of hundred and I prepared all the meat. Happy Day taught me the trade in one week.

The chief petty officer, Pusser Hill, was absolutely rigid on everything. When I was cutting up meat, up he'd stand watching me to make sure I was doing it right. When I was scrubbing up, he used to watch every little crack on the deck to make sure I got all the blood out. He said summat one day, I forget what it was, and I said summat back to make him laugh. 'What did you say?' he asked me. I didn't want to repeat it, cuz, from the tone of his voice, I thought he might put me on a charge, so I pulled a funny face instead. 'GET YOUR CAP!' he screamed. I had to double for'ard to get me cap and come back to be marched to the First Lieutenant on report. 'What is the charge?' the First Lieutenant asked.

'Silent insubordination, sir,' the Chief Petty Officer said.

'What form did this take, exactly?'

'He pulled a funny face, sir.'

'A funny face?'

'A look of dire disgust, sir. Like this.' He imitated the look I'd given him. I burst out laughing and I could see the First Lieutenant wanted to laugh as well. 'All right, all right,' he said. 'Take him away. Seven days No. 11s.' It got all round the ship. Blokes would say to me, 'Hey, Darkie, give us a look of dire disgust.' It got so common, even Pusser Hill used to get me to do it. Sometimes he'd laugh, then sometimes the bastard would scream 'GET YOUR CAP' and put me on a charge. Pusser Hill used to grin every time I walked past him.

We had a new officer come on board. He asked me, 'Where are you from, exactly, Turpin?'

I told him, 'England,' and he started laughing.

'What's funny, sir?'

'England, Turpin? You're black!' I'd noticed a twang to his voice.

'Can I ask where you're from, sir?'

'Australia,' he said. Now it was my turn to laugh.

'What on earth is funny about that, Turpin?'

'Well, sir, Australia, sir. You're white!'

'Just remember you are talking to an officer,' he said. I couldn't crib about any of my time in the navy. If I got into trouble it was because I deserved it.

Our first duties on HMS *Myngs* were patrols of the Norwegian coast. We'd set out from Scapa Flow, off the north coast of Scotland. Our skipper missed his way once and a message went out: 'HMS *Myngs* missing. Believed sunk.' The worst of it was, it was reported in our local rag and my mum read it. I came home on leave and she nearly had a fit when she saw me.

We were detailed at one time to shadow one of Germany's most feared battleships, the *Tirpitz*. We hit some rough water and our ship listed nearly 90 degrees. We chased the Tirpitz up and down the Norwegian coast and she took refuge in a fjord. We kept her pinned in there while RAF Lancasters tried to bomb her but she was under an overhanging rock and survived the attempt.

After a few months of Norwegian patrols, we were assigned to the Russian convoys, which meant sailing out of Scapa Flow up to Russia, to Polyarnyy – 'Pollyanna' to me – a naval base on the western side of the Kola inlet on the Barents Sea, part of the Arctic Ocean. Pollyanna's little more than a pile of snow down river from Murmansk.

We escorted merchant ships taking vehicles and tanks and aircraft and war materials up there. A 3,000-mile round trip. Cold?! It's further north than Iceland. The longjohns they issued us with were three-eighths of an inch thick. Lads regularly had to be sent up to chip the ice off the fo'c'sle. Just the spray off the sea was like somebody throwing a handful of needles in your face.

It wasn't just the freezing temperatures, the rough seas, the blizzards and the pack ice; there was the U-boats to worry about. They sunk a lot of our ships. We'd go for three or four days without any action, then all hell would break loose.

My mum used to worry for me that I was scared when I was on operations. I tell you, you didn't have time to be scared. But there were times when I really thought we'd be sunk. The seas were that rough, the boat would be going along tail down and nose up, and if you were going for'ard to aft, you had to tie your toggle to the lifeline or else you'd be lost overboard. The sea was that cold you'd be dead in a minute.

If you wore a steel helmet, you used to have to put layers of woollen underwear, or summat, in it to stop it freezing to your head and you used to have to wear a flannel mask when you was on lookout to stop your eyes freezing to the glasses. If you got a bit tense and you sweated, your sweat would freeze and you'd pull your eyebrows off.

We used to be turned-to on watch: 1st Dog, 2nd Dog, Middle Watch – all that. You had to scan 45 degrees and anything happening in your segment, you reported. I reported one of the ships we were escorting on fire once. HMS *Lapwing*, a sloop, on our port quarter. We were coming down the Kola inlet, trying to get the convoy in position, and there was a terrific BANG! The *Lapwing* had taken a torpedo amidships. Her back was broken. She split in half and went down. For a moment, she looked like two ships coming towards us. Of a crew of about 200, there was only about 40 saved. We weren't detailed to pick up survivors but we got one on board. He said he'd got in a little canvas lifeboat but the ones hanging on the sides of it gradually slipped away. Froze to death. A lad from Leamington was lost in that sinking.

Sometimes I'd be up there, on night watch, sitting in the gun carriage, traversing it round and round so's it didn't freeze up and it'd be so quiet and still I'd go in a kind of trance.

*

I'd saved some money in a little tin. My mum asked me what it was for. I told her it was to buy a train ticket to Heaven to see my dad. She told me trains don't go to Heaven.

*

When the next watch come to relieve me I said, 'I haven't seen anybody.'

'Who the fucking hell was you expecting to see, Darkie?'

I couldn't tell him I'd been half-expecting to see me dad. I had a bad bout of that in the navy.

The *Lapwing* sinking happened on one of our last runs to Russia. We got a 'ping' on the U-boat that'd done it and we depth-charged it for about three hours. We didn't get any wreckage but I like to think we hit it. Sometimes you'd see stuff coming up: somebody's cap, a suit, a slick of oil. It could mean a direct hit or it could mean they were sitting on the bottom waiting and had just released that stuff to fool you.

The U-Boats sent their torpedoes out in a fan shape – like a shotgun. The 'tin fish' left a white trail and if you could report it in time, the captain could take evasive action. We depth-charged a few subs in our time.

One day, we were dropping 'tin cans' on the subs when one of them went off too close to us and opened up a 47-ft split in our side. We were shipping water and had to put ashore while they done it up.

You know, I really swanked about in my naval uniform. When I come home on leave, Granny Whitehouse used to say, 'Here he comes, the bloody little admiral!'

12

Snowdrops and a Bowl of Maggots

I was in trouble with the Americans the whole bleeding time. They were stationed all around Warwick – mostly from the southern states: 'Whaaal, where y'all goin'?' an' all that. People think they must've been resented by the local lads because they were better off than us and brought nylon stockings and chocolate to turn the girls' heads but we didn't resent them at all. All's fair in love and war, innit? But, a lot of them resented me.

I went in the Castle Arms one evening and there's this girl, Olive Buckley, sat at one of the tables with a Yank. She'd got a harelip and used to talk funny. When the Yank sees me, he says, 'They ain't too pertickler who they have in the bars round here. Bloody niggers!'

'Oi, you ain't in the Deep South now, mate,' I told him, 'so keep your big mouth shut.' He narrows his eyes and says, 'You'd better back off, fella,' and Olive Buckley chimes in, 'Yeth, clear off, Jack.'

'Fuck you,' I told her. I know I shouldn't have said that but she used to court my cousin at one time. This Yank gets up to do summat but before he had chance to get started I kicked the table against his legs and let him have one on the nose as he fell forward. His nose split open like somebody'd unzipped it. I was gonna be in serious trouble if I got arrested. I turned to run out and, there, stood in the doorway, were two 'Snowdrops' – American military policemen – with their white helmets on. There was no back way out of this pub, only a yard with a toilet. I did the only thing I could do: I ran into the yard and stood waiting for them in the loo.

The Snowdrops come in twiddling their sticks and telling me what they was gonna do to me. I grabbed a mop that was leaning against the wall and jabbed it in their faces. I was holding them off but there was no way they were gonna leave.

I'm not proud of what comes next.

Never in my life have I ever fought with a knife but I was wearing one at the time and I thought I'd scare the shits out of them with it. I whipped it out and they immediately backed off and stood wider apart, looking serious. Now I had to swing the mop in a bigger arc to keep them both in range. I got one worked back a bit further and threw the mop at him as a diversion. He went to catch it, tripped over, bumped into the other lad and they both went down. I hopped over them, skipped out of the pub, ran up The Butts and dodged round the back of St Mary's Church.

Behind St Mary's, there's a big gate to an alleyway that leads on to Church Street. They call it the Tink-a-Tank, cuz when you run round it, it goes 'Tink-Tank-Tink-Tank' – that's what it sounds like.

The gate was left open all the time. It was dark and I was hiding behind one of the gateposts when I heard the Snowdrops approaching. One of them said, 'This path comes out at the top there. You go that way, I'll go this way, and we'll close in on the bastard.' I'd flung the knife away and there was no way I could take these two big fellas on with my fists, so I felt on the ground and found a heavy stone. I could just make out the white blur of a helmet coming towards me. BANG! I got the bloke right in the neck and he crashes down. I jumped over him: TINK-TANK-TINK-TANK-TINK-TANK down the path, up Church Street and along to Wathen Road. I got to No. 19, dashed in the house, snatched up me Burberry, snatched up me case, belted up to Warwick Station and jumped on the train to London. As soon as I was there, I sent a telegram home recalling myself, then I booked a bed in the Union Jack Club and that's where I spent the rest of me leave.

My mum used to say, 'Every time you come on leave, son, they send you these telegrams and have you go back. Why don't they let somebody else do the extra work?'

'Well, that's just how it is, Mum. We're the duty boat.' I used to tell her some awful lies to get out of it.

I never carried a knife again. I thought next time I'd very likely stick it in somebody. I used to get that worked up. You know what

I mean? I hated fighting but I used to go out, get smashed out of my mind, and I wouldn't actually know what I was doing. It was my fault, nobody else's. I don't walk around with a temper on me now like I used to.

Not all the Americans was bad. Down at Pompey – Portsmouth – I used to get on great with them but there was a lot of black ones down there, see? They'd be tap dancing up and down the Guildhall steps. They were brilliant at it. We used to get them to do it over and over again. Some of the white ones were all right, except for the ones labouring under the illusion they could do over here what they did in America: if you was black, they could kick the shits out of you.

I went nearly two years at sea without coming home at all. When I eventually saw my mum, she'd started straightening up and was walking better but summat else had happened. There was an old sod who kept pigs on the allotment at the back of us and a worm from his pigs got into my mother's bloodstream through the wound in her stomach and started eating away at the nerves in her eyes, making her progressively blind.

On 5 May 1945, the Germans suddenly surrendered and the war in Europe was over. HMS *Myngs* was ordered back to Portsmouth for a refit. One day they started changing the colour of the ship from dark Admiralty grey to light Admiralty grey. That could only mean one thing: the Far East. There was still the Japanese to deal with. We were concerned, cuz we'd been watching newsreels of the kamikaze planes. An extra gun was put in place of our destroyer's searchlight and off we went, from as cold as could be to as hot as could be.

The heat did funny things to the food. I sneaked some ship's biscuits into my locker and then forgot about them for a while. When I opened the packet and stuffed one in my mouth, it was full of weevils. I had to dash down to the showers to wash my mouth out.

One day we were preparing for the Japanese landings, formed up line-ahead in battle order about to bombard the shore, when the signal lamps started flashing all over the place: 'Action Aborted'. Everybody wondered what'd happened. It was 6 August 1945, and the Allies had dropped an atom bomb on the Japanese seaport of Hiroshima – the first atomic bomb used in war. On board HMS *Myngs*, we didn't hear or see a thing but the news was radioed through. The skipper broadcast it on the Tannoy and a big cheer went up.

Hiroshima looked like some kid had been playing sandcastles and walked all through them. A hundred thousand people were killed immediately and worse come after with radiation and disease. I thought, 'I don't want the world to explode, I like it here.' Three days later, they dropped another one and flattened Nagasaki, killing 75,000 people in one go.

Very soon after that, the news come through that the Japanese had surrendered. Huge roars went up all over the ship; there was yelling and dancing on the decks and we thought, 'Great, we'll be going home soon.' But, no, there was some clearing up to do and we were sent to Singapore, off the bottom tip of Malaya in the Indian Ocean.

We was the first ship in Singapore harbour after the Japs had surrendered. It was mostly Chinese that lived there and it had been occupied by the Japanese since, I think, early 1942.

The skipper, Captain Allinson, he was a great ol' bloke. I'd been sparring on the quarterdeck and he asked me, 'Are you going to fight professionally again, Turpin?'

'I would love to if I could get leave to do it, sir.'

'Come and see me when we get back to England. I'll see what we can do.'

Our Dick was still serious about his boxing. He'd come home on leave from the Middle East in March 1944 and took his first contest for more than three years – against Dave McCleave. That's a heck of a long lay-off and it turned into an eight-round slog that Dick lost on points; he'd KOd McCleave in the fifth round a few years before that. Dick resolved to train harder and blow the desert dust off his boxing but he was called to return abroad. It was nearly two years before he got back in the professional ring again.

Our Randolph was coming up to 17 and in the September of 1945 he signed up for the Royal Navy, too. We'd both run away to join the navy as kids and now we'd finally achieved it.

Randolph's reputation had gone before him, so they immediately snapped him up for the navy boxing team. He served his time as a boxer, really, but they trained him as a cook as a sideline.

He come to see me on board once when we was in harbour. He took a load of contraband with him when he left – enough to start his own business, practically – and they just waved him through the gate. 'Hey, that's ol' Turps. He give that Yank a right ol' spanking the other night.'

I anna used to bother about drinking until I was well over 18 in the navy. At first, I used to go ashore with the lads and I'd drink lemonade. They'd say, 'Sit on your own if you're drinking that!' and I'd have to pay for beer for them and they only paid for half a pint of lemonade for me, so I started drinking alcohol. Once I'd started, that was it. I used to get in some horrible states.

We'd go from one pub to another and from one fight to another. I hadn't used to get into long arguments. I'd say, 'I'm a trained fighter. Let's not argue.' Usually they'd back down but if they didn't, I'd keep talking and walking towards them until I knew I wasn't gonna miss, then I'd dig 'em. If I knocked them down, I'd ask them if they wanted to carry on. They'd say no, as a rule, and I could get back to me drinking.

I used to drink rum on the boat all the time. I shouldn't have, cuz some of the time I was still under 20 but one of my jobs was to fill the rum bottles down in the storeroom for the Rum Bosun. I'd sneak a tot or two by catching the drips off the pump and I used to come up from there three-parts cut.

Some of the things I used to do, I fully expected to get kicked out of the navy or sent to gaol. We was allowed to sell tobacco to the Chinese. Like, buy a half-pound tin for five shillings and sell it for ten shillings. What I'd do, I'd open up the bottom with a tin opener, take half the tobacco out, fill it back up with sawdust and get the chippy to solder the bottom back in. I made a bomb out there. The other lads used to say, 'How much are you charging for your tobacco?'

'Ten shillings. Why?'

'You seem to be making more money than anyone else.' We had some fun out there but you had to watch it, cuz the locals would do you soon as look at you.

In the main part of Singapore there was a place called The New World where they put on boxing shows. I thought it'd be a good way of earning beer money. The bloke that run it used to make me laugh. He'd say a number and hold up the wrong amount of fingers when he said it. 'How many rounds do you have to box here?' I asked him. He held up four fingers and said, 'Six.'

So I held up three fingers and said, 'I'll box four.'

I got a hiding the first time. Me nose and eyes were done, and me mouth was all cut. They give me £5 for losing. All my mates were saying, 'Good ol' Jack!' and getting stuck into all the booze I'd bought with the money. The worst of it was, I couldn't drink because my lips were that sore. I had to wait a fortnight for them to heal up properly. Then I went again.

The first time, I'd boxed in stockinged feet because I thought I'd be able to move around better but the ring floor was rough and it slowed me down. This time I'd put some boots on – sniper boots with a separated big toe for climbing trees.

The house fighter comes charging at me and backs me into a corner. He plants his left foot forward to get some purchase behind a punch and I slid my divided boot down his shin, CRACK! onto his instep, and followed it with a punch to the head. Gawd, I thought I'd broke his bleeding leg. He could hardly stand. I knocked him over with a nice uppercut and every time he got up I knocked him down again. Fifteen pounds they give me for winning. The boss says, 'You come back again. We got a lot of one like him you box.'

'No thanks, mate,' I told him. 'I'm retiring as the champion.'

There was another place, The Happy World, I went to with this kidda, Smith, to see a dance show. We sneaked into one of the dressing-rooms – out of curiosity, really. There's a kimono hung up, emerald green, with a big scarlet dragon on the back. Smith gets this kimono, folds it up and stuffs it up his jersey. The bouncer, a HUGE fella, seen us go in and he comes over just as we're creeping out. He notices 9-st. Smith now looks about 15 st. He grabs hold of him to see what he's got stuffed up his jumper and a fight breaks out. I jumped up and punched the bouncer at the back of the ear and he goes out like a light. 'Come on,' I said to Smith, 'we're out of here,' but, no, Smithy wants to go back and batter the bloke a second time. 'Knock 'em down and run,' I told him, but he wouldn't listen. The bouncer had come round by this time and appeared in the doorway. Smithy goes tearing back and he's wrestling with him in the street. The kimono's coming out of his jersey and if the naval patrol comes round we've got no chance.

I ran at the bouncer and belted him in the mouth as hard as I could, and me and Smithy legged it. My hand's hurting like bleeding hell. It's on fire. It felt like I'd splintered the knuckle. As soon as it was safe to stop running, I took a look and saw a large chunk of bone sticking through the skin. The moment we got back on board I went to the sick bay.

Top left: Quite a dandy, Daddy was! This must
have been taken in the early 1920s.

Top right: Our mum, in her 30s, bless her. She
was the best fighter out of the lot of us.

Above left: Dick as a 14 year old. It's obvious that a boy with the
surname Turpin is gonna be nicknamed after the famous highwayman.

Above right: Me and Randolph when I was seven or eight. I was
bigger than Randolph in them days. That's Stanley Llewellyn with us.
He found an unexploded First World War hand grenade at the
barracks. He was running along with it up his jumper, taking it
home, when it blew up. They only found part of his little sleeve.

Top left: George Middleton in the 1950s. George was more than just a manager to us.

Top right: Mick Gavin, our 'Mr Boxing'. This was Mick's publicity picture when he was fighting back in the early 1920s before the rules come in.

Left: Here he is, the bloody little admiral! Taken shortly after I joined the navy in 1942. I'm not wearing my hat correctly. I used to cop it for that.

Top: And here she is, HMS *Myngs*. I loved that ol' ship.

Above: 3 May 1947. My most important match and
my own promotion. I told you she was a beautiful girl.
(courtesy of *Coventry Evening Telegraph*)

DICK TURPIN (WARWICK)
MIDDLEWEIGHT CHAMPION OF GREAT BRITAIN
Sole Manager : GEORGE MIDDLETON, 34 Lee Road, Leamington Spa.
Telephone : LEAmington Spa 2779.

Top: Me, delivering a nice uppercut to Tom Cummings.
(courtesy of *Coventry Evening Telegraph*)

Above: The first black British champion,
my big brother.

Left: Salts was that impressed with the effect my outfit had on the audience he asked me to keep it in as a regular part of the public sparring sessions.

Below: A more conventional shot of me sparring with Britain's first black world champion, my babby brother.

Top: Me and Josie, outward bound, playing the quoit game on the *Queen Mary*.

Above: Me, Eddie Phillips and Randolph on the *Queen Mary*, homeward bound with straight hair.

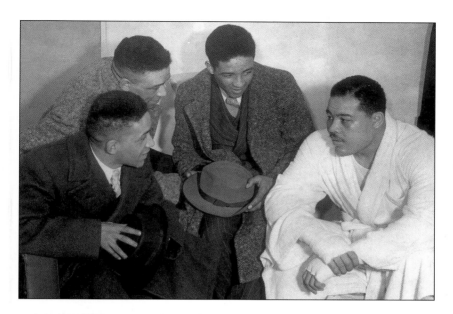

Top: Me and my brothers with our great hero Joe Louis,
taken when Joe come to London in 1952, I think,
to box some exhibitions and asked to meet us.

Above: Mum and Ernie having a night out
in Randy's Bar on the Great Orme in 1953.

Top left: Battling Jack in battle honours at a navy do in 1994.

Top right: Randolph cast in bronze in Warwick Market Square.
(courtesy of Dave Wright)

Above: The fighter and the writer. Me and Terry
at my place in Warwick. (courtesy of Lynda Fox)

Our doctor was an Irish bloke, a Lieutenant Commander, about 4 ft tall. He says, 'Will you fetch your hand over here, Turpin, and let me be after looking at it.'

'Yes sir,' I says. 'It's ever so swollen and painful.'

He examines it, 'Oooh, it looks like a piece of bone sticking out there, Turpin,' he says. He peers at it again and turns to his assistant, 'Pass me those pliers.' He clamps the pliers on the piece of bone and starts twisting and pulling. I couldn't believe it. I'm in bleeding AGONY! Suddenly, he pulls it free and waves it in the air. 'There you are, Turpin. There's your piece of bone – a front tooth. Now, Turpin, how did a fine front tooth come to be embedded in your knuckle, I wonder?'

'I've no idea, sir,' I told him. 'I don't bite my nails or anything.'

'It wouldn't have anything to do with the rumpus at The Happy World earlier on now, would it?' he asked me.

'The Happy World, sir?' I said, looking as innocent as I could. He was another one as used to grin at me whenever I walked past.

The Japanese had carried out a systematic campaign of rape and torture and murder on the people of Singapore. They killed hundreds and hundreds of them with bayonets, swords . . . they burnt them, hung them, machine-gunned them . . . *Anything* you can imagine, the poor bastards had it done to them . . . One job we were assigned to was releasing prisoners of war from Changi Prison . . . I ain't keen on talking about it. Some of the people in that place as weren't dead might just as well have been from the way they'd been looked after . . . Well, not looked after . . . The bleeding stench of it . . . There's some of it I won't talk about at all . . . These flies coming up off the bodies, that nearly finished me. They land on your face an' you're trying to knock 'em off . . . I was worried to death in case I caught something off them.

Our first priority was to send the Japanese back. Twenty-four thousand of them. We had to put them through the search tents, retain any watches and jewellery, and issue them with one vest, one pair of underpants, one pair of trousers and one shirt, and then put them on to boats that had been commandeered – fishing smacks an' all that. The Japs were just dumped off on the mainland and left to walk back. But these others that had been prisoners of the Japanese, the ones that had been there a while an' starved and tortured . . . diseased. I anna kidding, one night when I was on deck duty down there, I saw these horrors coming and I almost put me rifle and bayonet on me shoulder and marched away.

For some reason, it was the flies and maggots more than anything that did me. People think I won't eat rice because I don't like it but it isn't that. When someone puts a bowl of rice on the table, all I see is a bowl of maggots.

HMS *Myngs* had some really rough times but, it's weird, I can't remember that much about them. In war, you sort of switch your emotions off most of the time. We intercepted a German convoy once, off the coast of Norway. Blew it to bits. Sunk the bloody lot of them. It was near Christmas and all I thought was, 'Well, *they* won't be getting no Christmas pud.' I knew we was supposed to be fighting against evil but I don't think I ever fully realised the seriousness of what I was doing. I'd just turned 18 when I'd joined the ship.

Anyhow, both the Germans and the Japanese had been battered into retirement and us Turpins had scraped through it alive. Joan and Kath had helped the RAF by joining the WAAF, as they say. Joan was stationed up on Tyneside on the barrage balloons. Kath was stationed in Bristol. With her being younger, the war was nearly over when she joined. Randolph was on a peacetime ship, so he'd be all right. Ernie had survived his army service, too. But, evidently, we didn't all come through entirely unscathed.

My nephew, Cledwyn, Joan's son, told me he'd found out from his mother that Dick had been up a telegraph pole fixing some lines when an enemy shell had exploded near to where he was working and he got hit up the bum with some shrapnel. Dick more or less kept that to hisself. If that had happened to me and Dick knew about it, everybody in every bleeding pub in Warwick would've known.

I had been signed up for 'Hostilities Only' and in 1946 I was back in Pompey doing my finishing routine when I realised I didn't want to leave. I really, really loved the navy. I was never seasick and never sick of the sea. A factory life – being indoors, in one place, at one machine, with all the fumes and noise and dirt, for measly wages – had no appeal at all.

Dick had picked up his boxing again and knocked out Jack McKnight of Belfast in the first round. He had his finishing routines to do too, then he'd start boxing regular. I thought, 'Yeah, there's always my boxing.' But life on the ocean wave was definitely the life for me. When you're young and planning your future, you never allow for falling in love, do you?

13

Dark Threats

Betty Mary Quinney – what an absolutely beautiful girl! She come from out in the country – Mollington, near Banbury. She was living with her sister and brother-in-law next door to a pub I used in Leamington. I come out of this pub one night having an argument with two soldiers and a brawl started. I bumped into Betty a few weeks later and tried to chat her up. 'Weren't you fighting outside our house?' she said, looking disgusted, and wouldn't have nothing to do with me.

I was at the Palais one night and Bet come waltzing past with an RAF officer. I waved and she smiled. As soon as her fella went for some drinks, I shot across and asked her, 'Can I take you home?'

'No, thank you,' she says. 'I'm with somebody.' I pointed to my mates and said, 'See them blokes over there? If I don't take you home tonight, that RAF bod you're with, they're gonna kill him cuz that fella's no good for you and I'm the one you should be with.' She laughed and agreed to let me take her home. When I asked to see her again, she said, 'No. My friends have told me you're only interested in girls for one thing.'

'Have I tried to get fresh with you?' I asked her.

'No.'

'Well then,' I said. 'I'll pick you up here tomorrow night.' And to prove what a gentleman I really was, I shook hands with her and said, 'Until tomorrow then.' We used to laugh about that. She said I was the nicest bloke she'd ever met.

Me going as a regular sailor would mean delaying our wedding plans but all I'd have to do was clear it with Bet then I'd sign on the dotted line. There was one more leave before the end of my war service. I'd explain it to her then.

'What do you mean put the wedding off till you come home on leave *again*?' she said. We were out for a stroll. Bet stopped walking and turned to face me, 'I thought your service was finishing.'

'That's just it, duck,' I said. 'I love the navy and I'm thinking about signing on for 12 years.'

'If you stay in the navy, Jack Turpin,' she said, 'we're finished.' She reckoned she'd never see enough of me an' all that. I was disappointed but the outcome of a battle between Betty Mary Quinney and the Royal Navy was a foregone conclusion – the admiralty would be fighting well above its class. With my navy career scuppered, it was down to Plan B.

You often hear it said, 'The only thing square in boxing is the ring.' It wasn't that way with George Middleton. He used to tell his daughter Josie, 'Say your prayers every night and always tell the truth,' and that's the way George thought. I wrote to him asking, 'Can you fix me up with some fights, please? I'm ready to take up my boxing again.' I got a letter back saying that he'd arranged for me to fight a lad named Percy Pateman in Birmingham on Saturday, 21 May 1946, and he hoped I was training properly.

My training schedule at the time was mostly to go ashore with the lads, get pissed and pick a fight with somebody. Nobody drank like I did in the navy. If I come home on leave for 14 days, I was 14 days in a stupor. Same with smoking. I was hardly a moment without a fag in me mouth. As soon as I was gonna go back boxing, I quit both.

I took George's letter to the First Lieutenant. 'Your service is coming to an end, Turpin,' he said, 'but your welfare is still our concern. I'll take this up with the skipper.' He was worried that I was gonna be used to make somebody a pile of money. After he'd had a word with the skipper, he contacted George and I was granted leave for the fight.

We were busy returning hunks of meat and sacks of spuds to the stores: up the ladder, along the forecastle, down the ladder – good for fitness – but the skipper did better than that. Blokes on punishment were offered the choice of sparring with me instead of scrubbing decks, or being swung out over the side painting the ship. I had no shortage of sparmates.

The Saturday arrived and Mick Gavin come out to look after me. As usual, my pre-fight nerves started the ol' Fight or Flight Fandango and I wondered why the hell I was letting Mick glove me up. I took a couple of deep breaths and strode out into the auditorium.

From my corner of the ring, I glanced across at Pateman. He was a few pounds heavier than me but taller and not so well built. The referee called us to the centre and says, 'I want a good clean fight. When I say, "Break", I mean break but don't drop your hands. Defend yourself at all times . . .' an' all that, and then, like they always do, said, 'Shake hands and come out fighting.' I put a glove out to Pateman. He touched it and stepped back quick, like he thought I was going to sock him one then and there.

Back in the corner, I says to Mick, 'I think he's nervous of me.' Mick looks over to where Pateman's seconds are bent over their boxer shouting in his ears and says, 'Nervous? I can see him shaking from here.' That was all I needed.

The gong went and I come out of the corner at 200 mph: jab-jab-jab, feinting and dodging; jab-jab, overhand rights, straight lefts, uppercuts, crosses, all the time moving forward, arms going like pistons . . . and nothing making contact, cuz Percy Pateman had got on his bike. Everything he was attempting to throw back was either well short or well wide. We were more like two blokes separately shadow boxing than fighting. At the end of the three minutes, I complained to Mick, 'I might as well be in there by me bleeding self.'

Mick says, 'Jaysus! You're going like a bloody express train, Jack. Slow down. Take your time.' When Mr Boxing told you summat, you tried to listen.

On the gong for the second round, I walked calmly to the centre, squared up, feinted with the left and sent over a cracking right cross. It was one of the sweetest punches I ever threw: BOOOMP! Pateman went down like a sack of wheat and, I tell you what, the most surprised person there was me. I stood in a neutral corner while the referee conducted a count that sounded like the Royal Warwickshire Regimental Band playing for the King on his birthday. I'm drinking it all in when it started to dawn on me I'd got no feeling in me right arm.

When the count had climbed to ten, I run across to my corner with my arm dangling. 'Mick, Mick,' I said, poking at it with me other glove, 'it's broke!' Mick pulled and pummelled my dead arm till the life slowly needled its way back into it.

'That was a great punch, Jack,' Mick said, 'but you hit him on the side of the head and that's why it hurt you. Next time aim for the chin.' I could hardly wait for next time.

Four weeks later, I was on leave again for an eight-rounder in Brum with Wilf Stacey – a good boxer but like an octopus. He kept wrapping his tentacles round me. 'What's the matter,' I taunted him, 'scared to fight me?' – I was doing all that fancy stuff, talking to 'em, putting them off their stroke, way before Ali come along. Stacey complained about it and the ref stopped the clock to give me a ticking-off but I managed to wriggle free of him often enough to win on a wide margin of points. It was looking like boxing wasn't a bad choice at all for me and, although the day of my demob was a day of mixed emotions, I was looking forward to seeing more of Betty.

The navy fitted me up with my demobilisation suit: a dark-blue, pin-striped, double-breasted, big-lapelled number, with grey shoes and a grey trilby hat to go with it. I wondered if they were gonna give me a bleeding revolver an' all. Dressed like Lucky Luciano, I left the Royal Navy for good.

I got down to some serious training for my first contest in civvy street since the war. Brum again, up against a lad named Billy Peach, and it was a peach of a fight. I knocked him off his tree – out for the count in the first round. Mick Gavin was still on at me though: 'You're like the Flying bloody Scotsman, Jack. PACE YERSELF!' It was ages before I really got the hang of that. George was delighted. He believed I had something special.

He booked me down in Cirencester – a great little boxing town – to box Hal Bagwell, a kidda from Gloucester who'd only been beat once in 74 contests. I thought, 'Hey, George, you might be being a bit ambitious for me with this one.' See, George was learning as well. But I was on a roll, wasn't I? Mick was on about me starting too fast, so I'd take me time for this one and I had ten rounds to do it in.

My fight plan went by the board on the first bell. Bagwell tore into me like I'd been getting fresh with his girl. I give as good as I got and almost had him over with a right to the jaw in the fourth. In the sixth, I had him trapped on the ropes just as the bell went. I felt I'd swung the fight my way but, I anna kidding, he was a bleeding handful. He stayed strong all the way through the fight –

in the eighth he had me down three times and I only just survived the round. I come out in the ninth determined to play it defensive. I'd already proved I could hurt Bagwell; I might even get in a winning punch. But Hal floored me with a ferocious left to the solar plexus. Bent me in bloody half! I couldn't believe the pain. I went down on me backside and couldn't get up.

Randolph, on the strength of his brilliant amateur career, was as certain as anybody could be of a gold medal at the London Olympics that was coming up. It would have been a dream come true for Gibbs and Stefani. Randolph had won the Leamington Boys' Club their first national title in 1943: Junior 'A' class 7 st. championship of Great Britain. The next year, he won them Junior 'B' class 9 st. 7 Championship of Great Britain. The year after that, he made the record books by being the first ever to win the Junior and Senior ABA titles in the same year: Junior 'B' class 10 st. 7 and Senior welterweight. He fought those contests within three weeks of each other and his birthday come in between. That can never be beat, cuz they've changed the rules now. He was the youngest ever, at just turned 17, to win the Senior title.

In that same year, he fought for Great Britain against the Americans at Wembley. It was on television, this was. The star of the American team was a kidda called Harold Anspach – a Golden Gloves fella – tipped as a future World middleweight champion. Randolph put paid to him with a right-hander that lifted the kid three foot off the floor and I never heard of Harold Anspach again.

Randolph won the Royal Navy championship and the Imperial Services middleweight title. In 1946, he took the ABA senior middleweight title.

There was NOBODY around at amateur level that posed any threat to Randolph. An Olympic gold medal would've rounded his amateur career off perfectly but the boxing papers were predicting he would follow his brothers and turn professional. Inspector Gibbs and Ron Stefani were pleading with him but the press had got it right. There was nothing Randolph wanted to do more than to follow Dick and me and live by the glove.

All the boxing managers come wriggling out of the woodwork: 'If you sign with me, Randolph, I'll give you this, an' that' – holidays, famous trainers, quick ways to titles . . . What Inspector Gibbs wanted him to do, if Randolph was determined to go professional, was sign up with Vince Hawkins' manager, who he thought was 'most reliable'. Hawkins' manager, the cheeky sod, actually offered to pay for Randolph to have elocution lessons. Lick said, 'No thanks. I'm back-streets, me, an' back-streets I'm gonna stay.' Ron Stefani was always quoting that. We hated people trying to make out we were summat we wasn't and Ron didn't understand. Some people were surprised to find we was well mannered. It used to rattle me, that – cuz I'm black, I shouldn't know how to behave? No. There was only one bloke we trusted.

Fighting Turpin No. 3 launched his pro career with a middleweight contest on 17 September 1946, against Gordon Griffiths, on the undercard of a Jack Solomons promotion at Harringay. Randolph still had 18 months of his service to go but the navy gave him leave for his debut and all the boxing reporters turned out with their pencils sharpened, waiting to see if he was as good at professional as he was at amateur.

The headlining fight was a light-heavyweight bout between British champion Bruce Woodcock and World champion Gus Lesnevich, the 'Russian Lion' who was actually American. It was a contest with a lot of interest attached to it because of Freddie Mills, who was a very, very popular British boxer. Freddie had taken a right shellacking from Lesnevich earlier in the year in the same ring. Freddie had too much guts for his own good sometimes. Then he'd took a fight against Bruce Woodcock too soon after his beating from Lesnesvich, got another shellacking and lost his British title. Everybody wanted to see Woodcock teach Lesnevich a lesson and Harringay Arena was sold out.

Randolph was immediately plunged into the big time to have his first contest in front of 10,000 people. He more than rose to the occasion. He was AWESOME. He waded into Griffiths and battered him out of the ring nearly. The referee had to stop the fight before the end of the first round. Woodcock boxed brilliant and put Lesnevich's lights out but Randolph's was the fight of the night.

He'd completed the family trio. We'd all won our debut fights inside the distance: Dick in four rounds, me in three rounds and Randolph in one.

The Turpin brothers were actually now feared by other boxers. The newspapers regularly published photos and articles on us, calling us 'The Fighting Turpins' or 'The Coloured Batterers From Leamington', but most often 'The Dark Threats', cuz we were beginning to make the British boxing system look stupid by knocking over boxers as were lined up for English titles we were the wrong colour for.

George wrote to the British Boxing Board of Control and asked them to allow Dick to be considered for the British Empire middleweight championship. He got a letter back saying 'No'. They said they'd seen him lose a fight against Johnny Best at Marylebone and didn't think he was ready.

We could hardly believe it. What was going on? In the fight they was referring to, Dick had to retire halfway through with a damaged hand and in the whole of 1946 he'd only lost TWO fights out of TEN – that one and a very doubtful points loss to Johnny Boyd, who he KOd in the fourth when they were rematched a few months later. Out of the eight he'd won, seven were inside the distance.

'Bugger 'em then,' Dick said, 'I'll just batter all the blokes as the Board's got in mind for titles until they CAN'T refuse me a shot,' and he asked George to line them up for him.

In Wharf Street, Warwick, was Nelson's gelatine factory. They extract it from the boiled-down skins and bones of animals and use it for jellies and sweets. It stinks a bit. We used to sneak in there as kids and pinch a handful. This fella, Arthur Batty, was chief buyer for them. He had a word with Mr Nelson about whether he could have a derelict part of the first floor allocated as a gymnasium for this young Warwick lad named Dick Turpin who was going to make a big name as a boxer. We'd been training at the Rose and Crown in Leamington up till then and Arthur had come to see us and asked if he could help train Dick with some new methods he'd dreamed up, and he wanted his own gym to do it in.

Arthur'd been a sergeant with the Chindits out in Burma. His dad was manager of Smith's paper shop, where Dick had worked delivering papers when he was about 14 or 15, and they lived in the flat above it. Arthur went to university in Edinburgh to study to be a doctor but his dad died, so Arthur come back to Warwick and never finished his studying. He took a course in physiotherapy and bodybuilding and, out of that and what he'd learned about being a doctor, he invented his own system of weightlifting and bodybuilding.

As soon as he got permission to use the building, he scouted round the factory for bits and pieces he could make use of. He turned pulley wheels into weights; he got some metal tubes, put them in the floor, put springs on them and a bar across, and you'd lie underneath it and push up and down to develop your legs. The wooden floor was uneven, so Arthur went off scavenging and come back with a big roll of rubber conveyor belting and we're all there nailing it to the floor. He topped it off with a cheap quarter-size portable ring.

He opened it up as The Nelson Gymnasium. We paid him tuppence-ha'penny a week each, I think it was, for training sessions, and he started helping us. All along the line he was getting more equipment – gloves and bags and speedballs.

Dick was having hand trouble almost as soon as he'd started back fighting. It got so bad he thought he'd have to quit altogether but Arthur said, 'No, we can sort that out,' and fixed Dick up with little different gadgets and exercises to heal and strengthen his hands where the doctors couldn't. Within six months, Dick had got his punch back.

Most people in boxing were against building your body up with weights. They reckoned it affected your mobility. Arthur proved, if you did it his way, you'd have your strength and it wouldn't affect how you could move around the ring. Dick took advantage of it and so did I. Arthur was dedicated to it hisself and his build was very similar to Randolph's – but Randolph was a *fanatic* at it.

If anybody lifted a weight 40 times, Randolph would do it 50 times. He would compete with you over absolutely anything. He reached a point in weightlifting and bodybuilding where he looked like a heavyweight – getting on for 6 ft tall with muscles like King Arthur's suit of armour – but he was still an 11 st. 6 lb middleweight, as agile as ever.

Yeah, Arthur Batty. He was quite a fella. Out of that homemade back-street gymnasium in Warwick, this little old cow town, come champions.

14

Call Me 'Battling Jack'

Coventry, Birmingham and London were all bomb craters and derelict houses – streets like rows of rotten teeth. Britain was a dreary ol' place in 1947. Everything was scarce and everything 'cept fish an' chips was on ration. If you saw a queue, you joined it, cuz there must be summat at the end of it.

Winston Churchill had took us through the war as Prime Minister but then it was Clement Attlee. Labour. There was gonna be some big changes: nationalisation; the Welfare State. But, at that moment, Britain was in the doldrums and so was British boxing.

We had nobody apart from Freddie Mills who could win World titles. Freddie took a British version of the the light-heavyweight crown from Len Harvey in 1942 but lost it to Gus Lesnevich after the war. Joe Louis was in his tenth year as heavyweight champion; Rocky Graziano held the middleweight title; Sugar Ray Robinson the welterweight; Willie Pep the feather . . . See? All Americans.

That year I had my most important match. My own promotion. On 3 May, I married Bet at St Mary's Parish Church at the bottom of The Parade, Leamington, and I wouldn't have missed it for the world, even though I nearly did. It was our Dick's fault.

Dick was best man and he insisted we went for a quick drink first. We come out of the pub on time but Dick decided he needed another quick one before he'd be ready, so we went back in and when we come out again he had to go back in again, and by the time we got to the church we were late and crowds of people were already there. Ooh, a huge crowd! It caused traffic jams. As soon as we were married, me and Bet went to live with my mother in Wathen Road.

Randolph got married before I did – in January that same year. He'd been going out with her for quite a while. Mary Theresa Stack. We used to call her 'T'rese', cuz of her middle name. She was a great girl. Beautiful. She still is. Randolph was 19 then. T'rese's brother Michael was one of George's fighters and that's how they'd met.

They got married at the Catholic church at Leamington and Randolph give me a rollicking afterwards cuz I was talking while they was getting on with the ceremony. And laughing! – they give Randolph this little stool thing and he put it underneath him and sat on it. The ol' priest come along and patted him on the head and explained, 'You kneel on it.' I couldn't get over it. I kept bursting out laughing and every time Randolph looked over at me, he starts giggling an' all. Dick had got married before both of us to Emily Warsgrove, the girl next door in Wathen Road.

George was fixing me up with fight after fight, night after night but some I got another way. I'd be training with Dick and he'd say, 'I'm boxing down at Oxford on Monday, Jack,' or wherever it'd be. 'Bring yer kit an' come along.' If anybody dropped out, I was ready to step in. That's why some fights I had don't show up on my record. They showed up in me pocket though.

I was still nervous before a bout but when I come up against Arthur Marriott, I was SHIT scared. He had hair sprouting out all over the place, a big scowl . . . He looked like he was on his way to tear down the Empire State building and had stopped off to rip me apart first. Mick sensed my fear and come to the centre of the ring with me while the referee was giving instructions. It's the one and only time he done it. 'Don't worry,' he told me. 'You've beat gorillas before.' I beat Arthur on points. You know you can't go by looks but it always affects you.

In March 1947, me and Randolph were at the Albert Hall on the undercard of a contest between Al Phillips and Clifford Anderson who were fighting for the British Empire featherweight title. Anderson was a black fighter from my dad's place, British Guiana. They were the sort of opponents I had my sights on.

Al Phillips was a highly rated boxer but not in the same league as Cliffy, and Cliff give Phillips a 15-round lesson in the art and science of boxing. When it was over, the referee raised *Phillips'* arm in the air.

I ain't akidding, it was like somebody telling you what you'd been seeing hadn't really been happening. The crowd went BER-SERK! Randolph says to me, 'You should have Phillips, kid. You could stop him,' and George fixed it up for me to fight Al Phillips on Dick's card at Wembley.

I was chuffed. Phillips was the shining light of British feathers and, of course, the current holder of the British Empire featherweight title. Me beating him in a non-title fight would rocket me up the ratings. But at the last minute it's, 'Oh, Al's hurt his ankle training.' They sent his chief sparring partner, Dave Sharkey, as a late replacement.

'Right,' I told George. 'Sharkey's stepped into Phillips' boots, so he's gonna have to take what I'd got planned for Phillips.' Sharkey was lucky, though. With me only just getting married, I was worried I'd left me strength in the bedroom, if you see what I mean. I kept the fight long range, doing all the things Mick Gavin was always on about I should be doing – nipping in and out banging him with every punch in my repertoire which, by then, was quite a few. I give Sharkey such a whipping.

The boxing papers said I'd boxed brilliant and was well on my way to a title but I was still angry cuz I believed Al Phillips pulled out for tactical reasons, knowing I could take him.

George told me, 'Cheer up. I'm going to send you on your honeymoon, Jack. Take your wife with you.'

'It'd be some honeymoon without her, George,' I said.

Our 'honeymoon' turned out to be bed and breakfast for three days in Gosport where Randolph was stationed, so I could help him train for his next fight. George fixed me up with a fight of me own on the middle night.

After a night of newlywed passion, I had to get up at six in the morning, run along to the bay to meet Randolph, do ten or twelve miles of road work, come back to the digs, have a bath, get dressed and have me breakfast. Randolph would come in for a chat, then he'd say, 'I've got to get back at twelve and do the rest of me chores, so come down the barracks at half past five and we'll do the sparring.' I'd spar with him and go back to the digs. 'Some honeymoon this is,' Bet said. 'But I do like it here. Where are we going this evening?'

'I'm gonna have to go to bed, duck,' I said. 'I'm bloody

knackered.' Poor old Bet. She done so much for me and put herself out so much for me.

On our last night, the landlady suggested we all went for a drink at the local pub. T'rese was down there with us. We sat at a table – Betty one side of me, and the landlady, her old man and T'rese on the other. I asked the landlady, 'What would you like to drink? You old fucker.' Bet looked really shocked.

The landlady snaps, 'I *beg* your pardon?' Her old man wasn't a fighting bloke and he glanced nervously at the door.

'That last bit wasn't me,' I said, killing meself laughing inside. Then the voice come again, 'You old fucker.' This time the landlady seen my lips hadn't moved. It was an old mate of mine from when I was stationed down there in the navy. I looked behind me and there he was in the corner. I ran my fingernails across the bars of his cage: 'What-ho, shipmate.' The parrot cocked its head to one side, studied me for a minute, blinked and said, 'You old fucker.'

Randolph's fight was with Jury VII. It was beautiful to watch – the most perfect fight Randolph ever fought. Well, after the second round, anyway. Jury was from Africa somewhere and the seventh son. He must've been one of the hardest fellas in the world. Randolph had come straight up to the Albert Hall after night duty. He'd had a bit of a sleep on the massage table but I was worried because I didn't think as how he could be sharp enough to box.

In the second round, Jury hit Randolph with the most terrific right cross I've ever seen and Randolph went down like a felled tree. It was the first time he'd been put down in the professional ring and he was really hurt. He managed to rise on the count of eight. Him and Jury stepped towards each other and threw right-handers simultaneously. Jury's missed and Randolph's connected. Jury's whole face seemed to collapse. He dropped to his knees. I thought, 'Christ! Randolph's bloody killed him.' The blow had stretched his neck a good ten inches. Jury got up and come walking forward at Randolph with a murderous look in his eye. That was the only time I've seen Randolph showing a bit of fear, cuz that shot should have finished anybody off. But from then on, Randolph didn't put a foot wrong. I tell you, if you could have took a film of it, you could have used it to train any young boxer coming into the game.

When we got back to the dressing-room, Licker was crying. I said, 'What's the matter?'

'I've let you down,' he said. 'He knocked me out.'

'Did he heck!' I told him. 'He knocked you *down* but you got up and boxed perfect. You give him a real big hiding.' Randolph showed me his right hand. It was bloated up to twice its normal size. 'That ain't from hitting him on the head,' he told me. 'That's how hard I hit him on the chin.'

Dick's mission to force the British Boxing Board of Control to sit up and take notice of him got off to a stuttering start with a KO loss and a draw. He dug deep and got hisself on a winning streak, notching up 18 straight wins against progressively better opposition. Eight were achieved inside the distance. Surely the British Boxing Board couldn't turn their blind eye to me elder brother now?

Al Phillips met Clifford Anderson in a rematch for the British Empire featherweight title on 1 July 1947 – another farce with Phillips getting the decision again – and *Boxing News* come out predicting Phillips would be defending his title against Ronnie Clayton next. The British featherweight title was vacant, with Al Phillips rated No. 1 contender and Clayton second. Bert Jackson, Johnny Cusick, Ben Duffy and Gus Foran were all up there. I hadn't got a mention. Vince Hawkins was top of the middles, cuz he was British champion. Mark Hart, Albert Finch, Jimmy Davis and Ginger Sadd were all up there. The cruncher was that Randolph was ranked second and Dick, unbelievably, hadn't got a mention either. Yet, when the three of us were on a show at Coventry later that year, Dick completely out-pointed the British champion Vince Hawkins in a non-title fight.

Dick could have actually claimed the title for that fight, cuz the MC made the mistake of announcing their weights – both inside the middleweight limit – and that would have made it official if Dick had bothered to pursue it. I wonder what the Boxing Board would've done about their colour bar then?

They could p'raps afford to recognise Randolph's talent for the moment, cuz he was under 21 and too young to be considered for a British title. Randolph beat Jimmy Ingle that night. You know? – the older brother of Naseem Hamed's trainer, Brendan. Randolph's wife's dad put money on Jimmy to beat Randolph. That's what he was like.

I was on the undercard and I had a problem with my opponent, Tony Brazil. Three times he'd punched me low. I kept saying, 'If you don't keep them punches higher, I'm going to start screaming.'

He took no notice, so I see another one coming, stepped back so it'd miss and fell down rolling about and kicking me feet. Mick Gavin leapt into the ring, picked me up and carried me back to the corner. 'Serve the bugger right,' he whispered. Mick made a big show of massaging me stomach and me legs, and Brazil got disqualified.

Back in the July of 1947, me and Dick was over at Stratford at an open-air do down by the river. I was fighting a Welsh kid, Les Turner. They often introduce old fighters to the audience as a warm-up to an evening of boxing and this particular night it was Jimmy Wilde. He'd been a good fighter way back – 'The Ghost With The Hammer In His Hand', cuz he used to knock people out and his arms were that thin you'd think he'd break 'em if he hit anybody – but he was little and fat then.

Wilde started telling stories about when he fought on the boxing booths: 'I fought this bloke an' knocked him out; I fought another bloke an' knocked him out; I fought this other bloke an' knocked him out . . .' The end of the story, when he'd been going on for about two hours, was he'd gone home and his wife asked, 'Where the hell have you been?' and when he told her, she knocked him out.

I'm waiting and waiting and he's droning on. I says to Mick, 'I'm cold. I'm getting out of the ring.'

'All right,' Mick says, and throws a blanket round me and we walk off.

Les Turner comes round and asks, 'What you got out for?'

'Cuz I'm sick of waiting and it's chilly.' Wilde stops spouting and Turner's waiting for me to get in the ring. 'No,' I says, pointing the way. 'After you.'

The referee's giving us instructions: '. . . if one of you goes down, the other one goes to the farthest neutral corner . . .' and Turner's muttering to me, 'You've got a swelled head, you have, Turpin.'

'Not as swelled as yours'll be when I've hit it,' I told him, and in the fourth round I showed him Jimmy Wilde and his wife wasn't the only ghosts around with hammers in their hands.

My next fight was in Liverpool. I don't know what it was with Liverpool but the audience was always really hostile. The Scouse lads on HMS *Myngs* were terrific with me but up there it was different.

I was fighting a local lad, Terry Riley. Riley kept punching well below the waterline and the referee was ignoring it. In the third round, I complained. 'He's hit me four times in the bollocks and you've done nothing. You a relative of his or summat?'

The referee got mad, saying, 'You don't want to go before the Board, do you?'

I thought, 'Bleeding great! I've been consistently fouled and he's threatening to have me licence taken off me.' So I said, 'No, but it looks like a family deal to me.' He nearly stopped the fight there and then.

'Keep your mouth shut, Turpin,' he said, 'and box on.'

'OK,' I thought, 'I'll sort Riley out meself.' The next time we were in close and I was on the blind side of the referee, I tried a head-butt and missed. This woman in the audience shouts, 'WATCH HIS DIRTY BLACK HEAD, TERRY.' She turned out to be Bessie Braddock, their local Member of Parliament. See what I mean? I shouted back, 'BOLLOCKS, YOU OLD BASTARD,' and tried another head-butt in a corner but missed again and skinned me forehead on the top rope. Riley saw blood on my forehead, realised what I'd tried to do and threw hisself on the floor clutching at his own completely unmarked head, wailing and moaning, making a real meal of it. The referee stopped the fight and give me my first ever disqualification. The Scousers cheered themselves stupid.

The promoter come up to me and said, 'It took me an hour to talk Mrs Braddock round from complaining to the Board about you.'

I told him, 'You should see me foul protector. It looks like a load of Bootle dockers have done a bleeding clog dance on it.'

People were always punching me in the balls. I could've understood it if I was 7 ft 10 in., or summat, but I'm only a little fella.

Where me and Dick had to travel all over the place, Randolph, with him being the bigger draw, the majority of his fights were in London and he always got a lot of newspaper coverage. In the October of 1947, Licker fought Mark Hart at Harringay and after six rounds of good boxing, the ref found them equal. It was the only draw Lick ever had. I know Licker was gaining strength and would've taken the fight if it'd gone on longer but the papers made a lot of it, hinting that Randolph was losing heart cuz his older brother was in his way.

George left Lockheed to concentrate on Randolph's career. With the boxing going like it was, he could afford to do without the factory. He'd got a grocer's shop as well. I'd always do all the work I could get and Lockheed give me my job back.

One time recently, I saw Nigel Benn on television advising Audley Harrison to keep busy. He suggested a fight every six months. Nigel was giving good advice there, cuz Audley didn't seem to be doing nothing, but I couldn't help smiling about what's 'busy' now compared with when we was fighting. In 1947, Dick had 20 fights and Randolph had 13 fights. I had 30 recorded fights – near enough as many as the other two put together and summat like a fight every 12 days. With other fights, sparring and the boxing booths in between, I was practically boxing in me sleep. I was the busiest featherweight in the country and the boxing writers called me 'Battling Jack'.

When we was first married, Bet used to do the road work with me. My usual routine was ten or fifteen miles a day but with Bet my distance went up another ten or fifteen miles because I'd have to keep running back to see where she was. She'd say, 'Carry on. I'm coming along.' We'd get to the top of the Saltisford, near me mum's, and I'd sprint to the house. Bet would try to keep up with me. I said to her one day, 'You're looking a bit peaky.'

'I should think so,' she said. 'I'm three months pregnant.'

1947 was a pretty good year for the Turpin brothers but it was an absolute milestone year in British boxing, because that was the year the British Boxing Board of Control was finally forced to drop their restrictions on black British fighters.

15

Colour Bar OK/Colour Bar KO

They blamed it on Jack Johnson – a great hero of mine and Randolph's. There'd been race riots over him in America. I ain't akidding, he could punch a hole in the side of a battleship. He was a terrific defensive boxer. He could fight, and he fought clean. He was from Galveston in Texas and the first black man to win the World heavyweight title.

Johnson was boxing back in the early 1900s and the last thing most white Americans wanted then, with it being the most prestigious division, was a black heavyweight champion. They never even tried to hide it. They'd shout to Johnson's opponents, 'KILL THE NIGGER!' Trouble was, they couldn't find anybody as Jack Johnson couldn't beat. The other trouble was, he wasn't meek and mild outside of the ring like they thought a black man should be.

If you was a black boxer – there or over here – people would see you boxing a white fella and you wouldn't just be two athletes competing in a sport where one of you happens to be white and the other of you happens to be black; it'd be all the white men in the world fighting all the black men in the world, sort of thing.

Like with my dad, Jack Johnson was only three or four generations away from slavery. White people from a slave tradition had to believe they was better than black people, because if they wasn't, how could you justify slavery? The other thing is, if you've treated people like shits for hundreds of years, you'll be worried about them paying you back, won't you?

A 1922 statement from British Government House in reference to a proposed bout at a London venue between Battling Siki from French West Africa, who had just taken the World light-heavyweight title from Georges Carpentier in Paris with a sixth round knockout, and a white fighter called Joe Beckett:

> 'The view held by the authorities is that in contests between men of colour and white men the temperaments of the contestants are not compatible. Moreover all sorts of passions are aroused. Such contests, considering that there are a very large number of men of colour in the British Empire, are considered against the higher national interest and they tend to arouse passions which it is inadvisable to stimulate.'

The newspapers called Siki the 'championzee' and a 'jungle fighter' – like he was a gorilla trained to box. The bleeding cheek. He was actually a city fella. He'd never been near a jungle in his life.

Whichever way you looked at it, when a white man boxed a black man, most people saw it as a race war. They couldn't sidestep Johnson, though, because the colour bar in American boxing wasn't official. Some white champions and contenders were willing to fight him. Mostly cuz they thought they could teach him a lesson.

Up until 1929, British boxing was controlled by the National Sporting Club in London. You mustn't forget the betting that goes on in boxing. The NSC regularised the weight divisions and tried to make sure fighters were matched properly. The award they gave boxers for winning a British title fight was a Lonsdale Belt. It's like a fancy gold watch big enough to put around your waist – well, too big really – on a red white and blue watch strap. They named it in honour of their president, Lord Lonsdale, and where the watch face should be, they put Lord Lonsdale's face.

Jack Johnson come over to London in 1908 chasing a Canadian heavyweight, Tommy Burns, and, when he got here, Burns had gone to Australia. Johnson hadn't got no money to pay his fare out there so the NSC paid it for him on the condition that if he won, he'd come back to London to defend his title against a

British heavyweight. It would've been big money for them. Well, Johnson went over to Australia, won the title and went straight back to America.

If you look at it, see, why did the National Sporting Club do it? Not to help Johnson but because they could see something in it for theirselves. Jack Johnson was closer to slave days than I am and I know how I feel sometimes when people ask me to do them a favour and I do it and then when I ask them to do summat for me later on they walk away. I think, 'Bastards! They still think they've got us by the tail and they can whip us when they want to.' And I s'pose that's what Johnson thought. The NSC resented him for letting them down, so they took it out on black men over here and banned them from contesting British national titles. A.F. Bettinson – they called him 'Peggy' for some reason – he was the bloke most strongly behind it in the beginning.

Boxing was getting very, very popular and the NSC's Covent Garden gymnasium wasn't big enough for all the people as wanted to come to watch the fights, so they spread out and put tournaments on all over the place. They must've spread theirselves too thin, though, cuz they started going broke and the British Boxing Board of Control took over.

It sounds like a government department, doesn't it? **'THE BRITISH BOXING BOARD OF CONTROL'** – but it isn't. A gang of businessmen set it up, some of them from the old NSC, and it still controls professional boxing here today. Nobody can make money out of boxing without going through the British Boxing Board of Control. Every pro boxer has to pay for a licence from them, so do managers and trainers and match-makers and referees and promoters. The Board takes a cut of the boxer's purse, a cut of the promoter's money and another cut where there's TV fees. On the other side, they took over supplying the Lonsdale Belts, which they let you keep if you win it three times at one weight, and they appoint and pay for the referees and the timekeepers; they supply the gloves and bandages and inspectors and medical officers. When they set themselves up, they made a load of health and safety improvements to safeguard professional boxers. But they kept up the colour bar on their national titles.

REGULATION 31, PARAGRAPH 4:

Contestants must be legally British subjects born of white parents; must be resident, not less than two years in the British Isles, of which the first twelve months must be continuous . . .

Even the Americans who were very much against black people hadn't gone as far as writing it down. It's funny, innit, as long as you were white, you could actually have been born outside the British Isles and still be qualified.

Keeping up the colour bar mainly hinged around one fella: Charles F. Donmall, General Secretary to the Board. He said it was only right that a small country like ours should have championships restricted to boxers with white parents. Otherwise we might be faced with all our British titles being held by coloured 'Empire' boxers. He told the Board, 'No coloured man will ever be British champion.'

Some people still find it hard to believe you can be black and British at the same time. When I was a kid in Leamington, people would see me, a little coloured boy, walking down the road and they'd think, 'I wonder if he speaks English?' They'd speak pidgin English to me and be quite surprised when I talked back fluent. British people are a great big pudding-bowl mix, aren't they: Romans, Normans, Saxons, Africans, Indians . . . part of someone from every place in the world, most probably.

Not all of them at the BBB of C thought the way of Donmall. Overturning the ban was raised regular at their meetings but was refused by the ones that set the rules. Even when a white fella, Harry Crossley – the British light-heavyweight champion – offered to let Len Johnson fight him for his title and some of the area boards supported it, it was turned down by the London one, the main one. That must have been around 1930, cuz Crossley was champion then.

Len Johnson was a mate of Mick Gavin's from Manchester. Len had beaten Ted 'Kid' Lewis at middleweight and Len Harvey at light-heavyweight – two British and European champions – but because he was black he wasn't allowed to take their titles off them.

From time to time, boxing managers pleaded with the Board to let one of their black fighters have a title shot – George Middleton, of course, and Freddie Mills' manager, Ted Broadribb, was another one but they was all turned down.

The newspapers were full of it. Peter Wilson, George Whiting, Tom Phillips . . . the big majority of boxing writers wrote against the colour bar, quoting the Turpin brothers as the example, and the pressure built up and built up and more and more people started making complaints and getting petitions up. A bloke called Barney Janner got one up that went all round the country. Boxing fans thought the ban was stupid because the only boxer who should be British champion was the one that was best out of everyone born in the British Isles.

A London solicitor took up our case for us. A Jewish fella. He said he could associate with us cuz he knew what it was like being persecuted. He argued that all five of us Turpins were born here. We'd fought for our country in the war and that should qualify us to fight for our country in the ring. Our mum's family was all British. Our dad wasn't born here but he'd been brought up British and it was fighting for Britain that killed him. The Second World War was against Hitler, wasn't it? The Nazis had all those ideas about race and now people over here was doing it. It was a big controversy.

Jack Solomons told the Board he didn't agree with the ban one little bit. He thought the British title should be regardless of colour but he saw some money in it an' all and jumped on the band wagon by putting on 'domino' fights, where black boxers fought white boxers, to rub it in and cuz he knew it'd get a crowd.

Remember that contest at the Albert Hall when Cliff Anderson tanked Al Phillips for the British Empire featherweight title and still lost? Referees are appointed by the Board, aren't they? There was quite an uproar. Even Phillips' fans were embarrassed about it. Scuffles broke out, and questions were asked in Parliament.

OFFICIAL REPORT – FIFTH SERIES PARLIAMENTARY DEBATES – COMMONS – 1947–47 – MARCH 17TH TO APRIL 3RD. COLUMN 231, PAGE 107.

Boxing Matches, colour bar.

104. Mr Gary Allighan asked the Secretary of State for the Home Department how many police officers were on duty in and around the approaches to the Royal Albert Hall on

Tuesday, 18th March, on the occasion of the Anderson–Phillips fight; whether he is aware that the decision under British Board of Boxing Control [*sic*] rules caused a public demonstration at the end of that fight; and if he will warn the board that they must discontinue the operation of the colour bar rule at their boxing matches, as its retention will cause a breach of the peace.

Mr Ede: There were 27 police officers outside the Albert Hall but none inside, and there was no demonstration sufficiently serious for the police to intervene. I understand that the trouble arose from a difference of opinion between the crowd and the referee on the merits of the boxers. I have no jurisdiction over the British Boxing Board of Control.

The Board of Control refused to change the referee's decision.

Arthur Batty at the Nelson took a very close interest in the colour bar. He used to put our boxing pictures and posters up on the walls there and he wrote his own notices as well – mostly our fight records and his own predictions about fights. He done it as an encouragement. When Solomons told George that the Board of Control was gonna meet to reconsider Regulation 31, George told Arthur, and Arthur wrote on the wall:

COLOUR BAR KO, ROUND 1, JUNE 1947

A month later, Phillips and Anderson met again and this time Cliffy got disqualified. Phillips knew Cliffy could out-box him but he wasn't short of a trick or two hisself. He'd turned away from body punches so's they'd land in the kidney area or got up on his toes so's to make 'em land below the belt as foul punches. It ended with Cliffy getting disqualified cuz the referee seemed too thick to see what was really going on. Cliffy was really fed up about that but he never moaned. He was ever such a nice quiet fella.

COLOUR BAR KO, FINAL ROUND, SEPTEMBER 1947!

It got so's everybody had had it up to here with them being against us winning British titles. When Charles Donmall left the Board of Control and Teddy Waltham took over, the colour bar was swept away and the rules got rewrote:

A contestant must be a British subject who was born and is normally resident and domiciled in the United Kingdom. Provided that a contestant shall not be excluded whose birth has taken place abroad during the temporary employment or residence of his father overseas . . .

Were we resentful of the colour bar? No, not really, even though we realised we were being prevented from getting further than Empire titles. Now it seems like a terrible thing but at the time we just thought it was a pity Dick couldn't compete for the British middleweight title, cuz we thought he'd most likely win it. We didn't spend much time thinking about it, though. That was just how it was and we accepted it for a long time; but, in the end, it was the fighting abilities of the Turpin brothers – Dick in particular – and all them as helped us, that finally KOd it. With the ban on black British fighters swept away, things was very, very much different.

16

Big Brother is Watching You

I opened 1948 with a row of nine wins, with less than half of them going the distance, and I was being ranked three or four amongst British featherweights. Ronnie Clayton held the British, the Empire and the European featherweight crowns, having beat Al Phillips on points. I didn't see how I could be denied Phillips now.

I went to see his manager, Jack King. 'When are you going to let me fight Al?'

King was straight about it. 'Not this week, next week, nor any week in the foreseeable future, Jack. You're boxing too well.'

I thought, 'What a bloody racket this is!'

I reported back to George. 'Look, son,' he said, 'you've been boxing wonderful and I'm sure the Board won't refuse us a shot at the Southern Central Area championship. It would be a title for you.'

'OK, George,' I said. 'Get it me.' He did and I bloody lost. Albert Bessell was the holder. All the officials there thought I'd won – except the referee. The crowd got up on their feet and booed the decision; the promoter told the referee, 'You want your fucking eyes tested.' Mick Gavin was so incensed he walked towards the referee saying as how he was going to tear him apart and George had to throw a towel over his head and lead him away. Poor old George. He had a hell of bad time going home because we thought he should've been angrier about it. Every time he went to say summat, we told him, 'Shurrrup!'

Dick was regaining recognition for his boxing. If he was second to any middleweight in Britain it was only to Randolph. Lick'd left the navy in the March and was being regarded as Britain's hottest new boxing talent.

Well, yes, there was that little bit of green amongst it. I used to see behind the curtains, if you see what I mean. Before the war, Dick Turpin had been the one to watch, then Randolph come along and now most of the attention was on our baby brother and people were talking to Dick about how great Randolph was. Dick thought George was that way with it an' all. 'Arrgh!' he'd say. 'It's bloody Licker all the time!' But Randolph thought the world of his older brother.

Who was the best of the two? Well, Dick was fantastic, scientific and a great rider of punches. He won quite a few fights on knockouts; but if you watched him when he hit them, they used to knock themselves out mostly. He'd get them coming to him when he hit them. His timing was perfect. He knew how to use the ring and he'd mastered defence. Randolph was the same but his edge was he was stronger. He could take someone out with either hand.

I remember Dick and Randolph boxed an exhibition match in Birmingham. It was like they was working to a script. I was spellbound. For the whole of the fight, neither landed a clean punch on the other, they were both that skilful at defence. Then, just before the bell at the end of the last round, Licker stepped in under Dick's left lead, clipped him on the chin and put him on the deck. Instead of leaving it at that, Dick leapt up off the floor and flew at Randolph like a bloody madman. He was raving, throwing punches all over the place and calling Licker all the names under the sun. Jack Solomons, George Middleton and Alex Griffiths jumped in the ring and pulled them apart. 'Calm down,' Solomons told Dick. 'He didn't mean to hit you that hard. You walked on to the punch.' Randolph just stood there while Dick was raving, catching the punches with his hands.

Me and Dick almost came to fighting a load of times – knuckles I mean – cuz Dick used to run Licker down to people. To hear Dick speak, they was feeding Randolph lemons. I'd say, 'You don't talk like that when you're taking your wages off of him.' Sometimes I'd walk in a room and Dick and Randolph would be sat there just staring at each other.

After that flare-up at the exhibition bout, Dick said to me, 'He was bloody lucky I didn't get him, cuz I would have killed him.'

'No,' I told him. 'You were lucky he didn't hit you back.'

'That's it,' he said, 'go sucking up to your brother.'

I said, 'No. I always looked after him when he was a kid. You didn't.'

A reporter come to Wathen Road to interview me mum. 'Mrs Manley, you have two sons, both middleweights, both potentially in line for the British title. Which of them do you want to win it?' It was a delicate situation for her, cuz she knew how Dick could be with Randolph. 'Well,' she said, 'I want them both to win it. I'm no connoisseur of boxing but in my opinion, Dick could have beaten all the opposition with one hand tied behind his back if he hadn't have been away at war. Randolph's too young to fight for the British title at the moment, so Dick should have the first try.' But she'd seen summat, summat that upset her: what if Dick held the title and Randolph, by the time he was 21, was number one contender?

She got Dick and Randolph together. 'One thing you must promise me. You don't ever fight each other. If you do, I shan't have nothing to do with either of you ever again.' She got the reporter back and had a photograph published of them shaking hands in front of her promising in no circumstances would they meet each other in the ring. We loved our mum and we would never defy her.

Randolph had whacked up a score of 18 wins and a draw since his debut but had a blip when he lost on points to Albert Finch in April 1948. It was a fight he should've won and everybody noticed he hadn't fought as well as expected. They wrote some crap about it in the papers, saying his heart wasn't in boxing no more cuz there was nowhere for him to go in the middleweight division if he couldn't fight his big brother. The truth of the matter was, he'd been fighting with a bum hand.

He'd got into a ruck in Stratford with some RAF blokes over some birds. One of the blokes started saying things about Randolph's colour, so he got given a couple of black eyes to match it. Randolph dusted two of them up then shot back to Leamington on the back of his mate's motorbike. On the way home, they skidded and come off.

I don't know whether it was in the fight or in the motorbike accident that Randolph's hand got done in but his middle knuckle stuck right out. It went down again but never completely. Anyway, before it'd healed, that's when he fought Albert Finch. It was a blip on his record but it didn't affect Randolph much because the second time he got in the ring with Finch, by God, he nearly killed him.

In spite of what Dick moaned about from time to time, George was looking after him terrific. He negotiated for him to contest the British Empire middleweight title at Coventry City football ground against Richard 'Bos' Murphy of New Zealand. We knew Murphy had been welterweight champion of his country and he'd taken the Empire middleweight title from Vince Hawkins at the beginning of the year; but as far as how he fought was concerned, he was an unknown quality to us. They have videotapes of the different fighters now but in those days we had to travel out to see them actually fighting.

Murphy was billed at the Albert Hall against Mark Hart, a kid from Croydon, and George suggested Dick went with him to watch Murphy fight. Dick snarled at George, 'What do I want to watch him fight for?'

George looked a bit taken aback, so I said, 'I'll come with you, George.' During the fight I was thinking, 'There's something queer about this fella Murphy.'

We're out in the country training Dick, and I says, 'If you listen to me, you can knock Bos Murphy out in the first round.'

Dick laughs, 'Hark at Mr Smart-Arse here!'

'Well,' I said, 'Murphy fights orthodox but he's a natural southpaw.' See, at the end of the Murphy–Hart fight, I'd told George, 'Tell Dick he's got nothing to fear from Murphy's right hand but he's got to watch his left hook.'

'What makes you say that?'

'He's a southpaw turned round.'

'Ooh, I'm not sure about that, Jack.'

We went to see Murphy. 'Can I have your autograph please, Bos?' I asked. Murphy took the bit of paper I offered him and signed his name with his left hand. George shot me a little smile. When we told Dick the story, all he said was, 'Huh.'

Come the fight, Dick went out, Murphy threw a right-hand, then a left hook that went over the top of Dick's head, Dick hit him on the chin with his right hand: ZZZONK! Murphy managed to get up but immediately fell down again. And that was it. Dick was the new British Empire middleweight champion in less than a round. I told Dick afterwards, 'I won that bleeding fight for you and you never even said thank you.' He was always the same, though, Dick was. He didn't need any help from anybody, sort of thing.

I was on that card of Dick's at Coventry, fighting Ben Duffy, a very highly rated featherweight. Beating him would be another big move upwards.

The eyeball-to-eyeball stuff boxers do when the ref's giving the pre-fight pep talk, we never went in for that much. We generally just shook hands and come out fighting. We even used to have a little chat sometimes: 'You all right?' an' all that.

It's ever so funny, you'd meet blokes in the ring and try to knock their heads off but if they read in the papers something had happened to you, they'd be down to see you, or there'd be a letter sent to your house. It's amazing how the friendships form.

I was on the radio the other week, at Birmingham, and this woman rung in saying about her dad who was a boxer on the booths. When he died, this bloke turned up at the funeral. He said to her, 'He was a great fella, your dad was. He knocked seven bells out of me at the Onion Fair.' She could hardly believe complete strangers would put themselves out to come to her father's funeral just because he used to box. Well, it happens all the time.

Ben Duffy had a different take on it this particular night though. He stood there insulting me, telling me I hadn't got a hope in hell. I laughed. I thought, 'That's quite a compliment, Duffy. You're so high up in the ratings yet you feel you have to resort to this sort of stuff when you take on one of the Turpins.' Every time we were in a clinch, he carried on: 'Murphy's gonna kill your brother Dick'; 'Randolph's an overrated slugger.' He said foul things about my wife which I won't repeat. He was going right through the family. I was thinking, 'Yeah, you carry on, kid, none of this is bothering me in the slightest.' Then, in the fifth round, he got on to me mum and the temper erupted in me like a volcano. I threw an almighty right to his head and sent him staggering . . . Oh, Christ! . . . I thought I'd broken every bone in my hand. I froze with pain and Duffy knocked me down. I was getting off the floor after a short count, still mad to get at Duffy, but the referee saw me give my injured hand a shake and stopped the fight.

My arm felt like it had been plunged in a cauldron of boiling acid. The pain was flaring out from where the small bones in my hand had been impacted up like a miniature mountain between my knuckles and wrist. Even now, over 50 years later, I feel like screaming with it sometimes. I have to put a glove over it in cold weather and some mornings my fingers won't work properly.

George whipped me up the hospital and they worked on straightening it up and whacked on a plaster cast to hold it in position. I was livid with Duffy. 'You've got to get him again for me, George,' I said. 'Anywhere, anytime, at any money!'

You often hear people, especially promoters, calling all sorts of fights 'historic' but Dick had a fight coming up that truly was. A fight later in our lives was tagged 'The Fight of the Century' but it should've been this one really, cuz it affected all British boxers for all time. It was the fight everybody had been arguing and campaigning and fighting and writing for our right to have, and it was the first time the British Boxing Board of Control had conceded to it. A black British man was going to contest the domestic title of his own country. British sporting history.

The current middleweight title holder was Vince Hawkins and he'd be making his first defence of his Lonsdale Belt and it'd be Dick's first defence of the Empire title he'd took off Bos Murphy.

When boxers have an important fight coming up, their managers like to get them away from their home town so's they can't be worried or distracted, or tempted away from their training by their family or their mates. Every bit of your energy should be directed towards your training. You have to have a place that's exclusive to you where you can keep other people out.

George had chosen a village hall in Bishop's Itchington for Dick's training. It's a few miles out of Warwick, near a disused airfield. My wife's sister lived in one of the huts there. I think that's where Bill Hyam crept in on the scene with ambitions about becoming our trainer. He lived out there an' all, or summat.

Me, Randolph, and three or four sparmates went along to train with Dick, and we trained hard, I tell you. Dick had only been back in the ring for two years. The war had badly interrupted his career and he was 27 years of age but he was back on his form and favourite to win. He'd beat Hawkins into retirement with a cut eye when they'd met at Coventry the year before and Randolph had beaten Hawkins on points three or four months previous but there are NO guarantees in the fight game. We'd had word Hawkins was training hard up in London and looking better than he ever had.

All three of us were on the bill with Dick headlining. Randolph was boxing Alby Hollister, and I'd got the rematch I'd pleaded for with Ben Duffy.

A few days before the contest, George told me, 'I'm pulling you out of your fight, Jack.'

'Eh? No you don't, George!'

'But you've still got that plaster on your hand.'

I went out, got a hammer, smashed the plaster cast off and come back. 'It ain't in plaster no more, George,' I said. Poor old George. The Turpins was most awkward buggers.

Mick Gavin understood why I had to take Duffy on. He advised me, 'Don't trade punches with him. Step in with two or three punches and step out again.' My hand felt like it belonged to someone else but I planned to box to protect it – unless Duffy said summat about me mother, of course.

Ben Duffy must have seen a different look in my eye as we faced each other either side of the referee. He never bothered with the insults. We got down to business and I battered his face with straight lefts for eight rounds – one, two, three and move away. I boxed his ears off! A landslide points decision. A big, big win. Now they'd *have* to give me a shot at the British title.

Randolph won his fight comfortably on points, too, and it was time for the main event.

Fifty-five thousand people paid a guinea each in the tipping rain at Aston Villa football ground on Monday evening, 28 June 1948, to watch history being made. It was a fantastic atmosphere in spite of the weather.

Lionel Cecil Turpin, nicknamed 'Dick' after the famous highwayman, stood and delivered. After 15 rounds of immaculate boxing against an out-classed Vince Hawkins, Dick was the new British middleweight champion. They clamped the Lonsdale belt on him and the crowd rose to their feet and cheered and cheered.

We helped our mum through the ropes to stand beside him. She hadn't seen much of the fight, cuz her sight had got so bad, but she knew what the result was and she was smiling as proud as only a mum could be who had three sons – three winners on the same night – two in the top bracket in Britain at their weights and one who'd broken the colour bar to prove hisself the best middleweight in Great Britain and, at the same time, to confirm hisself the best middleweight in the British Empire.

For the very first time, a Lonsdale Belt was around the waist of a black man – my big brother.

17

Like Driving at Really High Speed

Before Dick become British champion, me and Bet had a big occasion of our own: the birth of our daughter. She was the most wonderful thing you ever saw. The newspapers described her as having 'six jet-black cotton-wool curls, skin like wild honey and eyes like limpid pools'. Her arrival was announced on the wireless. We named her Georgina Elizabeth in honour of George Middleton and my mum, and George and Lily become her proud godparents. When the American film star Tyrone Power was at Warwick Castle to make *The Black Rose*, me and me brothers were invited up to meet the cast. I took baby Georgina with me. 'What a beautiful child!' Tyrone said and he carried her about all day.

Randolph and T'rese had a little lad: Randolph Adolphus junior. But Randolph's marriage turned into a bit of a grudge match and only lasted about a year. We were sorry, cuz we liked T'rese.

Us Turpins were getting very famous and what with our actual contests and being invited to box exhibitions everywhere and go to other gymnasiums as honoured guests, an' all that, and with the training we had to do, we spent more time out than we did at home. All the attention we was getting wasn't easy for wives. Like, Bet didn't come to see many of my fights because at one of the early ones she come to, as we were leaving the stadium a girl jumped out of nowhere and kissed me. Bet smacked my face for it and didn't seem interested in my boxing after that.

Randolph fell out with his in-laws and it ended up with T'rese turning as sour as her mum on him and bringing an assault charge against him. The court case was dismissed but their marriage was spoilt. It affected Randolph a lot.

My win against Ben Duffy wiped out the disadvantage I'd suffered by losing the Southern Central Area contest and put me up there again with the top featherweights. My winning mood carried on till I met Jackie Lucraft in London in November. It was a real humdinger from the first bell to the last. I'd thought I'd won hands down but the referee walked straight to Jackie's corner and give it him. I told George, 'Get him again.' I took some sweets round to Lucraft's dressing-room to show there was no hard feelings. 'But,' I told him, 'next time, it's your turn to bring the sweets.'

Dick was moving steadily up towards a World title and was pulling the money in. Trouble was, if people praised him he'd stand them drinks all night. He would have been very well off if he'd invested his money but he liked having it in his pocket so's he could splash it about.

Dick's next stop on the title trail was a final eliminator for the European championship against the Italian champion, Tiberio Mitri. Dick still suffered with his hands and it affected his contest with Mitri. He held him to a draw but it was gonna have to be re-fought.

I had another humdinger when I was rematched with Jackie Lucraft early in the new year. Toe to toe, but I felt like I never got going properly and expected it to go to Jackie but the referee raised my hand instead. I looked at Jackie and shook my head apologetically. Jackie honoured our agreement from the first fight and come round to my dressing-room with a box of chocolates. I told George, 'Get him again.' There had to be a decider.

A couple of weeks later we met in Bermondsey and were given a draw but I'd busted his face into such a mess, if you'd looked at his eye you'd have thought it'd come out. I went to see him in the dressing-room and a towel had been wrapped over his injury and pulled so hard there was a dent all round his head. 'What the fucking hell are you doing?' I asked his manager.

'Trying to stop the bleeding.'

'If you done that to me,' I said, 'I'd kick you in the nuts. Get him seen to properly.'

Me and Jackie were one each, one even. There'd gotta be a fourth fight. I told George, 'Get him again.' He did, but I had to wait a long time for it.

In February 1949, I fought a battle with a kidda from Blackpool and the outcome of it changed my whole attitude to boxing. It was at the Victoria Hall, Hanley, Stoke-on-Trent, and the kid was the Ronnie Clayton who'd beaten Al Phillips.

Clayton was British and Empire champion, a hard-hitter, hailed as one of the best British featherweights for years. In 1952, he was to be ranked sixth in THE WORLD. His management promised me, win or lose, so long as I was still on me feet at the end of the eight rounds, I could box him in the summer for the Empire title. It's not often you get the opportunity of actually losing a fight on points and winning at the same time, and I was thrilled. Of course, I might well win it outright.

In the first four rounds, I had Ronnie on the deck three times. I come out in the fifth looking for a finisher and caught him on top of the head. Me hand went absolutely dead. It was hanging by my side – all from when I'd broke the plaster cast off to fight Ben Duffy. I boxed the last three rounds blocking and countering with one hand. But, I finished the fight still standing.

It was close but the referee reckoned Clayton had come back and shaded the bout. A lot of people shook my hand and said, 'You won tonight,' but, whatever they or the referee made of it, I was still on me feet when the final bell went and I'd earned the right to fight for a top title. I was chuffed. I was confident I'd get the decision over Clayton with two good hands. I went to Clayton's manager to cash in on his promise. 'When will it be in the summer then?'

'He beat you, Jack!'

'Yeah, but you said if I "went the distance".'

'We said "if you won".'

'You fucking didn't!' I said. 'I won the first half of the bleeding fight and I could've beat him with two good hands and you know it.' So that was another one where they set me aside.

I got moody about it and George said, 'What's the matter with you?'

'Don't blame me, George. Blame you.'

'Why me?'

'Well, do summat about it. They won't let me fight for the title when I've earned the right. The *Boxing News* is calling for it. Everybody's calling for it.' George went to see Clayton's people but come back saying they'd said it was 'too risky'.

'We'll sue the buggers,' I said.

131

George disagreed. 'We haven't got the agreement in writing from Clayton's people,' he said, 'and we could never persuade a court or the Board of Control without it.'

'Well,' I said, 'if I'm not gonna get a crack at an Empire title or a British title, why should I kill meself training?'

'Don't just throw it all away, Jack, you silly sod,' George said. 'You're too good for that.' He used to get ever so mad at me – cussing me up hill and down dale – but I couldn't rally. I lost fights I should've won just cuz I'd started not giving two hoots. You can understand it: I'd been doing all the road work, I'd been down the gym every night of the week, I'd stopped drinking, smoking, staying out late and, at the end of it, all I could see was a big black mass – *I wasn't gonna get a crack at the British title*.

Dick went off to Trieste on the Adriatic for his rematch with Tiberio Mitri for the European middleweight title eliminator – Mitri's home town. Dick was in good form but lost narrowly on points. It was a setback, cuz he needed that title if he was to be taken seriously as a World contender. There was, however, another way open to him.

George arranged for Dick to fight a French fella, Marcel Cerdan, in a non-title fight, in March 1949. The Empress Hall at Earl's Court, this was. The reason it wasn't a title fight was cuz Cerdan was overweight and got fined for it, and the promoters hadn't come up with a big enough purse for it to be worth him putting his World title on the line. George thought if Dick won, he could work on a return with Cerdan's World title at stake.

A couple of years before, Cerdan had won the French and European middleweight titles, and the year before he fought Dick, he'd taken the World middleweight title from 'Man of Steel', Tony Zale. He was the biggest threat Dick had ever faced.

I'm in the crowd watching. Dick was terrific. He was actually boxing that well he was making Cerdan look stupid. But in the seventh, he was just that little bit slow covering up and Cerdan caught him with a short right-hander straight between the eyes. A puncher only needs that split second. Dick fell forward with his nose pouring blood and, at EXACTLY the same time, *my* nose started pouring with blood an' all. I don't know whether it was the tension of the fight, or what, but that's what happened.

I went with Dick to the physiotherapist, cuz he was having trouble with his nose after the Cerdan fight. It looked OK but it hurt like hell. This physio got him on the table. 'Hold his hands, Jack. It'll give him something to squeeze on.'

The physio grabs hold of Dick's nose and gives it a wrench, and the next thing, the table's on top of us and there's all three of us on the floor. Dick's thrashing his legs about and yelling and screaming, trying to break free, but the physio won't let go. He's twisting and pulling Dick's nose and I'm hanging on to his hands for fear of me own nose.

There was a long, dull CRAAAAACK! and Dick screams, 'FUCK!' The physio releases Dick's nose and Dick runs out of the room dragging me with him. Outside, he turns on me and says, 'For two pins I'd knock your bleeding head off!'

'What for?'

'You should have let go. I wanted to kill the bastard.'

'But he was helping yer.'

'Helping me?' he asked in disbelief.

'Well, what does your nose feel like now?'

He puts his hand up to his hooter. 'Oh,' he said. 'It feels great, kid. No pain there at all.' He straightened his clothes and tested his nose again. 'He's all right, that bloke,' he said. 'Good physio.'

Our son, John Matthew Turpin junior, was born early that May. Everybody asked me, 'Is he gonna be a boxer like his dad and his uncles?'

I told them, 'It's up to him to choose what he wants to do. I'll help him best I can whatever it is.' You can't force someone into boxing. If you don't really want to do it, you'll be no good.

I'd now got two wonderful children and a wonderful wife but me and Mosh Mancini, we was away boxing all over England, Scotland and Wales. My family used to think I was a stranger when I come home. If we'd had a dog, I think it would've bit me as a burglar.

George Middleton had built up the biggest stable of boxers in the Midlands – in England, I should imagine. Everybody wanted him to manage them because he was doing so good for us and because he was such a straight fella.

Oh, yeah, a couple of months after beating my brother, Marcel Cerdan lost his World title to Jake LaMotta, the 'Bronx Bull'. The film *Raging Bull* come from the book of his life story. Cerdan damaged his shoulder in the fight and his corner threw the towel in. He was flying out to America for the rematch when his plane crashed into a mountain in the Azores and he was killed.

The middleweight division lost one of its most shining stars when Cerdan went. He'd only lost four out of a hundred and nine professional fights and what he lost was on dodgy decisions. Boxing reporters said even the legendary Sugar Ray Robinson was avoiding him.

After the plane crash, it leaked out who Cerdan's girlfriend was: Edith Piaf. A famous French cabaret singer. The 'Little Sparrow'. With Cerdan being a family man, it caused quite a stink. Women were bound to be chasing him, though, weren't they – a top boxer with film-star looks? I mean, the bleeding cheek! You get punched to crap and then, cuz you've got a bird, everybody's got to know about it, innit? It annoys me, that.

Something else come out – in the 1960s, this was, when it come out – the Mafia, or some mob in America, had bribed or forced Jake LaMotta to lose against a fighter called Billy Fox. The deal was, if he threw the fight then he could contest for the World title against Cerdan. It's funny cuz LaMotta was worth a World title shot anyway. In 1943, he become the first boxer to beat Sugar Ray Robinson.

Dick successfully defended his British and Empire titles against Albert Finch, which meant he'd won a Lonsdale Belt twice. One more time and he could keep it. That's very prestigious, and they're worth a lot of money an' all.

Jack Solomons imported an Australian middleweight over here. Dave Sands. He talked in fanfares about him. 'There is nobody in this world he couldn't knock out,' an' all that. Sands was an Aborigine and only allowed out of his country for six months at a time, because that's how they treated black Australians then. Solomons wanted to get as many fights out of him as quick as he could.

Solomons sold Sands' fights on how he'd boasted about him, so everybody laughed when Sands got out-pointed in his first fight. Sands showed a bit more class in a couple of fights after that but he hadn't shown none of this dynamite he was supposed to be packing in both fists.

George accepted an offer from Solomons for Dick to defend his British Empire title against Sands. George was always a little bit in awe of Solomons and p'raps should have looked around for an easier fight for Dick, cuz Dick's hands were still bruised from the Finch fight. In fact, the date had to be rescheduled to 6 September cuz of them not being healed, but if Dick was on form, him and Sands would be a good match.

On the night, Dave Sands sprung out of his corner like a boxing kangaroo, knocked Dick down twice, then laid him out, all in a minute. Solomons was delighted. He wouldn't look such a twonk now to the British press who'd been saying he'd buttered up Sands' abilities. But it wasn't how it looked.

Boxing's like driving at really high speed: you've only got to lose your concentration for a split second and it can prove fatal. Dick's wife, Emily, had been rushed into hospital with a miscarriage before we'd left to go to London. It'd been touch and go whether she died or not. And Dick's mate, the stupid bleeder, when they let Emily out of hospital on the day of the fight, brought her up to Harringay. As Dick's climbing in the ring, his mate shouts to him, 'Emily's here.'

The referee's doing the spieling and Dick's looking for Emily. I yelled at him, 'LOOK AT YOUR OPPONENT!'

Mick Gavin says, 'What's up?'

'Emily's here.'

'Oh my God!' he says.

Dick comes out, still looking for his missus, and BOOMP! – goodbye Empire title.

Dick won his next couple of fights but his dramatic loss against Sands had took the edge off his interest. Like, when he should've been eating properly he'd set off for a packet of fish an' chips and a pint of beer. Well, you don't do that, not when you're boxing seriously. And you don't stop out late at night.

How did Randolph do in 1949? Eight fights, eight wins, with six inside the distance. It was like someone had suddenly opened a door at Land's End and let a wind in that was blowing down all our middleweights.

I opened the new year with an eliminator for another crack at the Southern Central Area title, against Ivor Simpson, in Cheltenham again. Things were going well until the seventh round when Simpson caught me with a full body-weight blow to the solar plexus. It was like me stomach had gone sailing out of the ring and left me legs standing with me head and shoulders suspended in the air above them, then they all collapsed in a heap. The pain was *excruciating*. I thought I was gonna die.

The worst KO comes from a slow build up of blows to the head. You get less able to defend yourself and slowly drop into unconsciousness. Your brain's loose on a stem, see, like a soft cauliflower, and when you get punched, it can bang against your skull and start to swell. If they don't reduce the pressure quick through surgery, you can die. Having your brain temporarily disconnected by a single, clean punch ain't a long-term problem. You go out like a light and when the light comes back on it's like it never happened – you've got no ill effects. A knockout blow to the solar plexus completely disables you. You don't lose consciousness but you can't breathe. Body shots take ages to recover from anyway but when you get hit in the ol' tripe, oooh. It put the fear of God up me. I just lay there and got counted out.

On the way home, there was George and Dick in the front of the car, me and Mick in the back. I kep' doubling up in pain and Mick pulled my feet up on his lap, pushed me down on the seat and then bent me head towards me knees to try and ease it but it was still killing me.

Bet was asleep when I got in. I tiptoed up the stairs, got into bed and drew me knees up to my chin. Then Bet moved and I had to put me knees down. It was just like somebody had got a stick and rammed it in me stomach. I yelled out with the pain. Next minute, the light's on. 'What's the matter, Jack?'

'Oooh, me stomach!'

'You've gone all white,' Bet said, and she run down the road to telephone for an ambulance.

I must have been delirious. I'm effing and blinding to this doctor. 'You ******, I'll never be able to ******* box again! You'll ruin me career, you ****!'

Next morning, he comes round the ward. 'How do you feel this morning, Mr Turpin?'

'Bit groggy, doctor.'

'In the navy, were we?'

'I don't know about you, doctor, but I was. Why?'

'There was something about your language last night that suggested you might have been.'

'Ooops! Sorry, doctor.'

'We had an emergency with you, Mr Turpin,' he said. 'Burst appendix. If we hadn't operated straight away, you would have been a corpse talking to me this morning.'

'What about my boxing, doctor? Is it finished?'

'How would a scar like that suit you?' he said, showing a gap of about an inch between his thumb and first finger.

'Absolutely great! Thank you,' I said, but I was still worried about the effect on my boxing. The appendix scars I'd seen on other people were like bleeding shark bites where their muscles had been slashed to open them up.

When George Middleton come in, I said, 'Have a look at me scar, George, for God's sake.' It was just like the doctor said: a neat little scar about an inch long. A fantastic job. He'd cut between the muscles so there would be no physical effect on me boxing. It did have a psychological effect on me, though. I kept thinking, 'If they hit me in the belly, I'll bust open.' When sweat was running down me leg, I'd think it was blood.

I'd been out of hospital three weeks when I fought again. Tommy Blears. He hit me in the solar plexus and I went down like a ton of bricks. It happened again against Johnny Rawlings. I was hanging over the bottom rope, gasping for air, and I see this reporter write, 'Turpin goes down with a terrific right to the chin.'

I'm trying to tell him, 'Yer bloody fool! It was the stomach!' but I just hung there with me mouth opening and shutting like a goldfish. I got up and finished the fight but all my confidence had gone.

Dick was still the reigning British middleweight champion but Randolph had closed right in on him in the ratings. Licker beat Pete Meade who'd gone the distance with Sands, and Solomons had ambitions to bring Sands back over here to challenge Randolph for the Empire title. Randolph was looking forward to avenging his big brother but it never come off, cuz Solomons was to find Licker a bigger fish to fry. A much, much bigger fish.

Dick and Randolph's vow to our mum not to fight each other was looking to get embarrassing. They were being regarded more and more as equal. So much so that when Solomons brought Baby Day over from America to fight at the Albert Hall, it was billed as: Dick or Randolph TURPIN *versus* Baby DAY. There was a question mark over Randolph being able to get his hands right for the contest. Dick was the one who eventually fought and he lost on points. Boxing records never show how close points decisions are. This was very close. A lot of boxing pundits believed Randolph would've won it outright.

Boxing fans would have LOVED to have seen a Judgement Day between Dick and Randolph. It was a popular pub argument, who was the best, and George was under pressure. He started playing with the idea of Randolph going up to light-heavyweight, or 'cruiser weight' as it's called sometimes. Lick could do it easy and not lose any of his mobility.

On the face of it, it'd mean Licker going in the ring with the current British light-heavyweight champion, Freddie Mills – one of those fighters you almost had to kill to stop. He was a big puncher an' all, Freddie. Licker was up for it but George thought it would be a bit of a take-on with Lick only being 22 and new at that weight division. Then Freddie talked about possible retirement, so George's plan was, if Freddie did retire, he'd ask the Boxing Board of Control to consider Randolph as a contender for the British light-heavyweight title. It would please our mum if her lads were in different weight divisions and it would be good for George, cuz he'd have a more lucrative stable to promote with someone at that extra division. If Freddie didn't retire, Randolph would have to stay middleweight and George would still have the puzzle of avoiding Dick fighting Randolph. It was Dick who eventually solved the problem.

Dick'd got a third defence of his British title coming up – the chance of winning a Lonsdale Belt outright – against Albert Finch in Nottingham. The setback with Baby Day, well, when you're boxing, a loss can make you more determined for your next fight. Dick was moaning a lot more, though, and didn't seem so interested in his training. It was important for him to hold on to his title for the money as well as for his own pride but, as it happened, Finch took it on points. In seven months, Dick had lost his British Empire title and his British title. He could've come back even from that if his heart'd been in it.

Dick always blamed the war for ruining his boxing and in some ways it did but Dick was never as dedicated to his training as Randolph was. We all used to go running ten or fifteen miles, three times a week. Dick used to come halfway round with us then go back home. If he'd trained like Randolph, there's no telling how far he could've gone.

Dick quit the ring in the summer of 1950 to become a full-time trainer with George's stable. Dick was already part manager of Randolph and he said he was gonna help make Licker the 'greatest fighting machine in the world'.

The big 'To be, or not to be?' of British boxing was resolved without my brothers having to meet in the ring and without Randolph having to go up a weight. They'd kept faith with our mum.

Dick had boxed professionally from September 1937 to July 1950. He'd had 104 professional fights with 78 wins (12 by KO) and 20 losses (4 by KO), and held 6 fighters to a draw. He'd been Midland Area middleweight champion. After several years out of the ring serving his country, he'd come back to win the British Empire middleweight championship and to smash down the British Boxing Board of Control's colour bar to become the first black British champion under their rules. Between March 1947 and October 1948, he had a run of 23 consecutive wins. He'd earned good money and a lot of respect from boxing and the British public, and he was still three months short of his 30th birthday. He'd come a long, long way from the £2-a-time fighter he'd first signed up as. I look at his photograph and tell him, 'I'm proud of you, big brother, even if you could be a miserable old sod at times.'

18

A Count in a Castle

The Nelson Gym was a scruffy ol' place but we loved it. It'd done us all right. But Bill Hyam come up with another proposition: Gwrych Castle, near Abergele in north Wales. I pronounce it 'Grick' but the Welsh say it like they're getting phlegm up. It's got all the towers and turrets you see in fairy-story books but it's not really that old.

What it was, Bruce Woodcock had been lined up to fight an American, Lee Savold, for the World heavyweight title and Woodcock's people hired Gwrych Castle as a training camp, cuz it was a nice out-of-the-way place and big enough for the public to come and watch. Hyam, who travelled round Wales as a salesman, saw the notice and called in. He told George about what a great place it was and George said, 'Yes. It's a good idea to get Randolph away from home to train for his fight with Eli Alandon,' and got into negotiations with the owner, Leslie Salts.

That's really how Hyam worked his way in, cuz Mick Gavin couldn't come up to Wales with having to look after his kids who were still at school. Hyam was full of tales. He reckoned he'd been in a sniper regiment during the First World War; Jimmy Wilde had been in the same regiment and he'd trained Jimmy and made him what he was. I don't even know if he ever did actually box. I do know he sold Piccadilly fags for a living and, as soon as he took over the training, a big black cloud come over the camp – and it wasn't cigarette smoke.

When Dick was working with Mick training George's fighters, there was no animosity there, cuz they both respected each other. With Hyam, it was different. He stayed with us for years but me and Randolph only ever did what Mick told us. Dick could've advised us a lot, cuz he'd been boxing longer than me and Randolph, but he rarely did. I think part of it was in case there was repercussions in the family if he gave wrong advice. Mick Gavin was our man.

George said he needed me up in Wales to train with Randolph. I'd always sparred with me brothers, cuz sparring with a featherweight is useful to a middleweight. It helps develop their speed. Also, George reckoned I kept everybody's spirits up. It worked two ways this time. I'd lost my confidence since me burst appendix and with Randolph hitting me that often in the belly I got it back.

The deal was, we were Salts' guests and, in return, the public would pay him to see us training and sparring. George give Bet her housekeeping, because I wouldn't take any wages for helping Randolph, and we moved up there in the early summer of 1950 after my losing fight with Johnny Rawlings.

The castle's got a big marble staircase, a load of bedrooms, dining rooms, smoking rooms, a billiard room and stables an' all that, surrounded by woodlands. Salts set a ring up on the hill. Holidaymakers were coming to view the castle and the old paintings, and there was the usual slides and rides and candy floss. Salts hung a notice up to advertise his latest attraction:

SPARRING FROM OUR PROFESSIONAL BOXING TEAM

We sparred there to packed houses every time, and visitors loved to have their photograph taken with us. I thought, 'I hope it's gonna be luckier here for us than it was for Woodcock,' cuz Savold had give him a right old spanking.

Leslie Thomas Salts appeared to be wealthy and it was obvious he fancied himself as a real gentleman – king of the bleeding castle. He was always pulling Randolph to one side and muttering things. He had a creepy sort of voice, Salts. Randolph trusted him implicitly. He was the only one as did.

People who'd worked for Salts in the past warned us about him. Rumours were flying around about him always being associated with dodgy business. I don't know how much of it was true. But

Salts wormed his way so far into Randolph's confidence that anything he said was the truth as far as me brother was concerned; and Randolph called the shots, so we had to go along with it. Personally, I couldn't stand Salts and Salts didn't like me. I saw him on the telly a year or two before he died. He was calling hisself a 'count'. That's very similar to what I used to call him.

I tell you, being a guest of his, you was worse off than being one of his dogs. Us sparmates used to have to go down town whenever we wanted a decent meal. Not only did we have a full schedule of training, Salts used to keep us up till two or three o'clock in the morning signing autographs. But Randolph was happy there and he saw Eli Elandon off in two rounds.

You remember my big brother lost his British middleweight title to Albert Finch? Well, Finch still held it and, after beating Elandon in the September, it was now me baby brother's turn to fight for it. We insisted on the Nelson for that. None of us liked being away too long.

Licker come to his peak at exactly the right time. On the morning of the contest, he says to Dick, 'Don't worry, kid. The British title'll be ours again after tonight.'

Oooh, Randolph really slammed into Finch. I anna kidding, he bounced him all round the ring. He laid him out in the fifth round and brought the British middleweight title back to Warwick – only the second black man to have won it. Family pride was restored.

I'm not sure if two brothers had ever won a British title at the same weight before but I do know two black brothers never had – and in sixteen months of each other.

I was doing all right meself. I won the *Boxing News* Best Performance of the Week Certificate of Merit for knocking out Harry Croker in the first round at the Pershore Road Stadium in Birmingham in December, and I avenged my disqualification against Terry Riley by beating him on points in London. It was a good win. Riley had been trumpeted as one of the up-and-coming ones.

Being British middleweight champion, Randolph was now a contender for the European championship and early in the new year he fought an eliminator against Eduardo Lopez, the Spanish champion. It was another of Lick's spectacular round-one KOs. Now he was all set to take on Dutchman Lucien Van Dam for the title in London the following month. Luc Van Dam was very much respected over here, because, a few weeks before, he'd put up a decent show against the biggest name in boxing: the mighty Sugar Ray Robinson.

Robinson drove a flamingo-pink Cadillac convertible about 50 ft long, stayed in the very best hotels and travelled about with an entourage bigger than the King's: George Gainford, his manager; a trainer; a doctor; a hairdresser; a spiritual adviser and a load more. He even had a midget comic, Jimmy Karoubi, to make him laugh. Robinson was so legendary that his reputation took the edge off his opponents before they even ducked under the ropes. Muhammad Ali revered him. Well, he was Cassius Clay then. Based himself a lot on Robinson, Ali did.

Robinson was born Walker Smith, in 1921, in Detroit, Michigan, and made his official pro debut in 1940. I say 'official' debut, cuz he'd fought for money before that when he was really supposed to have been amateur. As a kid, he won the Golden Gloves featherweight title. He started off professionally as a welterweight and won the 10 st. 7 lb World title then went up to middleweight.

When Sugar Ray Robinson met Lucien Van Dam, he'd only got one loss on his record in a hundred and twenty-three fights and that was the one against Jake LaMotta. Van Dam had lasted four rounds with Robinson and everyone thought that was a pretty good showing. Now, Luc Van Dam was to fight me brother. We got talked into going back up to Gwrych Castle to train him for it.

Salts moved the ring from on the hill down to the more spacious east lawn and nailed a new sign up:

COME AND MEET A BRITISH CHAMPION
AT SUNNY GWRYCH CASTLE

There was even bigger crowds now.

I was still back and forth doing the rounds of the boxing halls with Mosh Mancini – London, Blackpool, Birmingham – like, a fight every few days. Then, on 20 February, I was at Watford Town Hall to meet my old adversary Jackie Lucraft. It'd been two years since our draw and I was keen to sort out which of us was truly the guv'nor. I'm very happy to announce it turned out to be me truly.

Like I was telling you, Van Dam had lasted an impressive four rounds against Robinson. That night in Harringay when he raised his gloves to our kid, he lasted forty-eight seconds. He clumped down that hard on the canvas that Randolph run over to help him. The referee shoved him out of the way and sent for the doctors. The Dutchman had never been hit as hard as that before – not by Robinson or anybody. And nobody had ever won a European title as quick as that. It might be a record even now.

It was really funny, too, cuz Van Dam's wife was also his manager and she was a good-looking blonde piece. As she was stepping down from her husband's corner at the start of the fight, the crowd was wolf-whistling her and she lingered for a moment to smile at them. When she turned round to see how her husband was getting on, he was flat on his back – out for the count.

Soon after his fight with Van Dam, Robinson fought Jake LaMotta and took the World middleweight title back off him in a real bloodbath. With it being on 14 February they called it the 'Valentine's Day Massacre'. Thirteen rounds he did it in and Sugar Ray Robinson was the current champion of the world again at middleweight.

Randolph's victory over Van Dam had sealed Licker as being the number one contender for Robinson's title – as much as it was thought a British bloke could be – and Solomons hit on the idea that while Robinson was doing his European tour to capitalise on his World champion status, it would be the ideal time for him to come over to Britain to fight Randolph Turpin. Nobody in British boxing who'd caught wind of what Solomons was gonna try to do thought he could pull it off.

In between fights in Switzerland and Belgium, Robinson went back to Paris and Solomons called over there to throw his bread on the water. Robinson's reply to Solomons' invitation to name his price was: '$100,000 and not one cent less, Mr Solomons' – you know, to risk his title. At the sound of $100,000 – £30,000 – a fabulous sum of money then when the average weekly wage was £3 or £4, Solomons locked up his wallet and come home.

Robinson wasn't one of those that look for easy fights but he'd been over here and seen Randolph fight and he'd heard what Randolph had done to Van Dam, so why risk his title unless it was very worth his while?

Jack Solomons, being Jack Solomons, sat down, reworked his figures, shouted at a few people over the telephone and went back out to see Robinson and George Gainford, and agreed to meet their price – the biggest purse ever paid for a boxer to fight in Britain. Randolph's share was gonna be £12,000, less than half what Robinson was getting but a small fortune nevertheless.

As soon as Randolph was told, he come to me in the gym, saying, 'Hey, Jack, we're having Robinson, kid. What do you think?'

'For the World title?'

'Yep.'

'You'll kill him!'

'I'll do my best, my son,' he said. 'I'll do my very best.'

Solomons, George Middleton and Randolph announced to the press they'd signed the contract to meet Sugar Ray Robinson for the World middleweight title at Earl's Court, in London, on Tuesday, 10 July 1951.

It's difficult for people today to realise what a huge event in British sport the Randolph Turpin v. Sugar Ray Robinson fight was. It would be impossible to exaggerate it. The Second World War had been over for six years and, although Britain had won, it didn't feel like we'd won nothing. The country was broke. The bombsites were overgrowing with weeds. There was unemployment because industries like munitions weren't needed any more, thousands of demobbed servicemen were back in the job market and women who'd took over a lot of the jobs as part of the war effort wouldn't all go back to being housewives. And here was this Yank, said to be the best boxer in boxing history, extending his tour of Europe to fight a Turpin from the back streets of Leamington Spa and Warwick. The whole country was talking about it and the crowds at the castle were breaking all records.

With the benefit of Mick and George's guidance, I was finding my form and getting some enthusiasm back. I had a rhythm to my boxing and I was punching hard, fast and often. I raised my sights to the Midland Area featherweight title. But if I was boxing well, Randolph seemed unstoppable.

We were on the same bill in Leicester: me up against Eddie Moran – the referee pulled him out in the third round – and Randolph against an old adversary: Jean Stock. The Frenchman had beaten our kid when they'd met three and half years earlier but Randolph had bruised hands and it'd affected his training. If Stock thought he'd met the real Randolph Turpin that night, he was in for a shock. Randolph battered him until the referee couldn't bear to see no more. Randolph went to Birmingham next and knocked Billy Brown out in the second, then went to Coventry and knocked Jan DeBruin out in the sixth.

There was a circuit of venues we travelled round. You'd see the other fighters on the circuit all the time and become friends. You'd get to know how they worked. Like any other sport, there's always new ones coming up and you have to do your best to stay ahead of the game. You'd learn a few dodges to give yourself an advantage – little ways of bending the rules. These can be psychological dodges like I used: talking to your opponent, winding them up, making them reckless. Or plain illegal dodges like head-butting, low punches, following a punch through with your elbow or using your thumb in their eye. Dai Davies was one who used the illegal class and he used it on me.

I fought him in London, in the May of 1951. Davies got his shoulder up in one of the clinches to unsight the referee and punched me twice south of the border. My right leg started twitching like a bugger. It got worse as the fight wore on. I went back to the corner at the end of the fourth round and Mick said, 'Yer dragging yer leg, Jack.' The pain in me groin was bloody terrible. Mick looked at George and they threw the towel in.

I used to see Dai Davies now and then. I asked him once, 'What about those punches in the groin, you bastard?'

He put his hands up and said, 'They wasn't intentional, Jack.' But he grinned when he said it.

'Why did you do it twice then?' I asked him. He just grinned again.

I pleaded with George to get me another fight with him but the Welshman was always too busy and I never got a chance to wipe that grin off his face.

George and Solomons booked Randolph for a pre-World contest warm-up fight with Jackie Keough on 5 June at London's White City Stadium. Boxing writers said it was crazy booking Randolph to box so close to his World title fight but when he won easy and come out without a mark on him, there wasn't much left to say. One or two of them went as far as suggesting Randolph had more chance of winning the World title than they'd previously thought but they still wouldn't even give him fifty–fifty.

Robinson was an absolute professional. He was proud of the fact he never fought with a built-in excuse to lose. He liked a good time same as the rest of us but when he was boxing, he was on the road to box. The more fights you win, the more you've got to lose by losing. Robinson's fight record was outstanding and he was jealous of it. It was the very reason he could command such money and the very reason he could more or less pick and choose his opponents.

We knew Robinson had done his homework on Randolph, so we done ours on him. Not only did Sugar Ray have fast combinations and punch-variety but also one of the hardest, fastest left hooks in the business. We had other boxers working with us: Jackie Keough, Eddie Phillips, Pete Price, Stan Parkes, Ted Morgan and Big John Williams, but our secret weapon was an American fighter, Mel Brown, who come up to the castle to help Randolph combat Robinson's three-left-hooks-in-a-row he was famous for. Our routine was to try to get Randolph with Robinson-style left hooks. Left hooks, nothing but left hooks.

I ain't akidding, Randolph trained to such an extent he was at least three weeks ahead of hisself. Dick's main job became laying us out on a carpet as we were carried unconscious from the ring.

One day, I done pretty good in the first of my three rounds. I caught Lick with three left hooks. Then I remember going up in the air. Next thing, I was opening my eyes and looking up at the sky. I'd never seen the sky so blue, the trees so green, or heard the birds sing so nice. I thought, 'He's done it this time. He's killed me,' and I started crying.

Dick come over. 'What's up with you, you silly bugger?'

'Thank Christ for that!' I said. 'I thought I was dead.' I sat up and looked along the carpet: there's two heavyweights and a middleweight still stretched out and Stan Parkes just coming to. I said to Stan, 'He's too far ahead.'

'You ain't joking,' he groaned.

'We've gotta do summat, Stan.'

'Yeah, but if we tell him, "You'll have to ease up a bit", he'll say we're jus' trying to dodge a bit of hard work.'

'Well, we gotta do *summat*,' I said.

Me and Stan went into the town later that day shopping. We were walking through Woolworth's and there's all these great baggy ladies' knickers hanging up with elastic in the legs and big fat bums on them. It give me an idea. I bought a huge pair of the knickers, a massive big bra, some coloured ribbons and some lipsticks from the cosmetics department.

Next morning, I put the ladies' knickers over me boxing knicks, padded out the bra with a few vests and made garters out of the ribbons. I drew notices all over me with the lipsticks: DO NOT PUNCH HERE; OUT OF BOUNDS; DANGER – an' all that. I put a dressing-gown on and a load of towels round me neck and went down to the ring with the others.

When he saw me, Randolph said, 'Christ, Jack, it ain't that bloody cold,' but he never suspected anything. When it was my turn to spar, I climbed in the ring and stood with me back to Randolph. As soon as they called, 'Seconds Out. First Round,' I threw off the towels and dressing-gown and turned to face him. Randolph fell on the canvas laughing. Salts was that impressed with the effect it had on the audience that he asked me to keep it in as a regular part of the public sparring sessions.

Randolph come to the dressing-room when we'd finished sparring and asked, 'What was the knickers and bra all about, kid?'

'I don't think you realise how far ahead you are with your training,' I said. 'You're knocking everybody out. My bleeding head's swimming. You're sending me punch-drunk.'

'Oh,' he said, 'I'm sorry. I should've known, cuz I was feeling mean towards everybody.' He bent down to kiss me on the forehead. 'You're a good kid,' he said. 'Thank you.'

'I'm your big brother,' I told him. 'I should look after you.'

I had to slip away from the castle for a few fights. I drew against Jackie Summerville – very respected he was – and won a ten-rounder on points against Gus Foran in Liverpool. I spoke to Gus years later and he told me his manager had advised him against taking me on but he did so because he thought it would be a real feather in his cap if he beat me. I thought that was pretty good, cuz Foran had been ranked in the top ten in Great Britain when I hadn't got a mention.

Things were coming to the boil in the press over Randolph's forthcoming World title fight. The sportswriters were dropping big hints – not just that Solomons and his lackey, George Middleton, were over-ambitious but that they were sacrificing their young star for a quick fistful of dollars.

Well, you think about it: according to *The Ring* magazine, Robinson only had one loss in one hundred and thirty-six official pro fights. He'd been boxing six years longer than our kid and had ninety-three more pro fights. Randolph had never fought a contest of more than eight rounds and Sugar Ray regularly fought ten and fifteen-rounders. Tom Phillips of the *Daily Mirror* believed in us. He bet his shirt Randolph would win it. Almost everybody else was encouraging but not rating our chances. Len Harvey – British ex-champion – was another exception. He told Randolph, 'Don't worry what you hear about Robinson, Randy. Nobody's invincible.' All of us who'd been sparring with Randolph didn't doubt he'd win. 'You'll be coming back champ,' I told him.

'It'll be a good fight anyway,' he said.

The British people knew the Turpins were good – especially the young un – but against the best in America? They were thinking 'You're brave to take the fight, Randy. Good on you. We'd love you to win. You'll get a shellacking, of course, but hopefully you'll take it like a man.' That seemed to be our tradition in boxing then. It was like the Americans were expected to win at everything.

The bookies felt the same. A Robinson win was offered at 7 to 1 on. For Randolph still being on his feet at the end of the fight to win on points was 20 to 1 against; the odds for a puncher's chance of a lucky knockout was 3 to 1 against. Whatever people thought the outcome was gonna be, this contest was the most exciting sports event in British sporting history and the tickets for Earls's Court sold out in three days. I bet Solomons was cussing he didn't find a bigger venue.

We come down from Wales by train on the day of the fight. Steam it was then. We was in great spirits right up until George noticed Josie was wearing a green suit, which he thought was unlucky. To make matters worse, we'd had a meal on the train and someone spilt the salt. It got us all a bit more thoughtful.

When we arrived at Waterloo, it wasn't just Jack Solomons, Sam Burns and Ted Broadribb who met us, like'd been arranged, but hundreds of people who'd got wind Randolph was coming – trying to get his autograph, trying to speak to him or just trying to touch him. We were in danger of not being able to get away in time for the weigh-in.

People had been gathering in the street for hours hoping to catch a glimpse of Sugar Ray Robinson and the traffic got stopped in the process. Mounted policemen were holding the crowds back at Shaftesbury Avenue and we had to have a police escort through to Solomons' gym, and we practically had to box our way up the stairs.

All the razzle-dazzle of America came with Robinson. 'Hollywood Come To Town,' is what the papers said. It was like Britain was only in black and white, and America was in technicolour.

Sugar Ray was the life and soul of the weigh-in, cracking jokes with everybody. They loved him. Randolph was happy to take the back seat. He never ever thought of himself as being a celebrity, or great, or nothing like that.

The British Boxing Board of Control doctor OKd the champion and the challenger for the fight, then Robinson and his entourage went off to their hotels and we wandered up town. We had a few hours to kill before we were due at the arena and Randolph wanted to watch a film. We thought that was a good idea, cuz it would get him away from people bothering him. He spotted a picture house showing *Shane*, a cowboy film he fancied seeing.

The cinema was warm and quiet and I started to doze off. No sooner had me eyes closed than Randolph was pounding me on the back, 'Wake up, Jack. This is a bloody good film!'

We come out of the cinema and took the tube to Earl's Court. It was a beautiful summer's evening.

19

The Fight of the Century

July 10th 1951. Eighteen thousand people are packed into the exhibition hall at Earl's Court and hundreds are gathered in the car park outside. Twenty million are tuned to the commentary on the BBC Home Service. Them as can't be at the fight, and them as can't listen to the live broadcast, will be queuing up at the picture houses later to see it on the Movietone newsreels with them as want to see it again. This fight ain't just happening here; it's happening everywhere. It's Jack Solomons' biggest ever fight promotion and he's plastered his own face across the programmes and posters instead of the boxers' faces. The whole world knows him now. The £80,000 he's collected in entrance money is a British record.

Mick, George, Dick and me are walking down to the ringside to wait for Randolph to make his entrance . . . There's a big buzz of conversation . . . Now they're catching sight of Randolph in his white towelling dressing-gown and the cheers and applause and shouts of encouragement are getting louder and louder as he's threading his way towards us: 'Good luck, Randy!'; 'Do your best, son!' . . . Me brother's laughing and waving to the fight fans as he's climbing under the ropes, and we're clambering in after him . . . And here comes the man they've been waiting hours to see – 'the Black Prince from Harlem', the middleweight champion of the world, Sugar Ray Robinson – the greatest, they say, of all time . . . A fanfare of trumpets is going up to salute the great American but

151

you can hardly hear it for the roar of the crowd . . . Robinson is sweeping under the ropes into the ring . . . He's bowing to his fans on all four sides . . . you could take him for a movie star. Bronze and handsome, with neatly sleeked hair and an immaculately trimmed pencil-line moustache . . . He's slipping off his blue silk robe and doing little jigs and bits of fancy footwork in his corner . . . The ring lights are shimmering off his body, showing off the sculpture of his muscles . . . He's absolutely oozing confidence as though he can't imagine there's a man on earth as can beat him. His entourage are twittering and fussing round him and his midget jester Jimmy Karoubi is helloing the crowd and pulling faces and doing funny walks to keep his master happy.

Our kid is sat on his stool in the home corner. He doesn't look so bad hisself. Great, in fact. Like Robinson admitted to reporters at the weigh-in, 'Built like an oak tree.' We're grouping round him to block his view of the American camp so's he won't be put off by all the flash and glitter. 'Get out the way!' he's telling us. 'I want to look an' all.' Randolph's drinking it in with a huge grin on his face . . . He's turning back to us and shrugging his shoulders. 'Well,' he's saying, 'he's only got two legs, two eyes an' two fists, same as me.' . . . Mick Gavin's gripping me arm. 'Watch that water, Jack.' There's been all kinds of rumours about the Mafia trying to dope the water, so we've brought our own, factory-bottled, and I'm guarding it with me life. 'Don't worry,' I'm telling him back. 'Everything's under control.'

The referee, Mr Eugene Henderson, an ex-pro heavyweight from Scotland, is calling the fighters to the middle. He's reminding them of the rules and telling them he wants a good clean contest . . . It never ceases to amaze me how calm and collected me brother is before a fight. Any fight. Even this fight. Right now, he's looking like we've forgot to tell him the man he's about to do battle with is the champion of the world and he's under the illusion he's about to spar another three rounds with me up at the castle.

The conversation of the spectators is falling to a murmur. The tipsters are leaning back, lighting their cigars, just hoping the British boy will be a gallant loser and not embarrass everyone.

'Seconds Out.'

Mick's issuing a last-minute warning, 'Watch his left hook, Randolph.'

Sure enough, the first meaningful punch of the fight is a Robinson left hook to the head . . . Randolph's taking it and

152

countering with a hard right to Robinson's head. Robinson's looking scornful . . . Licker's shaking him with a sledgehammer right to the jaw . . . a left to the head . . . The crowd are sitting up straight. There's an authority in Randolph's boxing they ain't credited him with . . . The fighters are circling round each other . . . Sugar Ray doesn't seem so keen to rush in now . . . and the bell's ringing for the end of the round.

Randolph's won some respect from Robinson. He's coming back to us smiling as if to say, 'Like I said, kid, he's just a man, same as me.' I'm handing him the water and Mick's telling him, 'Yer doing great, Randolph. Yer doing bloody great!'

Round two, and Randolph's got his feet planted wide to give leverage to his punches. Robinson's picking up the pace . . . on his toes . . . letting fly with a vicious left hook that threatens to take Randolph's head off but he's seen it coming and lets it whistle safely by . . . Now our kid's on the attack, working off his jab . . . He's blocking a right cross from Robinson and banging home an uppercut. Robinson's shook up again . . . Licker's pressing and crowding, using his jab with copybook precision . . . Robinson's getting in a right over the top to Randolph's head. Randolph's shaking it off and countering hard, forcing Robinson to hold on.

Round two to our kid. Mick and George are well pleased. 'That left hand's doing terrific, Randolph!' Mick's saying. 'Keep doing what yer doing.'

Round three and Robinson's coming out firing with both barrels . . . a dazzling left hook to the face . . . and another . . . He's following up with a terrific right hook. An 'OOOOOOFFF!' from the crowd. Randolph's staggering backwards. This is what they've been expecting. This is where the great American takes over to give the British champion a masterclass in the art of boxing. Isn't that what always happens? This is obviously the beginning of the end for Randolph. 'Good luck,' they've been telling him. 'Good luck, Randy. You'll need it.'

Sugar Ray's got his swank back and the tipsters are looking smug but I've seen Randolph take better from heavyweights and I know he's not really hurt. He's grabbing hold of Robinson to avoid the follow-up and Robinson ain't strong enough to shake him off . . . Eugene Henderson's forcing them apart and warning Randolph for holding . . . Randolph's slamming a right into Robinson's head, sending him reeling . . . The American's clinging on and it's his turn for a ticking-off from Henderson . . . Robinson's missing with a jab as Randolph's sidestepping and whacking in a left hook to end the round.

Round four. Licker's thumping home combinations at close range and Robinson can't keep him away . . . It's dawning on the American corner their $100,000 is gonna take a bit of earning . . . Randolph's releasing a thudding left hook and following it with a right cross. Robinson's nearly off his feet as the bell rings.

The tipsters are shifting about in their seats. These are no lucky punches the Turpin boy's throwing. He's got class. Our kid's plonking hisself down on his stool and casually leaning back on the corner post with his legs sprawled in front of him same as he's been doing all the way through.

In contrast, Robinson really looks like he's in a fight. His hair's sprigged up all over the place and he's wearing the disappointed look of someone who's been woken out of a lovely dream . . . Mick's telling Randolph, 'Show him who's boss.'

Round five. Robinson's missing with another left-hand shot . . . He's taking a solid uppercut to the jaw . . . a right . . . a left . . . a right . . . he's being driven back . . . he's trying to reply but Randolph's leaning away letting the punches fall short . . . His timing's perfect . . . Another jolting left jab from our kid . . . Randolph's scoring again and again . . . Sugar Ray's being beaten at long range and short range, and can't find no reply . . . Randolph's whipping in another right cross to the head, and it's another round to the Leamington Licker. The crowd can see the Sugar's melting. A third of the way through the fight and Licker's taken every round.

Robinson's on his feet as the bell's sounding for round six . . . moving briskly to the centre . . . Randolph's jabbing well but he's taking a hard countershot from the champion . . . Robinson's missing with a wild left hook . . . Randolph's closing in, taking shots to the body . . . repaying them with a resounding right to Robinson's head . . . and another from Randolph . . . and another . . . and now a mighty thump to the solar plexus. Sugar Ray's looking very, very discouraged.

Round seven. Randolph's dictating the fight, knocking Robinson out of rhythm with his jab and landing some straight lefts to the face . . . They're in a clinch . . . body punches are going in from both sides . . . Licker's steady as a rock . . . Robinson's head and body are recoiling time and time again from Randolph's pounding fists . . . Robinson's breaking free . . . Oooooh! There's blood cascading down his face from a long gaping gash over his left eye. The crowd are on their feet yelling and stomping and cheering. The tipsters couldn't care less about their dented reputations no more – Turpin ain't just good, he's exceptional. The *British* boy could WIN!

Randolph's on to the wounded Robinson, dizzying him with two left hooks. The American's back-pedalling furiously and missing with every punch he's throwing. The blood's gushing from his eye like water from a kettle. He's grabbing holt of Licker to stifle the attack but the referee's breaking them up . . . Henderson's taking a long, long look at Robinson's left eye . . . He's motioning the fighters on . . . Licker's powering in, piling up head shots . . . Robinson's breathing deep, drawing on his reserves, trying to step on the gas and turn the fight round . . . He's managing to get in some telling shots to the head but the timekeeper's bell is sounding the end of the seventh three minutes.

The Board of Control doctor's standing on the ring apron, leaning over the ropes, watching the American corner. Robinson's cuts man is working feverishly to staunch the flow of blood from the champion's eye. If he fails, the fight'll be stopped and the World middleweight crown will be Randolph's – ours, Leamington's, Warwick's, England's, Britain's . . . Even if they do patch that eye up, Robinson's the underdog now.

Round eight. Into the second half of the fight and we're sending Randolph out thinking we might actually be in for an early finish. The Americans have done a superb job on Robinson's cut but a single punch could reopen it . . . He's trying to keep the fight at long range to protect his wound but Randolph's overpowering him and thudding in two overhand rights to the head. Sugar Ray's going into a clinch for a breather . . . He's wriggling out of it and getting in some leather of his own . . . Randolph's blocking a right and rattling the Sugar Man with a superb uppercut to the jaw, sending up a spray of Robinson's sweat to glitter under the lights . . . Sugar Ray is weary – very, very weary . . . the bell's going and Robinson's gratefully survived the round.

Round nine. The American camp know this is new territory for Randolph. They'll be banking on him weakening now. 'He's given his best,' they'll have told their man. 'You've ridden the storm. As long you keep that eye protected, Robinson, you'll be fine and dandy. Go take him out.'

The fighters are coming out jabbing . . . Robinson's light on his feet and getting through with some crisp shots . . . Randolph's countering hard with his left. 'The left hand, kid,' Mick's been chanting between rounds. 'The left hand.' And Licker's jab is taking a toll on Robinson – relentlessly knocking him out of his stride. Robinson can't solve my brother's crouching style: 'First I'm there, now I ain't; now I'm in range, now I ain't.' He's making Sugar Ray's reputation for the pinpoint accuracy of his punches sound like an old wives' tale . . . Licker's blocking some oncoming shots and bullying the champion into a neutral corner . . . He's shrugging off a hard right to his own jaw and backing Robinson onto the ropes . . . He's crashing a left into the champion's jaw. Robinson's knees are going east and west but he's willing himself forward . . . fighting from memory . . . Licker's in control, stronger by the punch and, what's worse for the champion's corner, Randolph's clearly loving every minute of it. Those hundreds of miles we've pounded together along the empty streets of early mornings are paying off. It must be breaking their hearts.

Round ten. Robinson is attempting everything he knows . . . feinting . . . dodging . . . trying to draw a lead from Randolph so's he can counterpunch; trying to lure him into a mistake . . . He's burst into action . . . but everything he's doing our kid's doing better. It's the American that's supposed to be the left-hook specialist but his is a pale version of Randolph's . . . Licker's leaning back, keeping his chin out of range . . . ducking under a right to slam a ferocious left hook into Sugar Ray's jaw. Robinson's feeling it down to his feet. His eyes are blasted and he's covering up, trying to clear the mist that's threatening to overwhelm him.

Round eleven. Randolph's coasting . . . taking it easy . . . jabbing Robinson at will . . . Now he's flying in on the attack, rifling in some hooks to the head . . . Robinson's nearly off of his feet . . . but he's saved by the bell. It's a very dejected World champion that's walking back to his corner.

I'm wild with excitement inside but keeping my mouth tight shut. You can't take nothing for granted in boxing and there's still four rounds to go.

Randolph's opening round twelve with a straight left to the jaw. Instead of cowing Robinson, this is jolting the champion out of his depression. He's replying with a lightning right to Randolph's head . . . and a right to his chin . . . He's pressing forward, hungry for that one decisive blow that'll confirm his title . . . Robinson's sending in another hard right to Randolph's jaw and he's back in the fight. Our kid's shaken but he's replying with some steamhammer straight lefts and slowing the American down.

Round thirteen. I wish I wasn't superstitious. Me brother's out-boxing Sugar Ray but the fight could turn on a single punch and Robinson *needs* that punch. The crowd's convinced thirteen's unlucky for the Americans tonight. They've started to sing 'For He's A Jolly Good Fellow' for Randolph . . . The World champion is drawing a deep, deep breath . . . He's lunging forward . . . sending in flurries of pitter-patter punches to Randolph's body . . . he's punching with more precision . . . He's landing one of his sweeping left hooks . . . Randolph's rolling with it, taking the sting away.

Round fourteen. The big danger is of Randolph falling foul of a Robinson haymaker in a careless moment but Randolph, so far, is proving too wise . . . They're in a clinch . . . exchanging short blows to the head . . . Henderson's calling them to break . . . Now Randolph's stepping up the pace. He's steaming in with combinations and Robinson's holding on . . . Robinson's coming back . . . he's launching punches on a wing and a prayer, desperately trying to hold on to his title . . . he's missing with a left hook . . . missing with a wild right . . . Randolph's landing some big shots to the head, reminding the American he's here on business . . . Lick's almost playing with Sugar Ray . . . The champion's fading fast . . . He's summoning up a little burst . . . Now he's trying to cling on but Randolph's bombing him back onto the ropes.

My hand's trembling as I hand up the water. George is telling Randolph, 'You're the new champion of the world, son.'

'Not yet I ain't, George,' Randolph's saying. 'There's one more round to go.'

'All you've got to do, Randolph,' Mick's saying, 'is keep moving and you've won.'

Round fifteen. The concluding round of the middleweight championship of the world, the Fight of the Century. Eugene Henderson's telling both boxers to shake hands. Randolph's smiling as his gloves meet Sugar Ray's . . . Henderson's waving them on and Robinson's exploding into action. His eyes are spitting fire. He's on the rampage. There's almost hatred in them punches now. I've got two rounds even and twelve clear rounds to Randolph. Robinson's heading for a landslide loss on points – a hunted man who can hear the baying of the hounds. His only escape is that one golden punch that'll wipe the slate clean, that will preserve the legend, that'll keep him in the money. But our kid's having the time of his life. He's keeping the fight at long range, taming Robinson with straight lefts . . . left . . . left . . . left . . . cool and calm. Right now, they could stick Sugar Ray twins in front of him and it wouldn't make no difference . . . The tremendous cut over Robinson's eye is weeping . . . He's trying some reckless shots, hoping for the miracle, but Licker's up on his toes dancing – unhurt, unruffled, unmarked and out of reach – and Robinson's punching thin air with the world crown slipping off his head . . . He's holding at every opportunity . . . Randolph's tying him up on the ropes and banging him around the body . . . hard, sapping shots . . . Sugar Ray's hanging on to Randolph and . . . There it is! There IT IS! THE FINAL BELL!

Me brother's patting Sugar Ray's cheeks with his gloves, putting his arm around his shoulders and taking him back to the American corner. The crowd are going crazy, 'FOR HE'S A JOLLY GOOD FELLOW, FOR HE'S A JOLLY GOOD FELLOW . . .' But it can't be true, can it? Just saying the name Sugar Ray Robinson out loud is enough to knock most boxers out. They said Jake LaMotta done well against him and he looked like he'd been carried out of a butcher's shop. Has the great Sugar Ray really been out-fought, out-boxed, out-generalled and out-punched by one of us Turpins from Warwick?

Our corner knew what the decision *should* be but would Eugene Henderson see it the same? Some people were so mesmerised by Robinson, we might have been like the little kid who's the only one as can see the emperor's got no clothes on.

'Who has won?' Raymond Glendenning, the BBC Home Service commentator, asked out loud, under his handlebar moustache. The wait was AGONISING. Then, Eugene Henderson strode over to the American corner where Randolph was still talking to Sugar Ray and lifted Randolph's arm high in the air. Glendenning's voice rose to a shout, 'TURPIN HAS WON! TURPIN HAS WON! TURPIN, RANDOLPH TURPIN, TWENTY-THREE-YEAR-OLD FROM LEAMINGTON SPA, IS THE NEW MIDDLEWEIGHT CHAMPION OF THE WORLD!'

'TURPIN HAS WON! TURPIN HAS WON!' echoed in the pubs and parlours and streets of every village, town and city in the land.

In Buckingham Palace, King George VI left his wireless set and went back to his dinner guests. 'Turpin has won!' he told them.

There was PANDEMONIUM in the exhibition hall. The ring was bulging with a sudden rush of spectators and reporters. George,

Mick Gavin, Dick and me were among the first in and we hugged and cuddled Randolph and rubbed his hair as we escorted him back to his stool. I cupped my hands round his face and give him a kiss on the forehead. 'You're a big man now, bab,' I told him.

'Oh ar,' he said, 'but I wanted to knock him out.'

In the dressing-room, Randolph put his arm around me and said, 'Thanks, kid, for recognising the fact I've now grown up.'

Joan and me used to protect Randolph like he was our baby. Joan looks the picture of innocence in her photos – a real lady. They used to say, 'Your Kath can fight' but they should have seen Joan when she got going. In spite of us all looking after him, Randolph had still grown up in his own way and now our baby brother was the greatest 11 st. 6 lb fighting man on the planet. I couldn't have been prouder if I'd done it meself. 'You were good,' Robinson told him. 'Real good. Just like everybody said you were.'

Good? Our kid had beat the boxer who was rated the greatest of all time. In a single night, Randolph Adolphus Turpin, the 'Leamington Licker', Britain's No. 1 sporting hero, the idol of the nation, had become an international celebrity. Like the boxing writer Gilbert Odd said at the time, 'Once in a while there's a fight that comes right out of the blue and shakes the world.'

Even after Randolph had got showered and dressed and we were leaving the hall, the spectators were still on their seats, arms linked, singing chorus after chorus of 'For He's A Jolly Good Fellow' and the crowd in the car park were singing and dancing to their wireless sets.

It was like food and clothes and petrol and sweets had all suddenly come off ration; like summer had suddenly come after a long hard winter; like the war was finally over.

20

You, Sir, You Look Like a Big Strong Fella

In the winters back then, dozens of halls put on boxing shows but summers were like a closed season. There was some open-air stuff but, basically, you'd be doing nothing but training and you'd get brassed off with it. Worse still, you wouldn't be earning any money. But the boxing booths was there. All the big fairs had one, starting in the early spring and travelling from town to town until late autumn when they wintered up, repaired and repainted ready for the next season.

Mick Gavin had done most of his boxing on the booths and he introduced Dick to them around the time me brother turned pro in 1937. I went along after I'd signed with George and later on we took Randolph.

The booth itself was a marquee tent put up around two carts bolted together, like the gypsies did for a stage at the hop picking, so's you'd got a good firm basis for a full-size ring – the old three-rope ring, eighteen to twenty ft square – about chest-high to the audience, with steps up to it. People paid two bob to see the fights and stood around the ring to watch. There were no seats. Only the boxers sat down, between rounds.

At the back of the booth, they'd have a caravan for the boxers to use as a dressing-room. The front of it, the bit the punters saw, was made out of all the fancy woodwork you see on the roundabouts and coconut shies, decorated in bright reds and greens and yellows and blues, with electric lights and golden scrolls, and painted pictures of modern and old-time boxers posing and fighting. The name of the proprietor would be over the top and there'd be slogans like: 'First Class Talent'; 'Every MAN Should Learn The Art Of Self Defence'; 'FROM BOOTHS TO WORLD CHAMPIONS', an' all that. The booths did make champions an' all: Bombardier Billy Wells, heavyweight champion of Great Britain; Jimmy Wilde, flyweight champion of the world; Tommy Farr; Benny Lynch; Jackie Brown; Freddie Mills and, of course, us Turpin brothers. I tell you, the best boxers in this country come off the booths.

WANTED

3 or 4 White and Coloured Boxers to travel with the finest Boxing Show in England. Good wages and sleeping accommodation. Can start at once.

Apply to ALF STEWART'S
BOXING SHOW, FAIRGROUND,
STOCKTON-ON-TEES.

The boss of the booth would employ half a dozen or eight or nine boxers, according to the size of it. All kinds and all weights – some old sluggers on their way out but mostly youngsters as knew a thing or two about using their fists and were learning more every day. The fights were made up from punters challenging the employed boxers.

Mick Gavin introduced Dick to Len Johnson on the fairgrounds. Len was a left-hander and one of the greatest boxers in this country in his day at middleweight and light-heavyweight. Dick was so taken up with the way Len boxed, it was all, 'Len Johnson this; Len Johnson that!' Len was a good few years older than Dick but they had a lot in common. They were both brilliant defensive boxers. They even looked a bit similar. Len was known as the 'Uncrowned Champion' and would've been world ranking if the colour bar hadn't existed.

Each proprietor stuck more or less to one area. The booth we fought on most was Hickman's Boxing Academy, who did the Midlands: Birmingham for the Onion Fair; Stoke-on-Trent for Hanley Wakes; Nottingham for the Goose Fair; Ford's Field over at Leamington; Oxford . . . all round we'd go.

Charlie Hickman would send a letter to George Middleton, or later on to Randolph, saying, 'We'll be at so-and-so next week. We've got a fortnight there' – or whatever it was, and wherever the fair was we'd go and earn some money.

The entrance doors and paydesks were on ground level at each side and in the middle there was steps going up to a platform. To get the volunteers from the crowd, the boxers got up on the platform, bare-chested or in their dressing-gowns, flexing their muscles and staring at everybody, waiting to be challenged, and doing the speedball and punch-bag stuff – Tockerty-Tockerty-Tockerty; BATCH, BATCH-BATCH, BATCH . . .

> *My troupe of champions will take on all comers.*
> *Who's gonna challenge my fighters now? . . .*

Kaiser Bates was the 'barker' for Charlie Hickman – he used to do all the spieling on the microphone. You could tell Kaiser had done a bit of boxing, cuz he had a face like a billiard ball – everything rounded off. He'd gee up the crowd:

> *Don't tell me you're all afraid . . .*

A voice would go up, 'I'll 'ave the little un!' – usually some six-footer – and I'd got to take him. You had to be prepared to take on anybody – all comers. We'd go in and if they lasted the three rounds they'd get the money – two quid, three quid or a fiver, according to the weight of the boxer. For me, a featherweight, they'd get two quid if they went the distance. For most of the others, it'd be three quid. For Randolph, it was always a fiver. If the challenger got knocked out, they got nothing but a pat on the back and we got a quid. There was no points system.

The whole place smelled of sweat and grass, floor resin and fags. When there was a crowd in, the air was thick with tobacco smoke and it all gathered over the ring. We used to have a couple of puffs on a cigarette before we went in. That was a trick of Mick Gavin's so's we wouldn't be coughing all the time when we got up there.

It was bleeding hot, I tell you, boxing under canvas, especially when the sun was blazing down and you were up there close to the lights. It was good for me, though, cuz I'd sweat buckets and lose so much weight I could eat as many cream cakes as I wanted and still keep under 9 st.

You, Sir, You Look Like a Big Strong Fella

Each boxer had to work for the good of the booth. If you knocked your challengers out too quick, you wouldn't get nobody else fancying their chances, so sometimes we used to carry 'em for a bit. We used to take fight after fight, from ten o'clock in the morning till late at night.

There were challengers that come to the fair with the intention of fighting and ones who didn't know they were gonna fight till they got there.

> *You there, the big fella in the red jersey. Don't you fancy your chances with any of my lads?*

'I'll have the fella in the middle.'

I'd think, 'Oh, no, not another bleeding heavyweight.'

P'raps they'd got a nice-looking girl with them and they'd see the boxing booth and wander over to watch the fighters on the front waiting for challenges and the girl would point to one of the boxers strutting about, and ask her boyfriend, 'Could you beat him?'

'Easy!'

'Could yer really? Oooooh!'

> *Yes, you sir, in the green jacket.*
> *Show your girl what you're made of . . .*

Then he'd have to prove it if he wanted to make a name for hisself with his girl. Those were the ones I used to like, cuz they always made a mistake trying to be flashy.

It depended on what time the blokes come in to do the challenging. If it was after ten o'clock at night, you could lay bets they was gonna get their heads knocked off, cuz they'd come straight from the pub and got to feel ever so brave and think they could take you. I told one bloke I'd knocked out, 'You don't want to drink before you come down next time, mate. You're liable to get killed.'

> *Aren't there any men in this town?*

It didn't happen often but occasionally you didn't get no challengers at all. You couldn't let people as had paid to come in have nothing to watch, so we took lads from the gym down there.

163

We'd plant six or eight of them out in the crowd waiting. If it didn't look like you were gonna get anybody, the boss would give the thumbs-up and one of your mates would challenge you just to make the show. Some boxers say it was mostly those kind of fights on the booths. Well, it might have been more so on some than others, 'specially for the bigger weights, but there was never a shortage of challengers for little fellas like me.

Anyway, because the kid from the gym is one of your mates, he's 'kept' and does the three rounds without getting knocked out and Kaiser Bates, who also done the refereeing from outside the ring, like when boxing first started, would snatch up his microphone:

> *Did you see that? That was a real good fight! I'm going*
> *to give him his £3 now, and I'm sending the hat round so*
> *that you can show your appreciation.*

That way you'd get your nobbins. Once the crowd seen how well the kid from the gym's done in the ring, you'd get three or four more idiots coming along. That's how it worked. They called those fights 'gee' fights, cuz they gee'd up the audience. Afterwards, in the caravan round the back, you'd split the money with the bloke you'd boxed with.

There used to be one lad at Hanley Wakes up in the Potteries who was a favourite 'safe' of ours. I forget his name. He used to wait until there was a big crowd and he'd be staggering around, waving a bottle of booze and shouting to someone in the crowd, 'HEY, YOU! IS IT TRUE THE TURPINS ARE HERE?' – glug, glug, glug from his bottle. 'Boxing?' he'd say. 'Those Turpins don't know what it's all about. They should have been boxing when I was at the top.' He'd fall arse-over-tip all over the place and the crowd used to follow behind him. He'd bring 40, 50, 60 people behind him as he come into the fairground, so we'd got a house without having to spiel. He'd climb on the front and shout, 'I'LL GIVE IT 'EM. THEM BLOODY TURPINS!' and take another sip from his bottle. There'd be a massive crowd around our place and nobody at the other places.

Of course, they all thought he was drunk and in for a right shellacking but all he had in the bottle was water. Mostly he'd pick on Randolph, and he wasn't much bigger than me. The first show of the night he'd just be slightly 'drunk' and we'd let him go the distance and take the hat round. It'd come back full of money.

'Right,' he'd say to Charlie Hickman, 'I'm going to get some fish and chips. When do you want me back, guv'nor?' Charlie would tell him, 'Give us another couple of shows. And don't forget, we want a real big crowd. You're getting knocked out next time.'

And the way he used to get knocked out you'd have thought it's a wonder he ain't dead. Randolph would hit him with a right uppercut and the lad would go over backwards – right over – and land on his face. Randolph hadn't hit him really. He'd get nearly to his chin and stop, and the kid would throw himself back: BOOMP! and lie there twitching. The way he twitched was fantastic. You see people getting knocked out in the ring for real and they twitch like that. The audience used to join in with the count – the crowd always started counting when lads got knocked down: one! . . . Two! . . . THREE! . . . getting louder and louder, and whistling and roaring and cheering when they got to TEN! What the audience used to do if the kid come back and picked on Randolph again was chuck money in the ring to him anyway. So he got a double nobbins. Sometimes Randolph used to let him keep all of it. That made sure he'd come back again with us. I anna kidding, he was terrific. That was the way we used to have to do it – make out we was knocking seven bells out of each other.

Some challengers would bring their own gear with them – boots, shorts, gum shields and everything. Others, we used to lend them the gear to box in and they boxed in their shoes or socks. We stopped lending gear after a while cuz they used to pinch it and it's costly when you've got to keep buying new knicks all the time.

I've read a lot of lies about: 'Randolph boxed with this booth'; 'Randolph was on the road with that booth', but whenever Randolph went out to the booths I went with him, so I know if they're telling the truth or not. We were never 'on the road' with any booth – never actually travelled with them. We just used to go out to them, spend the day boxing and come home at night.

I read an article where a bloke claimed Randolph went from this bloke's father's booth to fight for the World title against Robinson. How could he have done when we was all training up in Wales at Gwrych Castle?

Hickman's Boxing Academy was a family business. Charlie Hickman Senior had been a boxer himself and he run his booth with his son, George, who had been a boxer, too – a real athletic sort of fella. Mrs Hickman was always dressed in black with an old-fashioned black cloche hat clamped on her head. She used to stride about doing the towels and keeping things in order. There'd been another brother, Charlie Junior, who was the talented one. Charlie had been an amateur area heavyweight champion and won a golden belt at Crystal Palace but he died in an accident on the fairground when he was young. His wife, Lydia, stayed with the family working the cash desk. His sister, Florence, worked in the paybox an' all. There was a sister-in-law, a big busty thing, but she run the roulette. They had another sister, Annie, who used to get on the front and do the speedball stuff with us.

There's an art to using the speedball. You put it high enough to have to reach up to make you keep your hands up, and you hit it fairly lightly to get your speed, bouncing it against the top board, and every now and then you steady yourself to slip in your one–two's. You've got to make sure you hit it straight so it'll come back straight, otherwise you'll miss it. Annie had got it right off. You should've seen her do the doubles on it: BRRM-BRRM, BRRM-BRRM – like a drum. She was fantastic: BUMP-BUMP-BUMP – elbowing and everything. I'm sure she used to get jealous of us and wished she could do the challenges and all.

They were related to a knuckle fighter, Tom Hickman, nicknamed 'The Gas Man' cuz he was such a bright light in the ring – I'm going back a couple of hundred years here. The story was, The Gas Man beat an old man to death – not in the ring, in a pub fight – but was never charged for it, cuz the old man died so long after the fight. That was before the Queensberry Rules. Mind you, we didn't always take much notice of Queensberry in the booths, especially with the drunks. One was a good foot taller than me. I hit him on the chin and he went down. Suddenly, he lashed out at me with big bleeding boots on. I sidestepped him, caught hold of one of his boots, tipped him over and thumped him hard to make sure he wasn't gonna get up. Charlie Hickman said, 'You didn't hit him when he was down, did you Jack?'

'Of course not, Charlie. He was well up on his feet.'

Mick Gavin used to be with us all the time and he'd say, 'Don't try hitting this fella on the chin. Aim for the belly button.' I'd look at his belly hanging there like a balloon. 'And throw your whole body at him when you hit it,' Mick'd say, 'and step out of the way quick before he's sick on yer.' I tell you, he was always right: BLEOUGH! and flat on their faces they used to go. I just used to step out of the way in time. Mick used to call out, 'You've got that one, Jack. He'll not get up.' He was great, I tell you, Mick, the ol' fella there. When he died, a real character went.

It was through the boxing booths we met Eddie Phillips. A fighter called Dango Quinn had met him down in Bournemouth. He said Eddie was a good welterweight and Randolph had been his hero since his amateur days. Eddie had moved down from Edinburgh to Castle Bromwich, cuz his dad was a doctor from Nigeria and got a practice there. Eddie was travelling with the booth and when the end of the season come he'd have nowhere to live. Randolph brought Eddie back to stay at his place in Leamington.

I used to be able to make Eddie almost die of laughing. We all got on so great we used to introduce him as our fourth brother and people believed it – right up until he opened his mouth that is, cuz he'd got a broad Scottish accent. Eddie loved the Nelson Gym. He reckoned it was like the Sparta in Edinburgh where he'd trained before meeting us. He'd been a mate of Sean Connery's and used to spar with him. He signed up with George and, outside of the family, he become Randolph's chief sparmate. He thought the world of Licker.

There was another couple of booths we used to go to – Johnny Gage's, who done Banbury and Oxford; Bob Parkin's, who done mostly London; and Sam McKeowens, who Freddie Mills was with – but we was mainly at Charlie Hickman's. Other fighters I remember on there were Tommy Icke, a flyweight from Birmingham; Larry Parkes, a middleweight from the Potteries; Stan Parkes . . . but, I tell you, it didn't matter which booth we went to, they used to be double chuffed if the fighting Turpins went on the front. The three boxing brothers. We drew the crowd. Randolph could actually pull a crowd on his own, and if there was somebody stupid enough to challenge him you could bet your bottom dollar there'd be tentfuls of people paying to see it.

The booths was a great way to keep fit. And on top of that, you had to take it pretty seriously because you didn't know when these idiots challenged you whether they could box or whether they was gonna come in there and just try and kick you in the nuts. One of our lads got booted between the legs. I ain't akidding, his balls come up like coconuts. We had to rush him to the hospital. When he come back, he says, 'From now on, every one of them as challenges me, not only am I gonna knock 'em out, I'm gonna give 'em a right lacing beforehand so they can't do what that bastard done.'

'Well,' I said, 'it's him you've got to get, not anybody else.'

The thing was, nobody would challenge if you beat somebody up that bad.

A heavyweight called . . . well, I better not give you his real name cuz it might upset his family, who probably think he was a hero . . . from up Tyneside . . . I'll call him 'Geordie Garside'. And if there is a boxer called Geordie Garside, it definitely ain't him. I anna kidding, he was as evil as sin itself. He was well over 6 ft with big arms and a massive chest. He had thin legs, though, with knees like cricket balls.

We'd got a challenger one night. This lad had clearly never boxed before. I swear if I'd have told him to put the gloves on his feet he would have done. Garside tied him up in the ropes and hit him everywhere: kidneys, in the groin, back of the neck – a brutal and sustained attack, and we never did that. I saw Garside afterwards. 'You ain't a boxer,' I told him, 'you're a fucking animal.' He told me it was his ambition to kill somebody in the ring. Then he starts getting nasty with me. I'd got a big spanner in my jacket. I always carried it on the booths. I was only 9 st. and if some of those buggers come back for me after I'd knocked 'em out, I needed summat. I pulled it out and told Garside it was now my ambition to kill him out of the ring. We was standing there glaring at each other – Garside with his fists up an' me with me spanner – when Randolph come up killing himself laughing. 'Jack,' he says, 'don't be a bloody idiot. If the police find you with that spanner, you're gonna be in trouble.' I put the spanner in me pocket and Garside slunk off. He could punch but he was a street scrapper, a rough an' tumble fighter, a bully boy – no good against anyone with class. You can't do boxing in hatred and anger.

The Hickmans were great. Once you were in with them, you'd got friends for life but old man Hickman could be a miserable bugger. We was down at Oxford one Friday. I'd had six challengers. Not one of them weighed less than 11 st. – that's getting on for a third of my body weight heavier than me. Every chance I got, I got in fast and banged them as hard as I could in the belly or under the heart – they go down on the floor and they can't get their breath. Anyway, I'd stopped them all. The old man was worried I was putting off other challengers and he comes to me and says, 'Next time a straight comes, Jack, carry him for a bit.'

'Like bloody hell!' I said. 'Haven't you noticed the difference in the size of them to me?'

'Yes. But you know enough to mess them about, Jack.'

'Boxing's my trade,' I said. 'I've got to be careful. If I carry these big buggers I risk getting hurt. I might get a cut eye or summat.' It's all right somebody your own size but when they're bigger and heavier than you it takes a bit to mess them around. When Hickman kept on, I said, 'All right, I won't box no more today.'

'Who's gonna box then?'

'Get the others to do it.'

Besides his usual boxers, he had two Welsh boxers there that day. There was always others.

At Nottingham Goose Fair one time, we went Thursday, Friday and Saturday. On the Saturday, I had 14 straight fights, and they was all over 13 st. bar one of them, and the only one that weighed inside it was 12 st. He was only the second one to go the distance with me. The first one was that big, when I punched him to the body, me fists were sinking in the fat, and when I hit him on the chin he was rolling away from me. But this other kid, every time I hit him with a good shot he'd go down on one knee and wink at me. That's how he got the money. I asked him afterwards where he'd learned his boxing. He told me he was the reigning ABA cruiserweight champion of Great Britain. Stan Parkes said I was mad to take him on. But he never beat me, did he, and I got over £300 in those three days, including nobbins – absolutely fantastic money then.

We had some laughs an' all. One night I offered a bloke two sets of gloves: a set of 10 oz and a set of 6 oz, same as we used. He picks the 10-ouncers. He thought the bigger the gloves, the harder they hit. He didn't realise there's not so much padding in a 6 oz glove. When it was all over, Kaiser Bates says, 'You cunning little sod, Jack. You knew he'd take them big uns, didn't you?'

Although he never appeared to be, Randolph was very, very religious. If you'd gone in his bedroom at night, you'd have seen ghostly lights all the way round. He'd got figurines of the Virgin Mary, and Jesus on the Cross, and they was painted with luminous paint. He was ever so much into that.

We was down just outside Brum near an RAF station. This RAF bloke challenges him. The bloke strips off and he's got a great big crucifix tattooed on his chest. Randolph says to Mick, 'Oh, Christ! Can't you switch him?'

'Why?'

'I can't hit that crucifix.'

Mick looked puzzled. 'Well, hit him on the chin then.'

'Oh ar,' Randolph said. 'I never thought of that!'

Then this other lad who evidently boxed for the RAF – bigger than Randolph – was standing out there with his mates and I was stood behind them. He was going on, 'I'll have the darkie soon. I've been watching him, he's nothing.' Well, there's only Randolph on the top who's coloured, so it must be him he means. Then this bloke says to his mate, a sergeant, 'Have a wander around and see if you can get any of these fairground Johnnies to bet on me to stop him. Tell them you have a chum who'll stop him inside two rounds, and we'll split the money.' So his mate's going round asking.

The big mistake he made was to think that fairground fellas are yobs. They've got two bleeding brains, I tell you. They can stand and look daft as a brush, and talk daft as a brush, and five minutes later you walk away and find they've talked you out of your wallet.

I nipped round and told Randolph, 'There's a bloke out the front, about 6 ft – got to be around 13 st. – who's gonna challenge you. He's got a mate in the audience laying money he'll stop you in two rounds.'

'I'm going back out,' Randolph says. 'When you're next to him, scratch your head.' The boxers go out on the front again and I go and stand by the RAF bloke and give me head a good scratch. Randolph's got the fella fixed. Wherever the fella moves, Randolph's glaring at him.

Randolph used to box southpaw sometimes to kid them on – never as a professional but he'd boxed southpaw in three or four fights as an amateur. He was perfectly ambidextrous. He'd take a bet with you on the rifle range that he'd beat you. And he'd fire the first shot off orthodox, then he'd turn around and fire them off southpaw – firing as well left-handed as he could right-handed.

When you work on the fairground, you get to think like fairground people. Punters would go out, say, the night before, and see Randolph boxing somewhere, and the next night they'd come to the booth, see the posters, and say, 'Wow. They've got Randy Turpin on.' Randolph would come out southpaw and they'd say, 'Oh, that can't be Randolph Turpin. I seen him last night and he's orthodox,' and think it was safe to challenge him. I used to wonder, 'How thick can these people be?' The only way we could have done it was if Randolph had got an identical twin who boxed southpaw. Anyway, so far on this particular day, he'd been boxing orthodox.

They start off and Randolph comes out, southpaw, jabbing with the right hand. The RAF bloke hesitates. Randolph gives him another poke with the right. The bloke starts frowning. He's trying to get in with his own punches but Randolph's jab-jab-jab with his right hand, holding him off. The bloke's expecting left jabs and he was gonna slip 'em an' all that but he's getting slammed in the face with the right. You can see how confused he is – it's written all over him. Randolph's eyes are boring into the other bloke's eyes all the time. 'Any minute now,' I thought, 'there's gonna be an almighty BOOM! and it'll be all over.' But Randolph was taking his time. At the end of the round, this sergeant that was with the bloke in the ring comes down to the ringside and shows his bloke a big pile of money he'd collected for bets. That was it for Randolph. He comes out on the bell, still southpaw: BAM-BAM – then suddenly switches to orthodox: CRASH! BOOOOOMP! The bloke's lying flat on his back with his mouth wide open. I anna kidding, Kaiser Bates could've counted to 210. The uppercut that did him stretched his neck about two foot before his body moved. I said to Randolph afterwards, 'Did you have to hit him so hard?'

'Yeah,' he said. 'He shouldn't show off.' We carried the bloke, still unconscious, to the caravan. When he come to, he said, 'What happened?'

'You've just met Randolph Turpin,' I told him.

Later on, Hickman had a painting of Randolph one side of the entrance, a painting of the Gas Man in the middle and a painting on the other side of Freddie Mills. The painting of Randolph showed him southpaw. Bob Parkin had a painting of Randolph on his booth, too.

Oh, we used to have some fun. I mean, the thing was, on the fairgrounds there was loads of women used to come around. It's funny the way they all seemed to flutter around the boxing booth. Weekends especially. You couldn't miss. It was slung at you sort of thing. What used to amaze me was the age of some of them that used to hang around there. It wasn't only girls of 17 or 18. I've had women of 35, 40 – at least twice my age – chatting me up. Sometimes there was that many women and girls after the boxers that Mrs Hickman would chase them off. We knew birds there as used to hang around and anybody who wanted to let off steam with them could just give them a call. Anybody as boxed. Not many of the blokes refused. It's like these singers getting knickers thrown in their faces but even more so. I've seen two girls having a fight over who's gonna go round the back with one of the lads.

Mrs Hickman come to me one day and says, 'Jackie, why don't you bring your wife along.' So I took Bet with us. 'Hello, dear,' Mrs Hickman says. 'Sit in that place there.' She points to one of the cash desks, 'It's two-shillin' each when they go in', and got Bet working for her within two minutes. Bet said after, 'Do those girls always hang round?' She was always jealous, Bet was. I can understand it now but I didn't at the time.

There was a kid from the Nelson called Don 'Chick' Checkley. Another featherweight. Heavier than me but shorter. Me and him used to get in the gym and have a fight. I ain't akidding, it used to be real serious. It'd start off OK then one of us would give the other one a bit of a dig and it'd all kick off. At half past seven one night I knocked him down. We'd planned we was only gonna have four rounds but at the end of the fourth Chick shouts, 'One more round!' He was trying his hardest to get me back. Every time he looked likely to knock me down, I'd catch hold of his arms and lock him up. We kep' on and kep' on. It was half past eleven when we come away from the gym and that was only because Mick Gavin got in the ring and said, 'If you two don't pack up now, I'll beat the bleeding pair of you up!' Mick knew Chick wanted to get his own back and he knew there was no way I was gonna let him.

Arthur Batty used to say to Chick, 'Jack Turpin will win the featherweight championship of Great Britain and I'll train you personally to take it off him.'

I used to tell them, 'In your dreams!'

Mind you, Chick couldn't half punch. We had Chick with us on the booth over at Coventry one day and he knocked a bloke out who'd got five brothers. As soon as Chick had knocked the first one out, a second one jumped in the ring. Chick could see this bloke had revenge in mind, so, before he's had a chance to put the gloves on properly, Chick's knocked him out an' all. The third one he hit before he'd got through the ropes properly. The crowd didn't like that and a great mob of 'em rushed the ring. They was all pitching in. Kaiser Bates was screaming in his microphone, '*You are the HIGGERANTIST crowd I have ever seen!*'

In the end, all the boxers was up there beating back the crowd with full punches and everything, having the time of our lives. Brothers, cousins, mums and dads – a great tide of them coming at us. As soon as they got above the ropes: BOOM! – we knocked them down again. He wasn't as tall as me, Chick wasn't. He had big shoulders on him though, and he couldn't half hit.

You, sir, come on now . . .

Like I say, when you go on the booths you never know who you're gonna box or what they're gonna do. They'll come in with an elbow, head-butt you, thumb you – anything, and you've got to stand for all of that. You mustn't complain. Usually, you just bang away – punching them on the chest and head, and you're not really hurting them, cuz you're not picking a target where it's gonna hurt that much but it's gonna keep them off you till you take them out. You learn to think fast, move fast, pick your spots and, when you think you've put on a good enough show, you get them out of the way quick. Someone little like me had to learn some special punches for the 6-ft drunks that were fond of picking on us, like following through with the elbow or little tricks like standing on their foot when they tried to move out of range.

When Randolph fought for the World title against Sugar Ray Robinson, he promised Charlie Hickman that no matter what happened – win, lose or draw on the Tuesday – he would come to the boxing booth at Kenilworth the weekend after. And he did. Randolph was always an honourable bloke.

You've never seen nothing like it. They were coming in in floods. A squad of policemen had to be detailed to hold the crowd back to make a pathway for us even to get to the booth. There was that many of them they was paying their two bobs, coming in, getting pressed through the back of the tent and having to come round and pay again. The fairground blokes were trying to hold the back sheet down but it was like trying to hold the Atlantic back with a fishing net. Some of them must have paid six or eight bob to stay in the tent that day.

Hickman still charged two shillings, you know. Like, with Randolph Turpin, middleweight champion of the world, being on there you'd think he'd put the price up but he didn't. They would see nine rounds of boxing for that and yet, at Gwrych Castle, Salts used to charge about a fiver just to get in, and you was lucky if you got close enough to the ring to see the fights, cuz that many thousands used to come. Hickman kept it at two bob and they was coming in an' coming in an' coming in – in the front, and out the back! We was all bandaged up for fighting and having to work the doors as well. All the boxers made extra money that night putting odd bits under the bandages.

The fairground is a world of its own. Sometimes someone would think they'd won something on one of the stalls and the fairground bloke would say they hadn't and it'd turn nasty. Then the fairground bloke would shout, 'HEYROOB!' – I don't know how you spell it but that's what it sounds like – 'HEYROOB!' and immediately four or five other fairground blokes would be there sorting it. A bloke told me that heyroob has been the alarm since fairs first started. The fairground fellas were like a family. They'd always help you out.

Down at Hanley, Randolph knocked a bloke out and he took a long time to come round. When the booth had closed up for the night, we're walking towards our cars and half a dozen blokes appeared in front of us with lumps of wood.

'What's on?' I asked them.

'You bastards are about to fucking find out,' they said. We couldn't risk our licences or risk copping a big injury that'd put us out of boxing for a while, so I tried the alarm, 'HEYROOB!' Next thing, half the fairground's surrounding them and dealing with it for us.

Who's gonna challenge my fighters now? . . .

It was a great ol' life on the booths. Dick's eldest son, Howard, done a bit on them. Jackie Junior stopped off at a fair up in Newcastle on Tyne that had a boxing booth – Ron Taylor's Excelsior, I think it was. John was back in training after being out of the ring for a while and he boxed a few exhibition rounds for the crowd. This'd be 1973, '74, and it must've been one of the last boxing booths, if not the last one. It's all stopped now.

The British Boxing Board of Control tried a couple of times in the late '40s to put an end to it by attempting to make boxers think that going on the booths was too low for a professional and threatening them with suspension if they did. Some of them went down to Birmingham to ask what they were expected to do through the summer when boxing matches was few and far between. How else could they get their money? Eventually, the Board of Control got their way and stopped licensed fighters going. They said it was for health and safety reasons. First they said boxers could go on the booths but only to fight exhibitions. When nobody took any notice of that, they announced the booths was out of bounds altogether.

That was a real big mistake, because it's one of the best learning grounds going. Cuthbert Taylor, a coloured featherweight from the Rhondda Valley, what I learned from him was how to fight with your shoulders without moving your hands. He'd boxed World champions. The thing is, you get to do your learning and training and fighting all in one go. You get people you don't even know.

In the gym, you're sparring with somebody and it's very likely one of your mates and you go around socially together so you don't really try. But when you go on the boxing booths, you're fighting a whole range of different people and it's the unwritten law between you and the bloke as owns it that you won't lose him money.

Just for the record, I meet kids who say, 'Yeah, my granddad fought your Randolph on the boxing booths and knocked him out.' Well, me, Randolph and Dick NEVER EVER LOST A SINGLE FIGHT ON THE BOOTHS. The best anyone ever did with us was go the three rounds. If we couldn't tip 'em over quick, we used to carry them. It was mostly cuz we kept them that they lasted at all. All the other times we would've taken them out anyway if the fights had gone on longer.

Now they've stopped the booths, you watch, professional boxing's going to suffer badly from it. If I'd never gone on them, I wouldn't have developed as well as I did, because I learned to anticipate what a bloke was gonna do before he did it. You've got to get all that figured, cuz if he gives you a kick in the nuts nobody's gonna feel sorry for you. They're gonna start counting.

21

How Much Sugar Do You Take?

Leamington Spa decided to do an official welcome home for Randolph. His victory over Sugar Ray had affected boxing fans and non-boxing fans alike, and it was gonna be the biggest event ever round here. Just my luck, George had got me booked down at Bristol to fight Denny Dawson. Mick Gavin, as much as anybody, deserved to be at Leamington but he volunteered to come and look after me.

The fight promoter at Bristol congratulated us on Randolph's win.

'We're missing the do back home,' I told him, pulling my face.

'Well,' he said, 'at least you'll be able to see it on the television.'

He'd arranged for a set to be put in the dressing-room and they held up my fight till we'd watched it.

They come from miles an' miles to pay tribute to my babby brother. Twenty-five thousand people jammed the streets, waving and cheering and singing to the brass bands, all wanting to be close to the man who'd beat Sugar Ray.

Randolph was sandwiched between the Mayor of Warwick and the Mayor of Leamington in the back of a big black open-top Humber limousine. He was driven slowly up to the town hall steps, where they all got out, disappeared for half a minute, then reappeared on the balcony. There was a big banner stretched across it:

How Much Sugar Do You Take?

LEAMINGTON SPA WELCOMES THEIR CHAMPION
RANDOLPH TURPIN

There's streamers and bunting everywhere and Randolph's surrounded by VIPs in their suits and robes of office. Me mum's up there in her best hat. She'd listened to the fight on the wireless and was prouder than anybody. When we'd got back from London, she kept cuddling Randolph and saying, 'My babby's done it. He's the best in the world!' People were singing 'For he's a jolly good fellow' and shouting 'Good lad, Randy' and Lick's standing in front of five or six microphones, looking bashful.

The lads from 605 Squadron of the RAF at Honiley laid on a de Havilland Vampire jet doing victory rolls in the sky. Can you imagine that being done for a sportsman today?

Randolph starts reading a speech: 'It was a great fight on Tuesday and I am naturally very proud to bring the honour of the middleweight championship of the world back to England and Warwickshire. I must tell you how grateful I am to my manager, my trainer, my family and others who have helped me so much throughout my career . . .' Then he come over self-conscious and handed the speech to one of the mayors and went back to the microphone. 'Well,' he said, throwing his hands up to his face, cuz the cheers were s'loud. 'I'm not much at making speeches but you all know what I mean.' He give them a big wave. 'Thanks a million,' he said. He'd done his real talking with his fists in the Earl's Court ring.

I'd boxed Denny Dawson before so I knew what to do. Mick confirmed it: 'Fight your fight, Jack. Crowd him; keep pressuring him.'

I called to see Randolph the next day. I was living in Parkes Street at the time and Randolph was at Bridge Close. 'How did you get on with Dawson?' he asked me.

'Forced him into retirement. Seventh round,' I said and Randolph nodded and grinned. The first fight I'd had with Dawson had been up in Carlisle in 1949 and I'd got Randolph in my corner. He'd do more fighting outside the ring than I'd be doing in it – bobbing and weaving and throwing the combinations he thought I should be dishing out. I could hear him shouting all through the bout, 'Clobber 'im, Jack, fer Chrissakes! Hit 'im with the right hand. The right! The right!'

I'm thinking, 'Now why is Dawson moving away from me right hand?' I only managed to hold Dawson to a draw on that occasion. I could hardly throw a punch for laughing.

Randolph fancied a walk to the Cassino Milk Bar at the bottom of the town. We always used to be going there to meet our mates and exchange the chatter of the week. All the way, we was besieged by fans and as soon as we got inside they mobbed round us wanting autographs, wanting to be with us or just wanting to be seen with us. We'd got used to setting the trend. People had already started wearing the clothes we wore and doing the things we did and saying the things we said but now it was even more so and all the most beautiful girls were throwing themselves at the champion of the world.

Two or three days later, not to be outdone by Leamington Spa, Warwick's gonna do a parade with the Royal Warwick, the sea cadets and the army cadets. We'd gone out riding in the morning – we were crazy on riding then – and my horse, Bugwhist, had thrown me and run off. Randolph jumped over a fence after it and ripped the arse out of his jodhpurs. We managed to catch Bugwhist but it made us late with no time to go home and change.

The mayor and everybody's there and they're falling over themselves to shake Randolph's hand while Licker's turning round and round trying to keep his back to the wall so's they can't see his bare arse. We'd got to watch the parade and take the salute. They're all marching past, eyes right, saluting, and I'm doubled up, laughing meself bloody sick.

No one was more surprised than the Americans when their gravy train got derailed at Turpin Station. There's a big, big difference between the money a World champion can make and the money an *ex*-champion can make. Being reduced to the role of challenger was a position the Sugar Man and his crew didn't find so sweet.

They'd taken the precaution of putting a clause in their contract making it mandatory, in the unlikely event of Robinson losing, for a re-match to take place within 90 days and they were anxious to make it as soon as possible. Randolph's first defence was fixed to take place in America at the New York Polo Grounds on 12 September 1951.

I told George, 'Tell them he's sprained summat and can't go.' I'd have spun it out for two or three years but George wouldn't go along with it. I don't think British managers, then, could handle the big time like the Americans could. Solomons was closer to it. For instance, Solomons was quoted in the newspapers saying any fight arranged in America for British boxers involved paying some off the top to the Mafia. Well, George wouldn't have wanted to get mixed up in nothing like that.

Randolph had to rest from the first fight and get through the victory celebrations and get back in training and travel to America and get acclimatised and train some more and defend his World title in just 64 days. It ain't even legal now to have a return so quick.

Licker's attitude was, 'Look, Jack, they was good enough to give me a shot at the title. The least I can do is give them a shot back.' To him, it was another big payday and another opportunity to knock Robinson out. Him and Sugar Ray had a bit of camaraderie going. Licker had completely bossed him at Earl's Court, they both knew that. They also both knew Robinson would pull out all the stops to come out best in their next encounter. Randolph was saying, 'One of us will have to go this time!' and punching the palm of his hand and laughing. I thought, 'Well, Robinson's got the benefit of boxing in front of his home crowd with an American referee who's used to regarding him as champion but he has got that hem of eight stitches over his left eye to sort out.'

So, it was back to business. Robinson went off to the south of France to get some sun on his eye and we went up to Wales.

Salts erected a new sign:

COME AND MEET A WORLD CHAMPION
AT SUNNY GWRYCH CASTLE
HAVE YOUR PHOTO TAKEN WITH RANDY TURPIN

Visitors come in their thousands and kep' coming and kep' coming. We signed that many photographs it's a wonder we had any hands left to box with. Our arrangement was that the photograph money should to go to the Sunshine Home for Blind Babies, or any other blind institute. It would've amounted to a real tidy sum. I often wonder if Salts actually paid it.

Everybody – boxers; rugby blokes; cricketers; footballers; the newspapers; politicians . . . Anthony Eden, soon to be Conservative Prime Minister of Britain, was one of them . . . actors; musicians – was wishing us luck with telegrams, letters and messages on the wireless. Everywhere we went, people called across, 'Do it again, Randy!'

It was quite a thing for us to be going to America, cuz most people in the 1950s hadn't been out of the country except for war, and when Solomons said, 'You're on the fight card as well, Jack,' I was chuffed to death. To get a fight in the USA high on the bill of a World title fight gave me a real boost. I felt my star was rising.

We set sail from Southampton on 15 August, for our seven-day journey to New York, First Class, on board the *Queen Mary* – 80,000 tons of luxury liner. As well as Randolph and me, there was Dick, Eddie Phillips, George and Josie – Mrs Middleton couldn't come with us cuz she couldn't leave their grocers' shop. There was Jack Solomons and his wife Fanny; his brother-in-law, boxing promoter Sam Burns and his wife Sophie; Bill Hyam; Salts and his missus and daughter.

We'd ended up with as big an entourage as Sugar Ray Robinson, complete with our own, unwanted, version of his midget, Jimmy Karoubi, in the shape of Salts' six-year-old son Nigel. There was actually no need for Salts to come but it was one of those times when Randolph wouldn't be told.

The *Queen Mary* was like a floating five-star hotel. Well, you'd most probably have given it six or seven stars. I anna kidding, the food was fantastic. The First-Class dining room seated getting on for a thousand people and the waiters piled your plate up with as much as you wanted and called you 'Sir' at every verse end and the cabins was really comfy but, after a while, it got boring.

In the mornings, we done our road work on the decks and had breakfast. Then there was lunch and sparring in the full gym they'd got on board. In the evening, that's when you got dressed up for dinner – women in evening dresses and jewellery; men in white shirts, tuxedoes and dickie-bows. The Turpin brothers always dressed smart but we had our own style and that certainly wasn't being kitted out like bleeding penguins.

After dinner, we had to play games like passing the rubber quoit round when you was dancing. Whoever had it when the music stopped, then those two had to go off the dance floor. The couple left at the end would win a bottle of champagne. They used to do the same game with a ticket sometimes.

I acted as Josie's boyfriend and done all the dances with her – well, walked round with her. We were doing the ticket game and, after a few rounds of music, there's only me and Josie and one other couple left on the floor. They passed the ticket to me and I held on to it. As soon as the music stopped, the other bloke threw his arms in the air thinking as he'd won and never noticed me shoving the ticket in his pocket. The MC, seeing the other bloke celebrating his victory, asked me for the ticket. 'I anna got it,' I said, and stood there looking ever so innocent. The other bloke put his hand in his pocket and found the ticket, and me and Josie got the bottle of bubbly. He accepted defeat but he muttered 'Bastard' to me as he was walking his missus off the dance floor. I laughed for days over that.

We had to play stupid games all the time. They was having more fun down in the steerage than we were. Our Dick used to sneak down there to chat up the birds, and me, Licker and Eddie tried to join him a few times but we could never get away with it, cuz Josie Middleton stuck to us like an extra shadow. We were her big brothers, sort of thing. I was glad when we docked in America.

All cities are noisy but New York screamed its head off. As soon as we disembarked, they took us to the Edison Hotel on West 47th Street, near Broadway, where Solomons stopped whenever he was fixing up American fights, and we spent the first four days on what the newspapers described as a 'whirlwind' publicity campaign.

It really *was* like being swept up in a swirling wind. We was on the go everywhere. The paparazzi blew along behind us with camera flashlights like Cadillac headlamps. 'RANDY HITS THE USA' was on all the newsstands; there was TV appearances, radio interviews, newsreel items. The world and his wife wanted autographs. No matter where we went, there was a crowd of people taking pictures. You could lose your head in circumstances like that but George kept us calmed down. Good old George. He was like a little bit of home come with you.

As soon as we arrived at the Edison, we were welcomed by a coloured lady from Harlem – one of these society women whose job it was to greet all the coloured celebrities as come to New York. Next morning, we went to a breakfast party at her house. It was a fantastic meal with entertainment – blokes on drums, singing, an' all that. A big crowd of people was scattered round the room and she introduced us to a bunch of them and sat us down. In the opposite corner was a beautiful-looking girl, Adele Daniels, about the same age as Randolph, and this hostess was particularly anxious for Lick to speak to her. She told Randolph how much Adele had wanted to meet him and kept shoving them together.

Randolph was a very, very handsome fella. All the birds liked him and birds was always chasing after him but we were worried about this one. When you're training, all women are bad news and this Adele Daniels was too pushy. For three days, she kept showing up wherever we went and before we left for our training camp Licker had taken her out a couple of times on shopping trips. Dick mentioned to George how good looking Adele Daniels was. 'A bit too good looking,' George said.

Some people believe the Americans took us out to nightclubs and showed us a good time to weaken Licker's chances of trouncing Robinson a second time. I could've understood it if they'd tried but we weren't that stupid that we'd have fallen for it. Those first four days were hectic but there was NO nightclubbing and nobody ever tried to make us go to nightclubs. Randolph was totally focused on giving Robinson another great fight. He sneaked a workout the day after we arrived and he was in terrific shape.

They took us on a tour of boxing gymnasiums. They're like factories over there, turning out fighters in dozens. I'm not akidding, you spar with somebody and they try to kill you, hoping there's some big manager in there that'll notice them. There's so many fighters in America and only a few of them can emerge.

America in the 1950s was supposed to be a rough place for black people – the Ku Klux Klan, an' all that. I've seen pictures with notices saying 'NO COLOREDS' or 'COLOREDS ONLY'. There was segregated public transport; segregated washrooms and toilets and segregated restaurants. We never seen none of that. But then I suppose we was being guided to areas we'd be all right in. Having an armed personal bodyguard probably helped.

This massive big bloke comes into the foyer of the hotel and sees me standing there. He flashes a police badge at me, 'Where's Toipin?' he asks. 'He's under my care while he's here.' I thought, 'Bloody hell, if you've got have police protection when you come over here to box, I wanna go home.' Benny Shulman was his name. I think he had a few personality problems. I was watching a TV comedy programme one day that was taking the mickey out of Jewish people a little bit. Shulman said, 'You'll switch that goddam shit off if you know what's good for you.' Another time, I was lying down in me room and the door burst open and Shulman leapt on the bed and stuck his revolver in me mouth. I froze. I thought he'd gone berserk. 'Ha-ha,' he said, putting his revolver away. 'You was really shaking there, man.'

'Wouldn't you,' I gasped, 'if some mad bastard stuck a gun in your mouth?' He was ever so good, really. When we left America, he gave us a little gold police badge each.

The Randy Turpin Training Camp was at Grossinger Airport, 1,700 feet up in the Catskill Mountains, a hundred miles from New York. The airport was built on a plateau and Grossinger's itself was a massive big country club: a hotel with a restaurant, a golf course, a ballroom and everything. The countryside was great for road work and there was horses we could borrow for riding.

Randolph borrowed a big white horse and he'd go whooshing around the airfield, jumping the fences. Solomons and George'd watch with their hearts in their mouths. Randolph was mad about driving as well and he loved the American cars cuz they were automatics. He learned to drive over there.

They set us up a ring in one of the hangars and supplied four American sparring partners. The sparmates ate with us and hung out with us. One of them, Leroy Coleman, a middleweight contender, was also a great jazz tap dancer. I asked him to show me some moves and we went out on the boardwalk in front of one of the annexes. He done a few steps and I copied them. Next thing, there's a TV camera on us and it's going out across America.

Leroy told us he'd been winding up one of the American lads about the castle we trained in: 'I've told him you said it's haunted and, damn, he's terrified of ghosts!' I'd taken some 78 rpm records with me and one of them had ghost sound effects on it – spooky footsteps rising and falling, ghostly moans, shrieks and rattling chains. It was comedy, sort of thing. The annexe we lived in was mostly made of wood, so we made a small hole in the wall, passed a wire through it and fixed up a speaker under this sparmate's bed. In the evening, Leroy says, 'Hey, my buddy wants to know, do you really have a ghost in your castle?'

'As a matter of fact,' I said, 'we've got two.' His mate's eyes stretched open.

Leroy chimes in, 'Two ghosts in one castle. Man!'

'Yeah. One dressed in red and one dressed in white. The red one, she's all right,' I told them.

Leroy's mate said, 'How d'you mean all right?!'

'She comes and chats to us.' His eyes are getting even wider.

'Chats to you?'

'Yeah. She tries to get into bed with us but we push her out, cuz she's so bloody cold. It's the other one we don't like – the headless one.' Leroy's mate is half standing up now and his eyes are bugging out on stalks. One of the trainers comes round and shouts, 'OK, YOU GUYS. EVERYBODY TO BED.'

About twelve o'clock, midnight, I put the record on: tomp-TOMP-tomp – Oooh, OOOoh, OooOOOOoooh! AIEEEEEEE! – *Rattle-Rattle*. The bloke had actually gone to sleep but Leroy wakes him up: 'Can you hear something?' He listens for two seconds, leaps out of bed and dashes out of the room. There's a CRASH! BANG! and the sound of running feet. When me and Dick got round there, the door's hanging off its hinges and the fella's going up the road like a bleeding express train. We had a hell of a job getting him back.

We had intervals for larking about but, basically, as soon as we hit Grossinger's we drew up the sparring lists and got down to work. Boxing fans paid two dollars to come and see 'The Man Who Beat Sugar Ray Robinson' and Randolph put on a good show for everybody, having the time of his life. He was unbelievably fit. He was telling reporters he was sure he'd retain his title. He wasn't getting bigheaded or over-confident. He'd got the measure of Robinson in London and totally out-boxed him.

Sportswriters visited the training camps – ours at Grossinger's and Robinson's at Pompton Lakes – and reported progress to their readers. We were getting good write-ups but Eddie Phillips saw an article saying Randolph seemed to be going easier on his American sparmates than he did on us. He asked Licker about it. 'Well,' Lick admitted, 'I've been told if I hurt them they'll be taken away from me.'

I asked George, 'What fucking use is that? Practising holding back instead of working on his killer move forward?' but I didn't get anywhere with it.

We were all convinced Randolph would come back still champion, and everybody we spoke to was convinced Randolph would win, but it was like the betting men still hadn't cottoned on to the fact that Robinson could be beat and the odds went in Robinson's favour at 2 to 1.

The former champion didn't seem so confident hisself. When you've lost your title, you've lost a hell of a lot, and if you fail to regain it, your career goes downhill fast. At the weigh-in – we had to go to the New York State Boxing Commission Office for that –

Ray Robinson seemed actually nervous. Randolph was geeing him up, telling him, 'Come on, give 'em a smile, Ray.' It was quite a switch from how it'd been in London.

The fight, advertised as 'A BATTLE OF NATIONS', was the hottest ticket in town and sold out within hours. The Polo Ground was bursting at the seams – 61,370 people, including a big contingent of British fans. The money taken that night stood as a record for a non-heavyweight contest for years. Part of it was the two greatest middleweights in the world were about to battle it out and part of it was what I was telling you about, a lot of Americans still couldn't really believe Robinson could be beat, 'specially by an English bloke.

Dick was banned from Randolph's corner cuz of a rule about blood relations not being allowed because they get too emotional, so a lot more was gonna be left to Bill Hyam. I was unhappy about that cuz, all along, Hyam had tried to elbow his way past Mick Gavin and he never come up with anything like Mick did. Hyam would bowl in and say, 'What time are you lads training today? Because I'd like to see a bit of New York.' I used to think, 'Shouldn't you be telling us when we're training?' It'd be Mick, though, that'd be looking after Lick in the dressing-room, keeping people away so's Randolph could have his pre-fight sleep on the massage table and getting him ready.

I'd been matched for a six-rounder with Joe Wamsley, a dark-haired, pale-faced New Yorker of similar height and build to me. I couldn't have been more chuffed to be fighting in America and for a purse of $500 – the most I ever got paid for a single fight. The only thing was, I knew no British boxer since the war had won in America. Then somebody whispered in my ear, 'Wamsley's New York State featherweight champion.' I thought, 'Oh God, George, you might have started me off down the ladder a bit. New York State is a very big place!'

The Polo Grounds is open air but up in the ring it was sweltering. I felt good, though, and anxious to get the fight on. On the first bell, I moved quickly to the centre and straight in with a few sharp jabs. I found range and was punching hard, giving Wamsley summat to think about. Halfway through the round, I muscled my way out of a clinch and Wamsley went BANG! right on the top of my head.

Afterwards I asked one of the Americans, 'What kind of punch was that, for Christ's sake?'

He laughed. 'They've got a theory here, Jack,' he told me. 'If you hit any damn black man off the top of the head you'll knock him out. It's reckoned to be our weak spot.' The blow surprised me more than hurt me. I went down on one knee and took a count of six. On the order 'Box on', Wamsley started dancing round me looking all classy and I thought, 'Now you've asked for it!' I steamed in and punched him all round the ring. I bullied him. For the remaining five rounds, I kept the pressure up, punch-punch-punch, giving him no room to work. On the final bell, the referee come straight over and held up my hand.

'Jackie Turpin's windmill style upset Wamsley . . .' the newspapers said. I'd become the first British boxer since the Second World War to win a contest on American soil and I had all those dollars in my pocket. That was my job done – well and truly. Now for Randolph's.

I darted back to the dressing-room, grabbed Mick Gavin's overcoat, threw it on over the top of me boxing gear and dashed back to the arena. I found a place just behind the British reporters that would give me a good view of the fight – about 20 feet from the ring. I could see Bob Christenberry and all the other Boxing Commission people lording it in the front row. They'd got a star referee in, Ruby Goldstein, to supervise. He's leaning on the post in a neutral corner with his arms resting on the top ropes, waiting for the fighters to arrive.

Back in the United Kingdom, the clocks are coming round to three o'clock in the morning and the national grid is on overload nearly with all the wireless sets tuned in to the fight. They reckon four million people climbed out of bed over here to follow Randolph's first World title defence.

At the Polo Grounds, the MC announces the contestants and the challenger comes up the steps. Robinson's wearing another of his sumptuous robes with the hood pulled over his head. He ducks under the top rope and acknowledges the cheers of his home crowd and stands waiting for the arrival of the World champion. Randolph comes bouncing in wearing his ol' white towelling dressing-gown and, I tell you, they give him a real champion's welcome – cheered themselves daft. He winds his way through the spectators and bobs under the ropes.

The robe and gown come off. It's Randolph in the black shorts and Robinson in the white shorts. The crowd go quiet. The timekeeper's bell clangs and the fighters join in the centre of the ring. They're up on their toes, left feet well forward, circling round each other.

It's Robinson's job to take the fight to Randolph if he wants the title back. He snakes out his left hand in a rapid succession of jabs but they're inches short. Randolph's like a coiled spring. He moves to Robinson's right and slams in two left hooks to the head. He connects with the second one and follows it up with a couple of stiff jabs to the face and a thumping left hook to the body. Robinson grabs hold. The clinch is smartly broken up by Goldstein. Licker lunges forward, just missing with some serious lefts and rights. Robinson's feet are working fast trying to position himself to find an opening in Licker's defence. He throws a couple of big shots but he's punching air. Randolph jolts home some punches to the head as if to say, 'That's how it's done, Ray.'

Round two. Robinson's working anxiously. A lot of his shots are missing by miles and Goldstein warns him for hitting on the break. He manages to land a fist behind Randolph's left ear – it's the best shot of the round and Randolph's shaken but he recovers quick and he's as calm and relaxed as usual in his corner.

Round three. Randolph's making Robinson do most of the work and leaning back from the hips, keeping the ex-champ's flashing fists out of range. He knows all those wasted punches will wear Robinson down. Sugar Ray's sampled the weight of Licker's fists at Earl's Court and he's wary of providing Randolph with a clear target. He's warned for holding and, on the bell to end the third, Randolph cracks in a right to the jaw and Robinson sags at the knees and nearly goes down. Licker grins and holds out his arm to show his dazed opponent the way to the American corner.

For the next two rounds, they're both giving as good as they get. I'm thinking, 'You can see Mick Gavin didn't get the upper hand in training this time' – cuz Randolph's not working behind his jab but relying on his reflexes to avoid Robinson scoring.

Round six. There's a lot of clinching going on. Goldstein tells them, 'All right. All right. Step back. Clean break.' Randolph's still playing the waiting game and Robinson's getting frustrated. He tries to hit Randolph after the bell but Goldstein pulls him away and bundles him off to his corner.

Robinson's fancier and faster on his feet in the seventh but can't match Randolph at close range. He tries to tangle him up but ships a lot of leather to the ribs. Again, Randolph's proving the stronger of the two and the weight of his punches is slowing the Sugar Man down.

In round eight, Robinson's holding at every opportunity. Goldstein intervenes and breaks up a clinch; the Sugar Man gives Lick a wry smile and Randolph grins back.

Randolph comes out fresh in the ninth, swaying easily out of range of the tiring Sugar Man's combinations. At the end of the round, the referee's scorecard shows them four rounds each, one round even, but I've got Randolph ahead by at least three rounds.

On the bell to start the tenth, Licker rockets in on the attack. Robinson tries to subdue him by grabbing his arms but comes out of a barrage of close-range punches with the old cut over his left eyebrow burst back open. It's HORRENDOUS. You can almost see his brain ticking through it. It's not just trickling blood like most cuts you get in boxing, the blood is spouting out.

The crowd are on their feet. This is it! The fight's gotta be stopped! My brother is in sight of his second decisive victory over the man who'd once been hailed as pound-for-pound the greatest ever.

Goldstein calls the doctor over to look at the cut. Amazingly, the doctor nods the OK and Goldstein waves the fighter on. It's now or never for Robinson. He squares up to Randolph. His eye wound is pouting, the white of the bone is showing through and the blood's gushing. Licker holds back, shoots a brief glance at Goldstein to see if he's serious about carrying on and Robinson seizes the moment. He lands a thudding right into Randolph's jaw. Randolph bends forward to avoid the follow-up but Robinson grabs him by the neck with his left hand and rams Randolph's head down. With his left hand still pressing on Licker's neck, he brings a right uppercut off the floor and smashes it into his chin. He follows through with a full bodyweight shot to the kidneys – Robinson would at the very least have been warned for punches like that over here but Goldstein says nothing. Randolph's hurt. Gasping. He holds on, trying to recover. Goldstein breaks them up and Licker's forced to take up a defensive position on the ropes while Robinson moves in for the kill. Licker manages to nullify the first attack but Goldstein breaks them up again. Lick endures another fusillade of punches and comes back with a few shots but Robinson smothers them with a clinch. Goldstein yanks them apart and Robinson repeats his trick of pulling Licker's head down with his left hand while simultaneously delivering a vicious right uppercut to the jaw. Licker grabs holt. Goldstein wrenches them away from each other and Robinson sends over a hammering right and drops Licker to the canvas.

My brother's slumped on his back, arms stretched out, absolutely still. The crowd are up on their seats howling like wolves. The press photographers have planted their elbows on the ring apron and they're lashing tracer fire from their flashbulbs to immortalise the moment.

Goldstein starts the count: one . . . two . . . three . . . Four . . . Five . . . SIX . . . As the count reaches SEVEN, Randolph rolls himself up onto his left knee. Ruben Goldstein crouches over him: EIGHT . . . NINE . . . Goldstein's outstretched arm swings up to bring his hand down for the tenth and final number. As it reaches the very tip of its travel, Randolph gets both knees off the canvas and beats the count. Robinson's looking on in disbelief with blood cascading from his eye.

Goldstein grabs hold of Randolph's wrists, drags the resin off his gloves on the front of his shirt and orders, 'Box on.' Robinson leaps on Licker and batters him onto the ropes. Randolph sideslips but gets nailed against the ropes on the adjacent side and the ex-champion explodes into a fury of leather.

If there'd been a roof on the place, the roar of the crowd would've sent it over the moon. Licker's bent forward, half sat on the second rope, and he's rocking and rolling with the punches. He's making half of them miss, and taking the sting out of others, but there's punch after punch he can't avoid cuz they're fouls – down on the thigh bone; down the backside; the middle of the back; the back of the neck; the top of the head. Robinson's holding and punching, sending blows to the kidneys – everywhere except where he was supposed to – but he can't finish Randolph.

Licker just kept rolling, bent forward watching Robinson's feet. By how the feet were positioned to get leverage for the punch, he could anticipate where the next blow was coming from and slip it or roll with it. He could feel the weary, wounded Robinson's arms weakening.

All of a sudden, I see Licker move his feet and start bringing his hands up. I knew those signs. He'd do it in the gym. He'd roll back on the ropes and block everything that come at him then quickly move to one side and bring his hands up. You was in trouble then. 'Any moment now,' I thought, 'he's gonna explode and knock the shits out of Robinson.' Every American in the place sensed the danger at the same time. It was like someone had switched the sound off then back on again louder. Even Bob Christenberry got to his feet. Just as he did, an incredible thing happened. With barely eight seconds of the round to go, Ruby Goldstein stopped the fight and give the decision to Robinson.

In the bars of New York, people spoke of that last barrage of leather as being 'hundreds' of punches but Ray Robinson hisself only ever claimed it was 'thirty or so'. We counted them off of a tape of the fight, didn't we? Of the total three dozen punches thrown, a dozen are wild misses, or parried, ducked or sideslipped by Randolph; ten were blatantly illegal. Of the remaining legal punches, two or three were well-delivered shots but most of the rest had the sting taken out of them by Licker swaying to the side or leaning away from them like he'd been doing all through the fight. He was content to wait and clear his head and let Robinson wear hisself out with the frenzy he was in. The end of the round was close and there was no way Sugar Ray could come out for another with that terrible eye wound. Randolph was bringing his hands up to finish the fight still punching, cuz that's the way he'd want to win it.

If me brother had a fault with his boxing it was he hated holding. He could have grabbed hold of Robinson's arms and locked up. I mean, you can hang on as long as you like till the referee starts saying, 'Let go. Let go,' and then you can push them off. I used to do that regular. If they clinched Randolph, he'd mostly lift them off the ground and throw them across the ring spinning like ballerinas.

If Randolph had been in real trouble, he would've gone down on one knee and taken a short count. He could have actually fallen over and taken the longest count possible, cuz Goldstein couldn't have reached ten before the bell went.

It was very, very unusual for a World title fight to be stopped after only one knockdown. Goldstein said he done it to 'save Turpin from further punishment'. If he thought Randolph was hurt, why didn't he give him a standing count? Besides, Randolph hadn't got a mark on him and Robinson had a cut over his eye big enough to post a letter in.

People who were sympathetic to Ruby Goldstein said it was cuz an American boxer had been killed in the ring at Madison Square Garden the week before and Goldstein didn't want to risk a repetition. If Randolph had been getting hurt bad, you absolutely know that George and Mick would have pulled him out. Our champions have to knock 'em out in America to get a draw.

Anyhow, it was all over. The crowd was going wild. The ring was surrounded by New York cops and the MC announced:

> *The referee stops the bout. The time: 2 minutes, 52 seconds*
> *of the 10th round. The winner and the new middleweight*
> *champion of the world – Sugar Ray Robinson!*

I usually kept away from Dick or Randolph when they'd lost fights, cuz I'd have to spar with them and I didn't want to say anything that they might take out on me, but this time I went straight to the dressing-room. As soon as Randolph saw me, he said, 'Sorry I lost the title, Jack.'

'They robbed yer, kid,' I told him.

'It's just one of those things,' he said.

That's pretty much what he always said if he lost. He never tried to take anything away from anyone who beat him. 'You know as well as I do,' he said, 'Robinson never hurt me. The only lad that's ever done that is Jury VII. Remember?' We both smiled at that. Later on, he was more forthright about it. 'I could've won if I'd been allowed to carry on,' he said, but he wasn't cut up about it. Obviously, at the back of his mind he was thinking, 'Oh well, I'll get him next time.' I mean, it was officially one each now, wasn't it?

Randolph got paid a huge amount in America – for the fight and for the film rights – and the decider would make him the same as a millionaire today, if he wasn't one already.

A few days before the fight, this shipyard bloke with big shipyards all over the States come up to Grossingers for a word with Randolph. The upshot was, he wanted Licker to take out American citizenship and offered to sponsor him while it was sorted out. 'We know you can take Robinson,' the guy told him. 'And if you'll agree to become an American, we'll *guarantee* you'll win the fight.'

That was completely against Randolph's nature. 'No thanks,' he said. 'I'm British by birth and I intend staying that way.' Now, that shipyard bloke could have been talking a load of shit, so I anna saying you should draw any conclusions from it. I'm just telling you what happened.

I want to make it absolutely clear that Licker didn't hold a grudge over anybody or anything for his defeat. He wasn't happy about it but he accepted it. The next day, he told the press, 'To my people back home, and to all the British people, I'd like them to know I done my best but it seems that, this time, my best wasn't good enough.' He congratulated Sugar Ray Robinson on winning and said he genuinely admired him as a boxer and as a man.

Whatever went on in that ring, everything was fine out of it. Sugar Ray invited us to his bar in Harlem. There was dozens of blokes outside his place tap dancing. Ray went and done it with them. He was great at it. 'You could earn your living at that,' I told him.

It was like we'd been mates for years. He bought me a 7-Up and took me to one side. 'Your brother gave me a tough time,' he said. 'He really hurt me. It was do or die, Jack. I was lucky Goldstein stopped it.'

Ray took us to his barber's shop next door to his bar and we had our hair straightened same as him. I had mine done first. Dick laughed, called me a bloody idiot and then had his done. Licker had his done next.

Me and Eddie Phillips were walking down Broadway and we bumped into Duke Ellington. I got his autograph for Georgina and he congratulated me on my fight, said sorry for Randolph and give us tickets for his show in the evening. It was fantastic: the Duke Ellington Orchestra in full swing and the Duke playing brilliant jazz piano. I said to Eddie, 'I'm not knocking Warwick or Leamington but what a town this is!'

I tell you, in America, some of the gear blokes was wearing knocked your eyes out. You'd see a guy walking about in plus-fours, Scotch socks and a deer-stalker hat. I got Jackie Junior a two-tone suit with long trousers and shirts with ties to match. He used to suffer from hammer toes, so I went into Macey's and got him some handmade orthopaedic shoes. When I give him his clothes, he threw the lot on the lawn. 'I want guns!' he said, cuz Randolph had bought a pair of six-shooter cap guns for Dick's son, Lionel. I'd bought Gina a Red Indian outfit with a chief's bonnet. Jackie Junior hit the roof over his presents, so his uncle Randolph went out the next day and bought him a pedal car about 6 ft long with pump-up tyres. He'd wear his suit then – get all dressed up to drive his car. I bought Bet American clothes too.

Me and Reg Gutteridge, who'd covered Randolph's fight for over here, went to a tailor for suits. I chose a bright pinky-red one. It fitted in great in America but when I come home Bet said, 'You go out on your own in that!'

Reg announced once, on the TV, that it was some London kid who'd been the first British fighter to win in America after the war. George phoned up and Reg corrected hisself on air: 'I beg your pardon. Of course, it was Jackie Turpin who was the first. Sorry, Jackie.' I thought, 'That's OK, Reg, but I'd have thought that suit would've imprinted it on your mind!'

22

DEE-DAH!

You'll never keep up with the places we lived. I can't remember them all myself. We were practically gypsies we moved around that much. We all bought houses. Randolph bought a few – in Warwickshire and in Wales.

When he bought Bridge Close, along the road to Birmingham from Warwick by the railway bridge – a beautiful black-and-white detached house with a lawned garden and a summer house – T'rese had left him and he asked me, Bet and the kids to move in with him. You can imagine an old-fashioned English summer there surrounded by flowerbeds and big trees. It's where we used to go scrumping when the vicar owned it. Randolph bought our house off us and give it to our mum.

Mosh and his wife Maria moved into Bridge Close as well, and Joan moved in with her third husband, John Beston, and her kids, Cledwyn Randolph O'Connell, from her first marriage, and Daffydd John, who they'd adopted when they lived in Wales, as well as two of Dick's kids, Lionel and Howard – cuz if you looked for Dick's house, it was the one with the kids tumbling down the steps. He had six more besides them two: Michael, Bernice, Robert, Richard, Rebecca and Keith, and it used to get too much for Emily.

Joan's first husband, Mac O'Connell, died of heart disease and she married Pete 'Diver' Wilkins. He got that nickname cuz he'd leapt off a bridge and saved somebody's life. Him and Joan stopped getting on, so they got divorced and she married Beston. None of us was angels but Beston's language and his manners were vile. He was Cledwyn's stepdad. Cled used to say, 'Yeah. A step in the wrong direction.'

Randolph was devastated about Randolph Junior not being part of his life: that's why he always surrounded himself with kids and he absolutely loved them. He was very much the boss, though. When he ate with us, nobody would touch anything until after he'd helped himself to what he wanted.

We'd be away a lot boxing and doing personal appearances, so Randolph told Joan, 'You can keep house for me.' She always answered the door and if she thought you was gonna pester Randolph, you wouldn't get over the threshold.

This woman knocks the door one day and says, 'I've brought my daughter to meet Randy.' There's a young girl there with her. 'I think they'll get on very well,' the woman says.

'How old's your daughter?' Joan asks the woman.

'Seventeen.'

'Yeah,' Joan says, 'in three or four years' time. Now go away or I'll have the police here.' Things like that was happening all the time. Randolph was a magnet to women and Joan spent half her time chasing them away. He's actually had to barricade the doors and windows of his houses to stop them sneaking in. Girls he'd never met would turn up with his name tattooed on their arms but Randolph was protected while Joan was around. Nobody was gonna exploit her baby brother if she could help it.

When we come back from America, Randolph brought Randolph Junior an expensive gold watch. He tried to give it to him outside the Cassino. His mum was holding him and when Randolph showed him the watch, the kid spat at him. I said, 'Don't give it him, Randolph.' But he did.

'It ain't the lad's fault,' he said. 'It's only what they've been saying to him.'

My John, like, took the place of Randolph's own son, cuz the Stacks wouldn't let him see Randolph Junior. Randolph was going down to Eastbourne one weekend and John says, 'Can I come?'

'No,' Randolph told him. 'I'm going on me own.'

Half an hour after Randolph's gone, we notice John's missing. I rung the police at Reading, give them Randolph's registration and asked them to make sure John's with him. They flag Randolph down and John's not there. They're about to walk away when they hear a small cough and the copper says, 'Hang on a minute.' They open the boot and there's our John. I said to Bet, 'Just wait till he comes home!'

Randolph brought him back but not before he'd taken him shopping and bought him a complete new outfit. John comes in: 'DEE-DAH!' – throwing his arms out like he's a cabaret act.

I said, 'I'll give you bloody DEE-DAH!'

Randolph says, 'Oh, leave him, Jack.' He spoiled him rotten.

We was all on good money, especially Randolph, and we was desperately trying to get something done for our mum's eyesight. We took her to one specialist after another. Finally, we got her one with half the alphabet after his name – the most noted eye specialist in the country. We stayed in London three days while he carried out tests. Mum said, 'My eyes aren't getting any better. If they was, I'd let you lads carry on spending your money but it's not going to happen.'

The specialist confirmed it. 'Your mother's eyesight is irrevocably damaged,' he told us. The nerves of her eyes had been eaten away. Even transplant eyes aren't any good when the nerves have gone.

When we realised we couldn't do anything for our mum's blindness, we was determined to help as many other blind people as we could. We'd do exhibitions outside the Pump Rooms in the summer time and give the money to the blind home in Leamington. They invited Randolph to visit and he come back crying. 'You'd cry an' all, if you'd seen what I've seen,' he said. This nurse had given a little lad the job of showing Randolph round the garden. 'He's been blind from birth,' Randolph said, 'but he took me round the garden and touched every flower and told me its name and colour.'

When Randolph was at the peak of his boxing, he'd hire the ballroom at the Woolpack every Christmas for a party. They were fantastic occasions. It was invitation only and people used to fall out with each other trying to get invited. I should have sold tickets. I would have made a fortune.

Randolph come to me one Christmas and said, 'Present for you outside, Jack.'

'You must think I'm bloody stupid,' I said, thinking it was one of his leg-pulls.

He laughed and said, 'You are if you don't go outside.' I went out and there's this sand-coloured Hillman Minx parked right outside the front door with a big blue ribbon tied round it. 'Happy Christmas, kid,' he said, and chucked me the keys.

'I can't bloody drive!' I reminded him.

'You're having your first lesson now,' he said. 'Get in.'

Out of habit, I went and sat in the passenger side. Randolph tapped on the window. 'The driver's seat, you fool!' I drove round the block successfully but when we turned the last corner, the coalman was parked making a delivery. Randolph yelled, 'BRAKE!' I stamped my foot on the clutch and rolled three foot under the back of the coal lorry. I took proper lessons after that.

We always kept dogs but at Bridge Close Randolph added two monkeys. Joan made clothes for them. They got really well known in Warwick. They used to get on the railway track and the trains got in the habit of stopping to toot their whistles to clear the monkeys off the line.

When you become famous and in the money, all the parasites leech on to you claiming to be your best friend but they're really only friends with your wallet. Real friends tend to stay away, cuz they don't want you thinking they're like that and what you're left with is the arseholes. At the time, though, you can't see it. I wasn't on nearly as much money as my brothers, so it was worse for them.

After the Robinson return fight, Randolph had money coming out of his ears. The world was his oyster, sort of thing. Unfortunately, there was people standing on the seashore who were interested in threading his pearls on their own strings.

Randolph announced he was going to control his own finances. George'd countersigned all Randolph's cheques up until then. 'If that's what you want,' George said. 'But take my advice and put your money in the bank or invest it in something.' Of course, George meant in summat sensible and he done his level best to make Randolph realise that you don't box for ever and if you start making big money and start spending big money, you wind up with nothing.

Randolph got a reputation for throwing his money about, which he literally did sometimes. He'd throw thousands of notes in the air and say to me and Joan, 'Count that!' We'd never seen so much money in our lives. Joan would try to ration him with it but he'd tell her, 'I fought for it. It's my money.'

'Exactly,' Joan would say. 'YOUR money, Licker, nobody else's.' She tried desperately to stop him letting people touch him for it.

His trouble was he was too kind. If people spun him a hard-luck story, he'd feel sorry for them. I'd tell him, 'I'd let 'em bloody well drown if it was me.'

'It's none of your business,' he'd say.

His so-called mates! . . . Licker would say, 'We're going on holiday to Spain, or the south of France. Do you want to come?' And he'd find hisself paying not only for their tickets but their meals and everything else. He couldn't see it, though. He was such a nice kid. He loved the look on people's faces when he gave them something. I don't know whether it was a throwback to the way we was brought up, cuz if we'd got something and we'd got a friend who'd got nothing, we'd share with them.

There was a bloke in Wolverhampton had a hotel and a young son. He come up with a hard-luck story about how he's gonna lose the hotel unless he pays so much. Randolph lends him the money because he couldn't bear to see the little kid homeless. Then the bloke needs another loan. Another bloke had money off him for a pig farm. Another bloke borrowed £6,000 to buy a pub. Those are just some that come to mind. There were hundreds of others. In later years, he'd look back and say, 'It cost me bleeding money every time I shook hands with somebody, didn't it?' but he never really regretted doing it.

He had George's advice in one ear and Leslie Salts, who'd now endowed hisself with the title of Randolph's 'Business Manager', murmuring in the other. When he gave Randolph the word on a hotel on the Great Orme at Llandudno coming up for auction, Randolph agreed they'd buy it.

Randolph had fell in love with Wales from the first time he went there. Llandudno had become a very popular place for holidays: 'Queen of the North Wales Coast'. Salts persuaded Randolph to go halves on the property, which they would turn into a sports complex. With how brilliant Salts was at business, coupled with Randolph's name to attract the crowds, it'd be a sure-fire winner.

It turned out Salts already owned the Great Orme Tramway. He said the hotel and all the buildings would fetch £15,000 at auction, and him and Lick would put up £7,500 pounds each. They'd open up the golf course again. The auction was in July 1952 and Salts was the one with his hand in the air when the hammer come down.

There were 15 acres of land but no golf course, cuz that'd already been sold off for grazing. Salts actually got the land, the hotel and the other buildings for £10,000. Lick had put up his half of the estimated £15,000, so, as far as I can work out, it only cost Salts £2,500 for his half.

George always tried to look after us. He put a private detective on Salts and got a pile of papers on him and all the shady deals he got up to. But there wasn't enough to go to court with and Randolph wouldn't listen.

I think Salts knew the Orme was doomed from the start and only wanted it for short-term advantage. He told the council and the press that the place would be a huge benefit to Llandudno. He put in a miniature railway and an outside boxing ring, same as he'd had at the castle. Randolph named it the 'Summit Complex'; they turned the old public bar into 'Randy's Bar' and we all trooped up there to help get it ready.

23

The Folk on the Hill

Losing to Robinson hadn't affected Randolph's popularity one little bit. Everyone was looking forward to the decider between them. Solomons made several attempts to fix it up but the Americans kept refusing. We couldn't understand it. Both fights had been box office sell-outs. A third fight would have broken all previous records. So why didn't they want it to happen?

I believe Ray Robinson's reputation was bigger than he really was. I'm not trying to belittle him by saying that, because I believe his reputation was bigger than anybody could be. Randolph was completely undaunted by him and, on form, would've beaten anybody at the time and anybody ever since. Robinson, the legend, was a big draw whoever he was fighting. So why should he risk his title again, and why should the American Boxing Commission risk losing the title from America to Britain again? It was annoying, though, cuz it was looking like there wasn't anywhere for Randolph to go as a middleweight. Randolph could switch up and down weights with no cost and he never cared who they put in front of him so long as they were good, so George thought light-heavyweight would be a better option with the middleweight division bottled up.

The World light-heavyweight champion at the time was an American fella, Joey Maxim. Freddie Mills had held the title till he met Maxim at Earl's Court in 1950. Maxim hit him that hard, all Freddie's teeth shot out. George and Solomons thought it would be great if Randolph got the title back for Britain.

The first stop would be Randolph going in against Alex Buxton. The Buxtons were another family of fighters – four brothers from Watford. One of them was the first coloured officer in the British army. They were all good boxers.

Our kid had just been doing light training since New York and he'd been out of the ring for five months. A long lay-off knocks the rhythm out of your boxing and you don't react so quickly. Even so, Alex took some knuckle, I tell you. The fight never went the distance but it was long enough for Randolph to scuff the ring rust off hisself.

There was no rust collecting on me. 'You set 'em up,' I told George, 'I'll knock 'em down.' I was knocking real good fighters over like skittles and I wanted to carry on doing it. In fact, I thought I could knock everybody out – till I met Sammy Bonnici. He was a southpaw and they're always awkward for an orthodox fighter but he was just another one to flatten as far as I was concerned. All through the early rounds, Mick Gavin was yelling, 'Box him, Jack. BOX HIM!' but I took no notice. I was punch-happy.

I got a strict dressing-down from Mick after every round. After the fifth, he smacked me round the ear for it but I still kept going for the KO and I lost on points and spoiled my run. On the way home, I said to Mick, 'I'm sorry for not taking notice of you.' Mick never replied. He wasn't speaking to me.

A couple of weeks later, me and Randolph were at Harringay: me for an eight-round draw with Dan McTaggart, and Randolph against the champion of France, Jacques Hairabedian, for his second light-heavyweight contest. Licker saw the Frenchman off with a left and a right in the third round. His next stop on the road to the World light-heavyweight crown was to be a battle with Don Cockell for the British and Empire titles.

I told you that Randolph never cared who they put in front of him. Well, Don Cockell was the one exception. This was the only fight I have ever known that Randolph really didn't want. In fact, he was dreading it.

Trouble was, Don and Randolph were great mates and Randolph didn't want to have to hurt him or take his title off of him. But, if he wanted to go anywhere as a cruiser, the British champion was unavoidable.

Randolph boxed beautifully against Don. He worked off his jab and whenever Don attacked, Randolph retaliated with summat magical – just enough and never more than enough. He wanted the fight to be absolutely as fair as possible. When he'd got him backing up, he kep' telling him, 'Come on, Don, fight back, fight back.' Don had nothing to come back with and, with four rounds to go, Licker had felled him twice and the referee had seen enough. My baby brother was the new British and Empire light-heavyweight champion.

In the July of that year, I had my first encounter with Potteries featherweight Tommy Higgins, in Ipswich. I had Randolph in me corner and, as usual, he was shadow boxing like a madman outside the ring shouting, 'GET IN THERE, KID!'

Tommy Higgins cost me my two front teeth. It wasn't his fault. My gumshield slipped and we both went in with our heads down. I still managed a points win – it was either beat Higgins or get another thumping from Randolph when we got home for not taking his advice.

For Randolph, holding titles at two different weights was a great achievement but it didn't come without problems. The rule is no fighter can hold a title at more than one weight at the same time. Stupid, cuz it should be up to the fighter, but which weight should he follow?

Solomons was convinced Robinson would agree to the long-awaited best-of-three between him and Licker, and he finally managed to get a verbal agreement from Robinson's people, and then he got summat in writing. It wasn't exactly a contract but to Solomons, who'd honour a deal just closed with a handshake, it was every bit as good. The British Boxing Board agreed with him but the American authority said, 'No.' They went as far as saying Randy Turpin wasn't even the main contender for the title and should go through a series of eliminators first. How the bleeding hell they come to that conclusion, I'll never know. *The Ring* magazine at the time had Dave Sands as number three, Walter Cartier as number two and Randolph number one. The Americans went even further and warned Robinson they'd take his title off him if he got in the ring with Randolph, and ordered him to defend against another American.

The Empire middleweight title – the one Dick lost to Dave Sands over Emily – fell vacant and it was a great opportunity to get it back for the family. Randolph dropped down to middleweight and went in with George Angelo, a South African fighter.

The trouble with Randolph earning a reputation as a knockout puncher is that people expected him to finish his opponents off with a biff-bang every time he went in the ring. Well, you can't always do that and instead of sitting back and enjoying two well-matched boxers going the distance with each other, they get the idea they've been cheated. People like that are sensation-seekers not boxing fans and that's how it was when Randolph went in with George Angelo. The fight went the full 15 and the referee had absolutely no difficulty in giving it Randolph on points, but the press moaned that the fight had not been as exciting as they'd expected. We were proud of Randolph. The Empire middleweight crown was ours again.

Titles have to be defended within a certain length of time and people started agitating about Randolph's defence of his European light-heavyweight crown. The British Board of Control were good enough to give him a bit longer than the usual six months but the European Boxing Union weren't so big-hearted. They had George and Jack Solomons backed in a corner and George was forced to advise Randolph to relinquish his European light-heavyweight title in favour of his ambition to regain the World middleweight title.

Meanwhile, back at the ranch, Sugar Ray Robinson was getting cheesed off. His pride was driving him towards another fight with Randolph and he wasn't being allowed to do it. Since Licker, he'd fought and beat a Hawaiian fighter, Carl 'Bobo' Olsen, on points and he'd KOd Rocky Graziano in three rounds. But he was having to really cast around for worthy opponents and talked about going up to light-heavyweight hisself. 'Right,' George said. 'Whichever weight Robinson chooses, Randolph will follow.' Robinson went to light-heavy against Joey Maxim but he lost. It's a fine balance, innit? He could put the weight on for the punch and lose his speed, or keep his speed and suffer a weight disadvantage. Where Randolph could float up and down between weights with no loss to his punch or mobility, Robinson couldn't.

At the end of 1952, we got the news that Ray Robinson had got out his tap shoes and gone on the cabaret circuit. I told you he was a good dancer, didn't I? It was the first of a few times he retired from boxing. With him pirouetting off into showbusiness, the World middleweight title was now vacant. It was like a rainbow had come out and everybody's chasing after the pot of gold.

You might remember 1953 as the coronation year of Queen

Elizabeth. The whole country was preparing for it. But the only crown the Middleton stable was interested in was the one Robinson had laid aside. But at the moment, Randolph's still light-heavyweight, cuz nobody at middleweight wants to box him.

I'd got no shortage of opponents. In January that year, I was in against Tommy Higgins again – the curly-headed youth from Hanley that I'd took on points for the price of my two front teeth. It's an important contest because whoever wins it gets to call themselves Midland Area featherweight champion. Randolph had a light-heavyweight battle lined up two days later with the Belgian champion Victor D'Haes. As usual we trained together.

My plan for Higgins was to take charge, keep him busy with my jab, wade in with body punches to slow him down and then move in for the kill. With my fight being over 12 rounds, me and Randolph added a few miles a day to our road work, and Mick Gavin had me concentrating on body punches in the sparring sessions. Randolph knocked D'Haes out in the sixth round. My fight went a bit longer.

There was a real sting to Higgins' punches. It was obvious he wanted the title as much as I did. But he'd got no answer to my jab or my body punches or my stamina. By the time the fight was halfway through, I'd got the measure of him. I stepped up the fury and nearly had him over in the eighth and eleventh rounds. The upshot of it was, at 27 years of age, I became the Midland Area champion with a resounding points victory.

'A fitting reward to Turpin's tremendous contribution to the sport' was how one paper described it. I don't know about that but it felt ever so good to have a title at last. From now on I would be getting more money and bigger fights. Tommy Higgins said he wanted to meet me again but I told George, 'Make him wait. I'm a champion now.'

Our fame shot up another couple of notches with all the Turpin brothers having won titles and the press were referring to us as 'Britain's Best-known Boxing Family'.

There's a little film not many people know about called *The Day of the Fight* by Stanley Kubrick. Walter Cartier v. Bobby James. Cartier knocks him out. Well, I don't think Cartier would have wanted a film made of when he met Randolph at Earl's Court in March 1953, cuz he got disqualified in the second round – for low blows, I think it was, or for persistent holding – and I wouldn't have wanted a film made of my disqualification against Harry Ramsden a couple of months later neither, although it would've made a good comedy.

I was all over Ramsden like a rash. I'd knocked him down six times in as many rounds. I was enjoying knocking him on his back but he wouldn't stay down and I got carried away and made a genuine mistake. I hit him before he'd got off the deck properly and got meself disqualified.

Ramsden's manager was a right cheeky twat. 'It's time you retired, Jack,' he told me. I mean, his bloke hadn't won the fight; he'd been given it. He'd spent half of it lying down. But I didn't harbour any grudges. In fact, I give him some useful business advice. 'Have you ever thought,' I asked him, 'of the money you could make by renting out advertising space on the soles of Harry Ramsden's boots?'

We officially opened the Great Orme Summit Complex in April 1953. Easter Monday. Randolph booked Jimmy Wilde to cut the ribbon because Wilde was a particular idol of the Welsh. We had telegrams wishing us good luck from Freddie Mills, Bruce Woodcock, Dennis Compton . . . oh, from just about everybody who was famous then. After that, we done our training in front of the usual huge crowds but at the Orme instead of the castle. The only thorn in our side was Salts.

Once, he told the sparmates he'd sent their wages down to me in Warwick. I went up to Wales to sort it out with him. For a week, I'd approach him and he'd suddenly disappear. One day I hid till he was walking past and then grabbed him. I was with two sparmates. 'Mr Salts,' I said, 'Stan and Pete here say you said you sent their money down to me to pay 'em.'

'I certainly did not.'

'Yes, you fucking well did,' the lads said.

'No, no, gentlemen. You must have misheard me,' he told them. That's what he was like, see?

Gwyneth Price, Gwen, a farmer's daughter, come on the scene at Gwrych Castle. Her sister brought her to see us sparring and wanted them to have their photo taken with Randolph and it wasn't just the camera that clicked. Gwen wasn't beautiful like Randolph's usual women but he adored her. I didn't meet Gwen at the castle. That pleasure come later.

I'd been home from the Orme for a week to reintroduce meself to my wife and kids and I went back to the Orme the night before

I was due to be sparring. I parked the car and went up to the flats. Pete Price was in the living room and a girl was standing over by the window with her back to me. I raised my eyebrows at Pete: 'Yours?'

'No, no,' he said. 'Oh . . . er, Jack, this is . . . er, this is Randolph's new girlfriend, Gwen.' The girl turned to face me.

'Pleased to meet you,' I said. She give me a half-smile. She was a big strong girl with massive biceps. 'Oooh,' I said, 'ain't you got big arms! Do you do weightlifting?'

'Bloody cheeky thing, you!' she snaps, and storms out of the room.

I said to Pete, 'Is she always like that?'

Pete laughed. 'You should've just said hello an' stopped at that.'

'Why?' I said. 'She ain't the Queen of Wales or anything.'

About half an hour later Randolph comes in and says to me, 'Got your gear with you?' It was a bit of an odd question.

'Yeah,' I said. 'Course.'

'Well, get it out. You're sparring tonight.'

'What? I've just drove all the way from Leamington. I'm having a rest tonight. I'll spar the morning, afternoon and evening sessions tomorrow if you want but I ain't sparring tonight.'

'You'll do as you're told,' he says. 'Or pack your bags an' go.'

'Right-ho,' I said. 'I'll put me bags back in the car.'

He give me a mean look. 'Don't get smart, kid,' he says. 'Get your gear out ready to spar,' and left the room. That night was the first real hiding he give me.

I was used to getting banged all over the place but this time he seemed absolutely intent on doing me an injury. I hit the corner post; I bounced off the top rope and he met me coming off; he knocked me out through the bottom rope; out over the top rope . . . In the end I thought, 'Thank God those three rounds are over!' Next morning, I'm in bed and he comes round. 'Come on. Road work.'

'Eh?' I said, looking at the clock. 'It's half past five. We don't go till six.'

'We're going at half past five this morning,' he told me.

At half past eleven, it was time for the morning sparring session and the public were waiting. When it come to my turn, I hadn't even stood up properly before Licker knocked me onto the ropes. I bounced across the ring and out the other side. Then he got me in a corner and really started lashing out. I thought, 'He's gonna

break my ribs!' After I'd taken all I could take, I slid slowly down
the corner post, breathing out in a long gasp, to the applause of
the crowd. I hoped one of the sparmates would pull me out. Did
they buggery! Dick said, 'Come on, kid, up you get.'

I thought, 'Thank you, big brother, I wish it was you having this.'
Anyway the bell went and that was the end of my rounds.

I anna kidding, every breath I took sent a sharp pain shooting
up me chest. Bill Hyam acted as like a medico as well for us. He
started pressing on me ribs with all his weight, checking them
over. 'You're hurting me as much as him,' I told him. 'They're
broke.'

'No,' he says, pressing down on them again. 'They're just badly
bruised.'

'Tell him I can't box tomorrow, Bill.'

'No chance! You tell him.'

Eddie Phillips was always a good mate and twice he tried to tell
Randolph I couldn't box no more cuz of the pain I was in but
Randolph wouldn't have it.

Every time I went to spar, my heart was going like a tip-hammer.
For ten days, Randolph leathered me. I was beginning to get
buzzing sounds in me head. I went up to my room and lay down
on the bed. I thought, 'I've got to get out of here.' I packed me bags
and sneaked them in me car.

Randolph come to my room. 'I'm going out,' he said. 'I'll be
back in half an hour. Get ready for sparring.'

'All right,' I says, and I waited till he disappeared out of one end
of the car park and I got in me car and drove out the other end.

I'm blinding down the road in the Hillman Minx. I'm almost
into Chester when I catch sight of Randolph's car in me rear-view
mirror. I put me foot down: BRAAAAAAGH!, go steaming through
Chester and I'm just coming out the other side when he comes
past and runs me up on the kerb. I yanked on the handbrake and
jumped out as he come running up.

'Turn round and go back,' he says.

'No,' I said. 'I'm going home. You've got plenty of sparmates up
there, beat them fuckers up!'

'Get back in the car,' he says, 'and drive back to the Orme.'

'No thanks,' I said and then chucked him the car keys. 'You can
keep your car an' all.' I got me bags and I'm striding along the road
when BANG! he grabs me by the back of me neck, lifts me off me
feet and carts me back to the car and loads me up against the side.

'Get behind that bloody wheel,' he said, 'an' start driving back to the Orme before I throttle yer.' Randolph tagged behind me all the way to Wales.

We park up at the Orme and he follows me up to the flat. I sat down in one of the easy chairs and he stood in front of me. He stared at me for a long time. Finally he said, 'OK, kid. What's up?'

'I'm fed up with you trying to kill me. Every one of the blokes here has asked me what have I done to yer that you're taking it out on me like you do. I'm getting funny sounds in me head and I don't want no more of it.' He sat down.

'Look,' he said. 'I'm sorry, Jack, but you shouldn't have said what you said to Gwen.'

I thought back to the only time I'd ever spoken to her. 'What? Do you mean to tell me I've copped out this much all because I asked her did she weightlift cuz she's got big arms?'

'Ah,' he said. 'But what else did you say?' I repeated exactly what I had said and told him if he didn't believe me, ask Pete Price. He sends for Pete. Pete comes in looking worried. 'Pete,' I said, 'tell Licker *exactly* what I said to Gwen Price when you introduced me to her and no fucking lies.'

'Well,' he said, 'you says, "You've got big arms, ain't yer? Do you go weight lifting?"'

'What did he say after that?' Randolph asked him.

'Nothing.'

'Nothing?'

'Nothing. Not one word, Licker, honest.'

'Thank you,' I said. I was grateful to him for putting it straight. But Randolph still wasn't satisfied. 'Are you *absolutely* sure that's all he said, Pete?'

'Yes,' he said, 'an' I was in the room all the time, Lick. If she told you any different she's bloody lying.'

Things improved after that but nothing was ever the same after Randolph had met Gwyneth Price. Later on, Lick got secretly engaged to her.

Things had been happening over Robinson's vacated middleweight title. The European authority said the French had a middleweight champion, Charles Humez, who was the only real contender for the World crown. The British Board confirmed him as a suitable match for Randolph, who, in spite of what the Americans tried to make out, was the true number one contender. 'All right,' George said, 'Randolph'll fight Humez then.'

Bill Hyam walked out on us around this time. I think he got fed up with us taking no notice of him. The only thing Hyam ever did for me was lend me *Give Him to the Angels*, the book about Harry Greb. I must have read it 50 times. Harry Greb become my hero.

Solomons put on a real big show for Randolph's World middleweight contest at the White City Stadium on 9 June 1953. The programmes were in the shape of a crown and the tickets were another sell-out. Randolph fought great and took the fight on points to regain his World title. He was back where he should be: king of the middleweights. Now he had two silver globes with the world engraved on them for his trophy cabinet.

After the Orme had been going a while, Salts started to draw back from it and to leave more and more to Randolph. They had increasing little disagreements and it went on like that until Salts cleared off altogether. None of us had any business experience whatsoever and we'd be away boxing, mostly, and just going backwards and forwards up to the Orme during the summer, so our wives and kids used to stay up there and they all worked hard cleaning and selling ice creams and photographs – anything that could make a little bit of profit. We'd spar exhibitions when we could and we had 'DO A ROUND WITH THE EX-WORLD CHAMP' at weekends.

But you know how it is, Randolph suddenly had even more friends. They'd come up there, stay as long as they liked and never give him a penny. With Randolph being away so much he said to our Joan's husband, Beston, 'You run it for me. You're the manager.'

I'd end up in court if I told you what I really thought of Beston but our Joan thought the world of him. Even though he hadn't been treating her right, she trusted him. We knew everybody outside the family was on the take at the Orme but when we found out Beston was on the take too, we was disgusted. From being a hod carrier on the buildings, Randolph had lifted Beston to summat special. He'd given him a job that in his entire life he couldn't aspire to if he hadn't married our Joan and that's how he repaid it. The only honest thing he ever done with Randolph was admit he'd been robbing him.

Joan was shocked. Right up to the point Randolph come round

the house and broke Beston's nose for him, she'd believed Beston had been doing a good job. Beston's excuse was: 'Everybody else was on the take, so why not me?' Randolph made him go back and work for nothing to repay his debt but by then the Summit Complex was in too much trouble to be saved.

I've got well ahead of meself now, because before all that happened, the Americans dropped a big bombshell on us. They refused to accept Randolph's new World title. As far as they were concerned, they said, the World title was still vacant and cropped Randolph's win against Humez down to a 'European' title.

It was American power politics. In other words: money. They just didn't want the middleweight crown to stay in Europe. They said Randolph would have to fight for the World title again in their back yard against Carl 'Bobo' Olsen, the fighter from Hawaii who Robinson had beat.

I was gutted for Randolph because he had to get over the disappointment of being robbed of his true status and would have to prove he was the undisputed middleweight champion of the world yet again. But he took it all with his usual shrug of the shoulders.

Olsen was a plodder. He'd proved his endurance in the 15-round hammering he'd took when he'd failed to take the title away from Robinson but middleweights didn't come stronger than Licker, and Olsen lacked Licker's speed, flair and punch. The good thing about it was it'd be another big payday and another fight in America for us both.

24

All Your Fault, This Is

Madison Square Garden, Eighth Avenue, New York – the most famous boxing venue in the whole world. The same ring as Joe Louis boxed in. The same ring as Joe Louis never lost a fight in. And on the undercard of the contest for the vacant World middleweight title: Battling Jack Turpin, Hanworth Road, Warwick.

Ever since I was a kid I'd imagined meself boxing there. It was the proudest moment of my life when I sat on the same stool as Joe Louis's bum had sat on. Well, I don't know if it was *exactly* the same stool but I told everybody it was.

I was up against Jose Paniagua, a Puerto Rican featherweight with the thinnest arms and legs I've ever seen on a professional fighter. My American trainer, Jimmy August, told me, 'I've seen this guy take a thump on the nose that sent his eyes spinning. It would have flattened a middleweight, Jack, but all Paniagua did was hesitate for a split second and then start coming forward again. So don't try to knock this fella out. Concentrate on your boxing.' I took a deep breath. Paniagua was gonna be a tough customer.

Climbing into that ring was like going to church and being blessed. I didn't hear a word of the referee's pre-fight sermon. I stood breathing in the sound of the 20,000 fight fans congregated there for the evening's entertainment. I could feel the presence of all the famous people who'd fought under those same bright lights: Max Schmeling, Jack 'Kid' Berg, Harry Greb and, of course, the greatest of them all – the World champion heavyweight from Lafayette, Alabama, who defended his title no less than 25 times: Joe Louis, 'the Brown Bomber'.

The timekeeper's bell called for the bout to begin. I rose from my stool. I felt Joe Louis pushing me forward. I'm 63 ft tall, elastic, light as air, with thunderbolts in my fists:

Jab, Jab-Jab, Jab, Jab-Jab
Come off the jab with a Right an' Left
DOOMP! THWACK!
BOP to the head
Feint with the Left, cross with the Right
BIFF-ZZZONK
I'm DYNAMITE!
A pugilistic alchemist
Turning sweat into diamond mist
BIFF-BAM-BIPPITY
Block, twist
I'm Battling Jack, me fists can't miss!
BAM-BAM-BAM
ZIPPA-DOC-DING
Step back, slide, Hook . . . and Swing!
Sweet on my feet, sleek as a panther
'Cut to the jaw, slip the counter
The King of the Ring in a blaze of light
Hammering home with a BOOMING Right
Floating . . .
Dancing . . .
Under a smoking sky . . .

I could have boxed six million rounds not just six. I wanted those feelings and that fight to go on for ever but the contest was over and the referee come straight across and held my arm high in the air: a clear points win for Battling Jack Turpin in Boxing Heaven, Madison Square Garden, USA.

If my fight was a dream come true, my brother's fight was a nightmare.

It was the autumn of a hard year. I'd lost my Midland Area title on points to horizontal Harry Ramsden of all people. Randolph had been up and down weights like a yo-yo. He'd had his second

World title took off him. What we needed was a good rest not more fights.

We'd set sail on the *Queen Mary* from Southampton on 16 September and nothing had gone right the whole trip. We'd booked Cabin Class, Solomons upgraded us to First Class and Randolph had brought Frank 'Algy' Algar along as an extra trainer, which made things really awkward.

Algar was a regular seaman – middleweight champion of the navy till Randolph took his title off him. He served in submarines and got taken prisoner of war but was released just as Randolph joined. He come home on leave and trained with Dick and Randolph. He got that involved he stayed six months and got arrested for going AWOL when they heard his name given out on the radio as Randolph's corner man. He got hisself special leave to come to America.

Then summat happened that still gives me guilt pains. I blame myself because I didn't do anything after Randolph threatened me.

Me, Licker and Algar were doing our road work on the upper deck, first day out, and Randolph kept bumping into me. 'Why do you keep doing that?' I asked him.

'Doing what?'

'Bumping into me.'

'I'm trying to push you over the side,' he said, and give me another nudge. He laughed but it wasn't a proper laugh.

'No, come on, Lick. Why do you keep doing it?'

He stopped running, and put his face close to mine. 'Jack,' he said, 'shut yer bloody mouth or I'll shut it for yer.'

It was then I noticed. 'Oh, Christ!' I thought. 'He's gone cross-eyed.' How the hell the Board of Control doctor never noticed it I'll never know. I opened my mouth to say summat and Randolph thumped me in the belly. 'I'll break your bleeding neck, Jack, if you ever mention this to me or anyone ever again.' Algy Algar heard it all but he didn't say anything. He wouldn't have let on if Randolph had got a bleeding glass eye. I cried meself to sleep more than once over that because they can sort it out, can't they, a detached retina? That's most probably what it was. I should've told George and had the fight held up until Randolph got it fixed but I daredn't. At the same time, I realise that, as he was then, Randolph probably wouldn't have taken notice of George, even, and I would've got a good hiding for nothing. We done the rest of the running in silence but Randolph still kept knocking into me.

One of the first people to greet us when we docked in New York was Adele Daniels, wearing a big scarf. 'What-ho, duck,' I said, and whipped the scarf off her to tease her.

'Get out of my way,' she said, and snatched the scarf back and wrapped it round her neck quick. But not before I'd seen this big raw fresh scar it'd had been covering.

'Oooh,' I said. 'Somebody bite yer?'

'Go away,' she says, 'You're always interfering,' and pushed past me and went over to kiss Randolph.

The Americans didn't make so much of us this time – the difference between Randolph being a challenger and actually being World champion, I s'pose. We had Benny Shulman again and they did take us to the Polo Grounds as guests of honour to see Rocky Marciano beat Roland LaStarza and notch up his 45th win in his amazing 49–0 record. I swear LaStarza's head went round twice. I thought, 'They'll have to screw that bugger back on.'

Our training camp was back up at Grossingers and the next day we took the long drive out there and got settled in. I thought I'd go for a wander round the airport and strolled down this little road towards a hangar to have a look at the aeroplane. As I was approaching it, I could hear: DOOMP! – CHOO – DOOMP! – CHOO – DOOMP! – CHOO – DOOMP! . . . I walked in and all I could see was this massive punch bag – at least three foot in diameter and eight foot deep – and it's flying all over the place with great dents in it every time it was being hit. I sneaked round to see who was knocking it about and there was Rocky Marciano. 'What-ho Rocky,' I says. 'What are you doing here training? You only boxed last night!'

'Hey!' he says. 'It's Jack, ain't it? Come on over! I've come back here to loosen up, get things working properly again and start building up for my next fight.'

'Good God!' I says. 'Don't you have a rest between fights?'

'I let the others do that, Jack,' he told me. He must have been talking to George, cuz he knew that I was boxing nearly every week back home. 'Don't you just love boxing, Jack?' he said.

'Actually, no,' I told him. 'I hate boxing but I do it cuz, if I fight regular, I don't have to train all the time and when I have a fight I know I'm gonna get paid for it. When I go down the gym to train, I'm not gonna get nothing only p'raps a thick ear off somebody.'

214

He really laughed at that. 'Man!' he says. 'You're one funny guy.'

He was a hell of a great fella, Rocky Marciano. A real gentleman. He had very short arms for a heavyweight and had to walk through punches to get to his opponents – like suffer three or four punches to land one of his own, sort of thing. What he'd do was he'd batter their arms till they couldn't raise them, then hit 'em on the chin. We saw LaStarza when we went to get our licences from the New York Commission. His arms were in such a mess he had to have operations on them.

The Americans had supplied us with Jimmy August – the trainer I mentioned earlier – a stocky little guy who'd worked with Olsen and knew him well, and had worked with people that'd fought him. That's really important and we were lucky to get Jimmy. But Algy and Dick kept interfering and arguing with everything he tried to do, and it was upsetting George.

Randolph used to get these little blue patches sometimes and he started going off on his own a lot. Your trainer needs to be God. You can't be objective enough to control your own training. But Licker started taking no notice even of Mick who, to all of us, was the greatest thing in boxing. I did my level best to persuade Licker to at least listen to Jimmy August. 'He *knows* Olsen,' I told him.

'Yeah,' he said. 'But Algy's come all this way and that's it. Algy's looking after me.'

A miserable training camp is the last thing you want and Jimmy August was a real pro. 'Your brother shouldn't have all this bickering round him,' he said. 'I'll train you instead, Jack.' I was happy, cuz I'd got meself a good American trainer. After that, I didn't know much about what was happening with Randolph. I was busy getting on with my own preparations.

I had some good write-ups from the press guys but they were printing things about Randolph's attitude, saying he was moody and only working when he felt like it, which wasn't very often or for very long.

Randolph agreed he'd only boxed a couple of dozen rounds in three weeks but him and Algy insisted that was enough, cuz he was way ahead in his schedule and didn't want to peak too early. I wasn't so sure meself. He was weighing a bit light, which isn't a good thing against a puncher like Olsen. Then a stupid rumour went round that Randolph had been seen out drinking.

Randolph never really drank alcohol. Dick had taken to going off a lot without us and it was him who'd been spotted drinking, but the American press were too thick to notice the difference. If you ask me, they wanted it to be Randolph.

Teddy Waltham, representing the British Boxing Board of Control, was getting nervous about Randolph's training an' all, because Randolph was only taking notice of Algar, who shouldn't have been there at all with him not having a Board of Control trainer's licence.

Then the papers were full of Randolph wanting to retire from boxing after the Olsen fight – and they saw it as an explanation of everything. Randolph had mentioned something to that effect to George Whiting, a journalist friend of ours, and he'd printed it. Whiting was entitled to print it, cuz Randolph had actually said it, but I should imagine Randolph meant it to be in confidence.

Looking back, I believe it was just an idea Randolph was trying out for size, sort of thing, because Gwen wanted him to retire. When other journalists tried to confirm it, Randolph said he'd been misquoted. Here he was, all set to get the World middleweight title for, as far as we were concerned, the third time and he wouldn't want to retire without a few defences of it. He'd been done out of them before.

Licker kept insisting everything was all right but the odds lengthened in Olsen's favour. On the day of the fight, Randolph come in as the 3 to 1 underdog. But so what? That was no different from when he'd first challenged Robinson and look what happened then. I was still confident he'd come out on top and Sugar Ray Robinson agreed with me. He told the press he thought Randolph would 'win easy'. In my book, Robinson was the authority cuz he'd fought both Licker and Olsen, and he'd got the scars to prove who was the better of the two.

I hadn't been without problems meself. This welterweight kid the Americans supplied me and Randolph with as a sparmate had fought some of the top fighters and he couldn't half punch, but we'd been advised to ease off the pressure on this kid, cuz he'd been knocked about quite a lot. The first time he hit me in the chest, I went straight through the air – actually sitting down in the air. Jimmy August leapt in the ring, smacked him across the face and give him a right roasting.

After Jimmy give him a rollocking for punching too hard, he'd throw a punch and stop it just before it hit me. So, I'd got a welterweight sparring partner that me, a featherweight, wasn't allowed to hit too hard and who wouldn't hit me.

I complained to Jimmy, 'I can't spar with anybody that doesn't hit back.'

Jimmy says, 'He's heavier than you, he's more experienced than you and I'm not going to let him chop you up. Hit him, but go easy.' I couldn't go along with a farce like that so Jimmy got rid of him. Then I felt bad, cuz I'd cost this bloke his job and he must have been on rough times. Other than that, Jimmy August was brilliant with me and it all come out right in the end. Like I've told you: a dream come true.

I got great reports in the newspapers: 'Jackie Turpin has a hustling, bustling, bang-wallop style that suits the American audience.' They loved how I pressed forward all the time and threw a lot of punches. They also thought I was a bit of a character, which they like over there.

A bloke from one of the big New York stadiums offered to launch me on a big career in the States. A 12-month contract with options. I'd train under Jimmy August, with a guarantee of 12 fights, one a month. I was chuffed to death. Even if it only lasted the 12 months, with all that training and experience behind me I could come back to England with a trunk full of money and take the British featherweight title for sure. That'd be another dream come true.

I couldn't wait to tell Randolph.

'No you don't,' he said. They never give Randolph proper security in his apartment and the Yanks was sending all the press and everybody to knock on the door all night to keep him awake. He told George, 'Don't let Jack stop out here on his own.' George agreed. I was gutted.

When it come to Randolph's fight, he had George, Algy, Mick Gavin and Dick in his corner. They'd relaxed the blood relatives rule for some reason.

Licker flew at Olsen. For the first three rounds, he battered him with ferocious punches, totally controlling the ring, showing the world who was the rightful owner of the middleweight crown. He circled left, leaving Olsen staring wildly at where he suddenly wasn't. He done the same thing the other way about. He backed Olsen up at will and nearly had him down several times with big scything left hooks.

Give Olsen credit, not many boxers could have survived those early rounds. He was like a carthorse caught in a storm. When the thunder rolled, he reared backwards, then plodded forward again under another hail of leather. There was nowhere to go for shelter and the outcome of the fight seemed a foregone conclusion.

In the 60 seconds between the third and fourth rounds, summat strange come over Randolph. It was as if he'd been replaced by a pale shadow. He battled through the remains of the bout like a man trying to punch his way through a sea of mud. Olsen used him like a bleeding punch bag. Time and time again Randolph was trapped on the ropes and forced to cover up while Olsen clubbed him around the head. It was only our kid's bravery that kept him on his feet.

Whether Olsen's arms got weary or he decided Randolph was never going to go down from head punches, I don't know, but he suddenly switched his attention to the body. That was when the serious fouls started.

Every time Olsen sent over a looping right-hand that was supposed to be to the ribs, it was going round the back to the kidneys. The referee said nothing. I felt like leaping in the ring and giving Olsen a good kick in the nuts.

I saw Dick'd left the corner but I didn't take much notice of that, cuz it could have been over Randolph not listening to what he was telling him – or over anything or nothing. Friction had been building up mainly for reasons that came out later – but a corner man deserting you ain't gonna help your performance. On its own, though, it wouldn't explain the big change that'd come over Randolph.

The timekeeper's clock absolutely crawled towards the final bell. I anna kidding, Randolph was guts personified. He was taking brutal shot after brutal shot but absolutely refused to let Olsen finish him. In spite of Licker fighting at a hundredth of his ability; in spite of him being battered to the canvas in the ninth and forced to take almost the full count in the tenth, he come back to win the final round. But you didn't need to know nothing about boxing to know who'd take the decision. Carl 'Bobo' Olsen was the new middleweight champion of the world.

The papers were full of it. 'The Turpin Tragedy' one called it. They all said admiring things like, 'Even in defeat Turpin's courage knew no bounds' – stuff like that, but they all claimed he'd thrown the fight away with poor training. They knew Olsen wasn't normally in his class.

A lot of people have asked me, 'Had he been got at by the

Mafia?' – an' all that, cuz he'd never started off that well then faded.

You've got to know Randolph. He was a complex fella. I mean, he'd come to me one day and pour his heart out and the next day he wouldn't tell me a thing, and if I tried talking about what we'd been talking about the day before it'd be 'Shut your mouth' and he'd threaten to bop me. I could sometimes get him laughing and he'd forget what he was gonna smash me one for. Most of the time he wouldn't have really done it but other times he would've actually hit me. So, if he said 'shut up', I shut up. Sparring was different. That was his business. People used to say, 'Why do you spar with him?'

I'd say, 'Well, if it was your brother as needed sparring partners, wouldn't you spar with him?'

'Not if he knocked me about like your kid knocks you about.'

Even me mum used to say, 'You didn't ought to spar with him, Jackie. He hits you too hard.' Then, when Licker had another big fight coming up, she'd say to me, 'You are going to help him, aren't you, Jackie?'

Mick Gavin used to get on to me blind about it: 'Don't spar with him no more. You're jeopardising your own chances.'

'Randolph needs it,' I'd tell him, and that's how I used to look on it.

Like I say, Randolph wouldn't always share his worries with you, and exactly what had happened between those third and fourth rounds we never even got a chance to discuss cuz of all the panic that come later. He told the press, 'Any fighter who's got a load on his mind before a fight is past his peak before he gets in the ring.'

It was quiet in the dressing-room after the fight. Randolph had got showered and was getting dressed. When he'd put his trousers on he nipped into the loo and come out looking worried. 'Quick, kid,' he says, 'come and see this.'

I saw what was happening and immediately got hold of George. 'He's passing blood.'

'Get him back to the hotel as fast as you can,' George said.

George got the hotel manager to send a tarpaulin up to the bedroom. We spread it over the bed, put Licker on it and tucked the edges up around him and sent the waiters for ice, buckets and buckets of ice. Randolph lay there covered in ice till the bleeding stopped. He was obviously hurt really bad but I can't remember anybody sending for a doctor.

219

In the front of the Edison hotel was a milk bar that'd got the first jukebox we'd ever seen. Me and Randolph must've put a fortune in it. On the morning of 2 November – the day before we was due to sail back to England – Randolph was playing the jukebox when two plain-clothes cops come in from the NYPD, flashed their badges at him, shoved him back against the bar, handcuffed him and hauled him off to the Seventh Precinct. As Licker's being marched through the door, he turns to Dick and says, 'All your fault, this is.' Dick looked terrified.

Benny Shulman said, 'There's obviously been a mistake. I'll go down town and square it.' But he come back looking as bewildered as we was. Next thing we knew we were in court.

One American paper described the court case as 'among the most unruly seen in a New York court for many years'. You'd have screamed laughing if you'd went to it.

Randolph was charged with an alleged assault on Adele Daniels in her apartment – a 'cruel, vicious and bestial' assault. She'd got herself represented by a famous New York lawyer – J. Rowlands, I think – some bloke who'd got well known by defending in a big callgirl trial. He was a cocky little fella in a $1,000 suit with a silk handkerchief flopping out of his top pocket and a big red rose in his buttonhole. He wore a black homburg hat and carried a walking cane. I ain't akidding, he looked like summat out of a Batman film but the way he dressed was nothing compared with the fancy way he had of putting things.

The judge sat there the whole time with his feet up on the table. Our solicitor was in the middle of a speech when the judge interrupted. 'God dammit!' he told him. 'Will you shut your goddam mouth and let somebody else have a word.' I nearly got chucked out for growling when Rowlands called Randolph 'a beast of the jungle in human form'. The judge warned me, 'If you don't quit, you will be ejected from this court and arrested.'

'All right,' I said, and sat there biting me lip. The woman in front of me got a bollocking for doing her knitting. You absolutely never knew what they were going to come up with next. At one point, Randolph was called 'a killer with Mafia connections'. Poor old Randolph. His head was whizzing round from one person to another. He didn't know what the bleeding hell was going on. He still wasn't well from the fight, he'd just suffered a huge setback to his career, he was facing an inquisition from the British Boxing Board of Control and now he'd found hisself in court facing a possible American prison sentence. I mean, he hadn't done nothing wrong; but if it could go this far, where could it end?

Suddenly, however, the criminal charges against Licker were unconditionally withdrawn and Daniels' mob switched tactics. They decided to sue Randolph for $100,000 – about £35,700 then. Twice as much as he'd earned fighting Olsen. We was allowed to catch our ship back home on condition Randolph left $10,000 security against being called back to answer a civil case. Everything was nearly back to normal but the trouble with having so much mud thrown over you is that some of it sticks.

It seemed to be the only thing people wanted to talk about. There was a load of stories going round. One was based on the fact that people had noticed that Dick and Randolph weren't speaking. They tied that in with Randolph telling Dick 'It's all your fault' when he was arrested. They reckoned it was Dick as was mixed up with Adele Daniels, Dick that'd assaulted her and Randolph who was taking the blame for him. I can understand how the rumour got started but the rumour-mongers had got their stories crossed up. Besides, Randolph would never have covered up for *anybody* that'd hit a woman.

What Randolph blamed Dick for was for being a bigmouth telling Adele Daniels about his marriage break-up with T'rese. What Adele Daniels had accused Randolph of seemed to me to be almost word for word what T'rese had said. This second time with Adele Daniels was a lot worse, of course, cuz, you know what it's like, people as didn't believe Randolph had been violent to T'rese started to have doubts, cuz, hello, it's cropped up again.

T'rese was all right. We all liked her, still do, but it was certain of her relations that got at her. The few that really knew Randolph knew he couldn't do them sort of things. The truth was, although Dick liked Adele Daniels, he was more interested in this mate of hers, and it was over her that Dick and Randolph fell out.

You've got to remember that we was young and thousands of miles from home in a country where we were big celebrities and we had birds throwing themselves at us all over the place. I ain't saying that makes it all right; I'm just saying that's how it was. Dick was head over heels for this newly divorced women and he asked Randolph to advance him the money so's he could stay over in the States with her until her divorce settlement come through. Randolph told him, 'If you want to leave Emily, tell her to her face,' and refused Dick the money. With that, and all the other things about the training and the outcome of the World middleweight contest, that's why they weren't speaking.

You can imagine our journey back. It was like there'd been a death in the family – well, a mass murder. It was gone midnight when we docked at Southampton and we ran straight into a Mexican stand-off. Randolph wouldn't get off the boat till all the reporters had gone and the press wouldn't go till he'd give 'em an interview. George didn't want to speak to the press either. I think George was the most affected of any of us, cuz nobody had been believing him when he was defending Randolph. I mean, he'd been crying and he wasn't normally that emotional.

In the end, Dick went and spoke to them. Well, more like whinged to them. 'The trip's been miserable going out and even more miserable coming home, blah, blah . . . ' It was all over the newspapers the next day that him and Randolph had fallen out cuz Randolph had blamed him for everything that'd happened in New York and Randolph was upset cuz Dick had refused to go to court for him as a witness, an' all that, but nothing about the real reason.

George come out in the end. 'Randolph is certain in his own mind,' he told the reporters, 'that, free from worries, he could stop Olsen in eight rounds.' I would've said five.

Teddy Waltham, representing the Board of Control, called Randolph's training schedule 'unorthodox and inadequate' through having an unlicensed trainer.

What do I think is the reason for Randolph's loss to Olsen? It's hard to believe that it was woman trouble or the alleged lack of training or even eye trouble. It didn't look like he couldn't see punches coming. Olsen ain't that fast. I believe it had a lot to do with the effect of the kidney punches. Olsen had thrown a few early in the fight then really gone to town. As far as I was concerned, Olsen should have been disqualified for fighting dirty, cuz every chance he got, he'd push Randolph back on the ropes, put his head on Randolph's chest and start swinging the punches round the back to the kidneys. Not a word was said about it.

Some boxer in America said, 'That's another British hope that's got beat.'

'Hang about,' I told him. 'What about the Britisher that comes over here and beats both your blokes? Joe Wamsley was a New York State champion featherweight and Jose Paniagua was another of your top fighters. And don't forget,' I said, 'we're only a little island. You've got more to choose from than us an' we can still beat you.'

After we come back home, George took Randolph for a medical and found out he'd got an enlarged liver. On top of that, his eye was worse. He could see straight ahead but he couldn't see at an angle.

As far as I was concerned, the charge against Randolph had been a farce – I mean, at one point Daniels accused Randolph of punching her in the face. Randolph's lawyer said, 'This man has recently been the world's middleweight boxing champion. How is it you were not knocked out?' All she could come up with was, 'I guess God must have saved me.' Although the charges were withdrawn, the New York State Athletic Commission still banned Randolph from fighting in America indefinitely.

The lions in the Daniels den eventually become less hungry for Randolph's money and were willing, they said, to settle out of court for £1,250. We could've fought it but George said, 'It's only cigarette money.'

'You must smoke expensive fags, George,' I told him; but George was right, it was less hassle to pay the money and close it down.

Anyway, we come off the boat at Southampton and went back to Warwickshire. 'Cept for Randolph. He took a taxi to the Royal Hotel in Southampton to meet Gwen Price. Him and Gwen got married in secret at Wellington one Sunday morning. Our mum never really forgive them for that, cuz she'd kept asking Randolph if he was gonna marry Gwen and he wouldn't tell her, cuz he knew she didn't believe Gwen was right for him. Even though he'd fell out with our mum, he was happier than I'd seen him for months and months. But, the shadows behind him were getting longer and longer.

25

A Future in the Balance

Summat had started happening that'd never happened before. I was having trouble making the weight. All those cream cakes were catching up on me. I was 29 years old and I felt I was starting to knock on a bit for a boxer. I'd had my third toe-to-toe encounter with Tommy Higgins – there was lumps flying off us – but I'd struggled with my weight and Tommy got the edge. I moved up from featherweight to lightweight but I was having trouble maintaining that.

I was billed to fight Frank Parkes, the Midland Area lightweight title holder, up in the Potteries on 15 June 1954. I'll never forget the date. It wasn't a title contest but the deal was that if I beat Parkes I could meet him again for a shot at the area title.

I'd got 12 days to get from 11 st. to 9 st. 9 lb. I started training in long, thick woollen underpants – the sort we used on the Russian convoys, big thick sweaters and a couple of tracksuits over the top of that and a motorbike suit over the top of all them. I looked like the Michelin man come to town. I was running 20 miles a day and I kep' at it and kep' at it until the day of the contest.

At twelve o'clock, I was driven to a pub near the Victoria Hall where scales had been set up in the bar. I handed over my papers and stepped on to the platform. A quarter of a pound overweight. Now I had a choice: I could fight at the weight I was at and forfeit the £20 that'd been posted as a surety against me failing to make the agreed weight, or try to get the weight off.

Mick Gavin advised me, 'Go in as you are.'

'Nah!' I said. 'He ain't having no twenty quid off me. Besides, if I fight overweight, they'll say it don't count for a shot at the title.'

George said, 'Go and skip it off then.'

You're usually allowed one hour's grace to come within the limit but George negotiated an extra hour for me cuz I'd got such a lot to shift. I dashed out of the pub, skipped meself daft for two hours and come running back. For a few seconds it looked like I'd come in still over the limit by 2 oz.

I stepped off the scales and told everybody to stand back. 'I don't want nobody touching that bleeding machine,' I warned them. I waited for half a minute and carefully stepped back on the platform and held my breath until everything had stopped quivering. The official looked over the top of his glasses and read off my weight. 'Nine stone nine,' he said. 'Spot on!'

For five rounds, I knocked seven bells out of Frank Parkes. I was coasting it, enjoying meself. He'd got nothing he could bother me with and I was on for a landslide points win, if not a KO, and the bonus of a contest for the area lightweight title against the very same bloke I was handling with consummate ease right now.

On the bell for the sixth round, I stood up and . . . well . . . I just stood up . . . just STOOD there . . . I couldn't move out of me bleeding corner. Me hands flopped to my sides and I stayed standing there with my feet glued to the floor.

Parkes is throwing every punch in the book at me and I'm bloody defenceless. He can't believe his luck. He's grinning at his corner men before every punch he's throwing.

I was that weak I couldn't feel him hitting me. I didn't even have the strength to fall over. I'm thinking, 'For Christ's sake, Parkes, knock me down, you prat.' But, try as he might, he couldn't finish me off. It become obvious to the referee that I was unable to defend meself and he stepped between us. It's to do with your blood sugar, see. Everything goes on you.

I was depressed for days. I had a big decision to make. Finally, I went round to see George. 'I'm having real trouble making the weight,' I told him. 'The training ain't coming as easy as it used to. I ain't gonna box no more.'

'OK, Jack,' George said. 'If that's how you feel, son.' He knew I wouldn't take a decision like that lightly. 'What'll you do now?' he asked. It was the very question I'd been wrestling with without being able to come up with a satisfactory answer.

'I've got one or two ideas up me sleeve,' I said.

The idea I went with would have been better left up me sleeve, an' all.

I started a scrap-metal business with this certain fella. He seemed decent so I didn't see anything wrong with the money going into his account. Two years I did that for. Then, even though we seemed to be making money, the business suddenly went for a Burton. I took him to court but I ended up without a cent.

We come out of the hearing and he ran for his life. I chased after him but fell down the steps and the bastard got away. I thought, 'Never mind, Jack, you'll see him again.' I got me job back at Lockheed's.

The next time I saw my scrap-metal partner was at a boxing do. I tried to get him outside on his own. 'I've got a new car,' I said. 'Come an' have a look.'

But he clicked on. 'No thanks, Jack. Not today.' I never saw him after that. But all that scrap-metal business happened after I'd come back from Woking.

You don't know about Woking? Yeah, well, everybody's got a ghost in the cupboard. The official story was, if I stayed in Warwick, I'd be going down the gym and everybody would be on at me to come out of retirement and I might get lured back into boxing against my better judgement. But that wasn't it really. The real reason I left Warwick to go to Woking was cuz Bet had caught me out over a bird. An 'indiscretion' they call it, don't they?

To save a lot of scandal in the papers, we decided it'd be better if I left home so's Bet could divorce me for desertion and why Woking was cuz Jack Rowe, an ex-army boxing coach I knew through Randolph, lived there and he said I could lodge with him and his wife, Hettie. He told me I could get work at Vickers-Armstrong. 'Oh,' I said, 'they made the boat I was on.' I fixed meself up with a job as storeman, come back home and had a long talk with Betty.

'You *really* want me to leave, then?'

'Yes. I'm fed up with you.'

'In that case you can have a divorce.'

'You're being too nice about it,' she told me.

'What do you want me to do?' I asked her. 'Say you can't have a divorce?'

'Well, no,' she said, 'but I would have felt better if you'd put up a bit of a fight.' I never could figure what she wanted.

A Future in the Balance

I was coming up to my 30th birthday, my career was over as a professional fighter and I was driving away from my wife and kids, who I loved, to go and live somewhere I didn't want to go to. I said to meself, 'You're a bloody fool, Jack Turpin!'

26

Teach Me To Dance Like an English Man

My married life would have been completely different if only Bet'd taught me how to dance. She was a cracking ballroom dancer. And she could sing. She sang with a band. Her and the trumpet player used to have fights: 'Do you *have* to drown me out all the time?'

'I've got to be loud, I'm a trumpet player.'

'Well it wouldn't be so bad if you could play in key.'

The trumpet player also fancied hisself as a boxer at one time.

The church at Leamington had a wooden building on the side. The ol' vicar there was keen on boxing and he started a club in it. 'The Fighting Padre', they called him. He invited me down there to have a look and talked me into sparring with the trumpet player. We were mates, so I didn't think he'd try and get smart with me but, halfway through the first round, he lets go a big right-hand. I snapped back out of the way but another coat of paint and he'd have taken the skin off me nose, so I sparked him out.

The vicar said, 'There was no need for that, you know, Mr Turpin. I asked you to spar with Peter because I thought he might learn something from you.'

'Well, Vicar,' I said, 'I think he has.'

Bet did try to teach me to dance once. 'You've got two left feet,' she said. The thing was, at the dances I used to have to sit there like a dummy while everybody was taking her on to the floor and it set a little bee going in my bonnet. I used to say, 'It's all right. You dance, duck,' cuz she loved dancing so much. But I wouldn't get a look in with her in Leamington or Warwick unless I started a fight with somebody.

Randolph took us to a do at the Shire Hall for Anthony Eden the year the Suez Canal and all that blew up. I'm sitting with Bet and this bloke comes across and says, 'You don't mind, do you, Jack, if I ask your lovely wife to dance?'

'No,' I said, and he waltzes her off. Next dance, he's over again. 'Don't mind, do you, Jack?' I'm waiting for a drink at the bar and he's taken Bet back to her seat. He's talking to a fella who's standing a little way away from me. The fella says, 'That bird you're dancing with.'

'Oh ar, Jack Turpin's missus.'

'She's a bit of all right, ain't she?'

'I can have it away there anytime,' the bloke says.

I went back to Bet. 'Do you know that bloke as keeps coming over and dancing with you?'

'Not till tonight, no.'

'Oh, all right,' I said.

She looks at me. 'What's the matter now?' she said. 'You're looking evil.'

The bloke comes over again. 'Don't mind, do you, Jack?'

'Yes I do,' I said, getting to my feet. 'Fuck off.'

He just stands there, so I grabs him by the lapels. Randolph comes running over and knocks my hands down, puts his arm round the bloke's neck and walks him outside. He comes back after a minute or two. 'I give him a slap,' he said. 'What was it all about?'

When I told him what I'd overheard, he said, 'Oooh. Let's go back out and see if he's still around.' But the bloke was nowhere to be seen. I stopped going dancing for a while and Bet used to go to the Palais with our Joan. One night Joan said, 'You're coming with us tonight, Jack and Randolph. We'll get a babysitter and have a bit of a party. We had a great laugh, me and Joan, rock 'n' roll jiving. 'You dance like those Americans,' Bet said.

She taught Jackie Junior to dance – waltzes, foxtrots, the lot – but she still wouldn't teach me. I kept telling her, 'There's nothing worse than coming to a bloody dance and I've got to sit and watch everybody else dancing.'

'There's nothing wrong with that,' Bet said.

'Yes there is. I say I don't mind but I do bloody mind. I'm burning up inside.'

'But you've got nothing to be jealous about.'

'OK,' I said. 'You know those certain girls as sit along the balcony? How mad will you get if I keep bringing them down one at a time and dancing with them?'

'I shan't get mad.'

'Right. Next Saturday, you can dance with all those blokes who think as I don't mind, and I'll dance with them girls up there.' I'm not akidding, after the third one, Bet smacked me face.

'You were a rotten flirt the whole time we were courting,' she said. 'There was no need to cuddle up to them like that.'

'I was dancing like the Americans,' I reminded her.

'But you're not American, you're English.'

'Well then,' I said, 'teach me to dance like an English man.'

'I can't,' she said. 'But I'm really sorry, duck. I know how you feel now.'

I come home for a visit after a fortnight and it was funny cuz I didn't know whether to go straight in or knock on the door. I kept walking up and down the street and eventually Bet came out and said, 'Come in, you silly bugger.'

What I could never understand was I could go out somewhere and what I wanted to say to Bet I could say, in fun, to a complete stranger. I'd think, 'Why couldn't I tell Bet that? Cuz I'd mean it with her.' But a way of saying it never come to me.

I hadn't been down Woking long when a young amateur boxer approached me, Tony French. 'Please, Mr Turpin, come to our club and train us.' He kep' asking me and kep' asking me. Eventually I went down to have a look.

The gym was an old church hall. They'd got a couple of good lads there, so I said, 'Yes, all right. I'll train you.' They give me a free hand and all the equipment I needed. Bill Turner was the committee there virtually, and supported me all the way. The kids come to us in droves.

I anna kidding you, every one of them kids, anything I told them, was the absolute gospel. You could've brought the chief of police down there to tell them what I was saying was a complete load of lies and they would've called *him* a bleeding liar and thrown him out.

I took some of the young boxers to Brighton. Tony Brazil trained the Brighton club. One of my lads was putting a protective cup on and Tony comes up and says, 'Jack Turpin's your trainer, ain't he?'

'Yeah. How do yer know?'

'He's making you put a cup on.'

I overheard it and I told him, 'When I knew we was gonna fight your lads, Tony, I thought we'd better double up on the bollock covers.'

He laughed and said, 'It's all part of the game, innit, Jack?' I'd got him disqualified but it's ever so funny how they never held it against you.

After I'd been down Woking about eight months, Bet decided to join me. We rented a caravan on a site down there. I got a message at work one day to come home straight away. As I drove on to the site I could see all that was left of my caravan was smouldering stumps. I had pictures of my kids and Bet all shrivelled up and I'm bawling me eyes out. But they was all right. It was a right relief, I tell you. Bet's sister had moved into our Leamington house in Althorpe Street but she was just on the point of moving out to take over a pub, so it worked out well and we come back to Warwickshire and good ol' Lockheed.

The great thing was, in Woking, Bet had started taking an interest in the boxing. At first she just used to wash the strips and then she got more and more involved.

I started spending time at the Nelson and keeping up me road work, and I was eating better. I'd let me boxing licence expire but one week I got down to 8 st. 13 oz, my best fighting weight, and I said to George, 'I think I'll start boxing again.'

'All right, Jack,' he said. 'We'll apply for your licence.'

The Board of Control turned me down flat, so George said, 'We'll go and see them about it.'

Lo and behold, who should be sitting there on the committee but Frank Parkes. I asked them, 'Why won't you give me my licence back?'

Parkes chirps up, 'You're not good enough, Jack. I stopped you and I wasn't a big puncher.'

'Not a big puncher?' I said. 'You couldn't knock me off me feet when I was standing there motionless with me hands at me sides. The referee stopped me, not you.'

'Well?' he said, raising his eyebrows. He had such a smart-arsed look on his face I'd have liked to have had him in the ring there and then.

'I wasn't even dazed,' I told him. 'If I could've raised me hands, I would have knocked yer bleeding head off, especially when

231

you come whaling in like a big girl swinging her handbag.'

Some other official said, 'No mud-slinging, now, Mr Turpin. It's no use arguing. We can't renew your licence.'

'Fucking well don't, then!' I said, and I walked out. And that was it.

It'd never worked out that I'd been allowed a shot at the British featherweight title but I'd been high in the featherweight ratings for years. I'd got 131 recorded professional fights behind me: 88 wins (18 by KO), 35 losses (10 by KO, 2 by disqualification), 8 draws.

The only belt I won was awarded to me by Billy Mann, who run Mann's Coaches from Wolverhampton way. He was president of the boxing clubs around this area and said it was time I got some recognition. They got up their own version of the Lonsdale Belt and said my name should be the first on it. It was great of them and I used to show off about it but, to me, it was a poor substitute because I'd got my heart set on winning the British title.

I'd boxed countless exhibitions as a boy and as a man; sparred thousands of rounds in gymnasiums; I'd fought countless all comers in the fairground booths; I'd boxed in stadiums and halls up and down the country and abroad; I'd won the Midland Area featherweight title; I'd been the first British boxer to win in America after the war; I'd helped my big brother become British and Empire middleweight champion and my baby brother to become the middleweight champion of the world. All in all, I don't think that's bad for someone who just sort of drifted into boxing.

27

The Comeback Road

Just as I was bowing out of boxing, Randolph was planning a comeback. In May 1954, he'd suffered a bad defeat and lost his European middleweight title – in front of 40,000 people at the Torino Stadium in Rome – to Tiberio Mitri, the Italian champion Dick had lost to. I tell you, there was summat not quite right about this one.

I'd flew out there with him, Gwen and George. Dick and a mate of his, Tom Payne, went ahead of us by road.

Ninety-nine times out of a hundred, a boxer will start off with the jab but Mitri went straight in with a left hook. I suspect someone leaked it out that Randolph's eye was bad. The fight was over in 65 seconds. It wasn't a knockout. Randolph was actually ready to carry on but as soon as that hook landed the referee stopped the fight.

George wouldn't take any commission for the Mitri fight and he was adamant he didn't want Randolph to box again. But, how else could Lick earn the money he could get boxing? He'd lost a big part of his reputation but there was still crowds in London who thought he'd come bouncing back into world class. But no boxer can keep his title for ever and Licker decided to quit. He bought a house in Bodelwyddan, near Abergele, and moved up there with Gwen, planning to start a family together.

Deciding the right time to get out of boxing isn't easy. If you're broke, it's impossible. Randolph had been out of the ring six months when he asked George to go up and see him. Lick had spent so much

233

money, and given away so much money, he needed to make some back.

He was still fit. He had eye difficulties but he said he could cope. Him and George decided to give Randolph's boxing another go. As soon as George'd left, Randolph went clicking away on the ol' typewriter and wrote a poem for him. I've got a copy of it and I want you to print it fully as he wrote it, because journalists in the past have twisted it by printing only the last verse to prove Randolph's depression with boxing. It wasn't that way at all.

THE COMEBACK ROAD

_____

The comeback road is hard and long
the boys I'll meet will be hard and strong,
but my patience is good,
and my will power strong.

_____

I'll hear the bell
which means time to go
but I'll do my best, and I'll have a go
cause I've got someone to back me.

_____

The manager I've got
is the one for me
as I know he'll stick
In a real rough sea.

_____

They say I've finished
but I'll prove 'em wrong
and I'll have a go
Cause my patience, will power, and heart are strong.

_____

If I make the grade,
on that one big day
we can look at them all
with a laugh and say,

We've done our best
for the game we love
now there's no more kicks
and thats real good.

_____

So we'll leave this game
Which was hard and cruel
Then down at the show, on a ringside stool
We'll watch the next man, just one more fool.

_____

how's this Mid for a start, but dont think that I'm going to
be another one of those writing mad caps, as you've only
been gone half an hour, and I was thinking what a feller, to
come all down here, to get me at a gym, but like you said,
if it's not right the first time, we'll call it a day, but I'll try not
to let you down on the first time out, as with you with me
I'll feel confident of pulling it off, okay, so long now, mate,
see you when were at work again,

   Love from Gwen and Lick X X X X X

Randolph had slipped up to light-heavyweight permanent now. In
fact, he sometimes struggled with that and he thought he'd end up
going with the heavies, which he did but only in pirate fights.

People said Licker was finished but he did prove 'em wrong.
And the boys he met were hard and strong – but after nine months
out of the ring, he won his next two fights inside the distance
against top class fighters, Ray Schmit and Jose Gonzalez, and he
really took Alex Buxton apart for the British and Empire light-
heavyweight titles, winning the Lonsdale belt outright. Then come
the hard and cruel bit in the shape of Canadian fighter Gordon
Wallace.

Randolph put Wallace down in the fourth and the referee
started the count. Randolph turned and started walking off to a
neutral corner when Wallace jumped up off the canvas and threw
a punch over Randolph's shoulder into his ear, knocked him
down and the referee counted Randolph out. There was loads of
complaints over that and not just on our side. The referee hadn't
said 'Box on' and the punch come from behind.

Randolph wanted to quit boxing again that night. But his heart was strong and a couple of wins later, he was off to Germany to fight the German champion Hans Stretz. He lost on points against Stretz but it wasn't decisive by any means. Then he beat Arthur Howard and won the British light-heavyweight title a fourth time and come off the floor five times to do it. He had six straight wins after that, with only one going the distance, but his comeback suddenly shuddered to a halt when he met Yolande Pompey, the light-heavyweight champion of Trinidad, at the Alexander Stadium in Birmingham on 9 September 1958.

In the second round, Licker knocked Pompey through the ropes. Pompey tried to catch the top rope but missed. Lick grabbed his hands, pulled him up, got him round the shoulders and eased him into the ring. As soon as Pompey got to his feet, he hit Randolph with a right-hand to the ear. The result was horrible to watch. I've heard Harry Carpenter call it the 'Exit Waltz'. You know? When you're trying to stand up but you're half knocked out and your legs won't obey what you're telling them and you keep plunging forward on your face with your arms behind you like you're made of rubber.

Josie Middleton told me, 'When Yolande Pompey beat Randy, I cried. I was still crying when Randy came out of the ring. He stopped on his way back to the dressing-room and asked me why I was crying. I told him it seemed so sad he'd lost when I'd seen him beat better boxers than Pompey in a few minutes. Randolph smiled. "It's only a boxing match," he said. My dad told me he definitely wouldn't let him fight again.'

I wasn't sad. I was mad. When I got to the dressing-room, I said to Pompey, 'That's what you call fucking sportsmanship?'

He said, 'I'm sorry, Jack. It's got to be painful for you, it's your brother.'

'What's painful about it,' I told him, 'is a bloke's decent enough to save you getting injured falling out of the ring and you hit him when he's got both hands holding you up.' I turned to Randolph and said, 'I'd have let him break his bleeding neck.'

'I ain't a mean git like you, Jack,' he said. That was the only time I lost my rag with a fighter. I was always on to Randolph about helping people up when he knocked them down. Mick Gavin give me a slap round the face when I'd picked up an opponent.

'You could end your bloody career doing that,' he told me. 'An unconscious man is a dead weight. You could've rigged your back.'

George wouldn't take any commission for the Pompey fight either and for Randolph's health and safety, and his own peace of mind, he called it a definite day.

Randolph had a couple more fights, pirate fights – nothing to do with George or the Boxing Board of Control – against heavyweights who were willing to have a go for the money rather than being blokes who'd earned the right to fight him – but he was officially retired.

'The Leamington Licker' fought 75 pro fights, with 66 wins – winning an amazing 49 inside the distance, and 17 of those in the first or second round. He only had 8 losses and 1 draw.

From being a poorly little boy who'd nearly died three years running from bronchitis and pneumonia, he rose up to become the World middleweight champion twice. He wasn't in the slightest bit bigheaded about it. I used to do his bragging for him and, as you might have noticed, I still do. I used to do his complaining for him an' all, and still do. I know he was my baby brother but you'd be proud of any British sportsman as had done what he'd done, wouldn't you?

28

Bradford Football Ground, 1963

It's the main event of the evening: a heavyweight wrestling contest between Lord Bertie Topham and Randy Turpin.

Turpin, in black trunks, accompanied by his second carrying a water bottle, walks to the centre of the pitch and climbs in the ring. They're followed by Lord Bertie, wearing a top hat, a monocle and a cape bearing an alleged family coat of arms. In Topham's wake is Ponsonby – a bowler-hatted valet bearing a glass of wine on a silver tray.

Ponsonby waits until the cheers and boos of derision of the crowd have subsided, then rekindles them by dusting his lordship's corner with a silk handkerchief. 'Oh, how dirty, my lord.' It's the young Northern School of Music student's first time out as Ponsonby and he's performing his £3-a-night role with gusto.

The referee attempts to get the wrestlers to the centre of the ring to perform his obligatory inspection of their hands and boots but he's dismissed to wash his own hands by Ponsonby before the valet deems him fit to come near his master.

The contest begins with the fighters performing a routine sequence of holds and throws. Lord Bertie's constant flouting of the rules has the crowd baying for his blood. With a toff's disdain for the oiks on the terraces, he seizes Turpin in a headlock and thrusts his opponent's head through the ropes. 'Ponsonby!' he thunders. 'Hit him on the head as hard as you can with your tray.'

Ponsonby reels back as though struck by an invisible hand. Bert never mentioned this in the script. Looking less than well, Ponsonby slowly makes his way to the front of the ring and stops before the proffered head of Randy Turpin, ex-World champion middleweight boxer and undefeated British and Empire light-heavyweight champion. As he draws back his metal tray, Ponsonby's past life whirls before him then, all too quickly, screeches to a halt in the present. He stammers a brief prayer to the god of good-natured ex-professional-boxers-turned-wrestlers and . . .

CLANG!

The blow delivered, Ponsonby drops his tray and makes off across the pitch. Turpin shakes himself free and follows in close and apparently enraged pursuit. Round and round the pitch, in and out the goal posts. 'Ponsonby! Ponsonby!' roar the crowd, delighted by the prospect of this lackey of the upper classes getting a public trouncing but Ponsonby shows an exceptional turn of speed and Turpin loses ground and returns to the ring.

'Hey, lad. I wouldn't like to chase you over a mile,' Turpin said, by way of compliment to the young musician, after the evening's entertainment.

'I was running for my life, mate,' the weary student ruefully replied.

– From a conversation with jazz clarinettist and marathon runner Eric Newton, Ponsonby, 1963–4.

In the early '60s, every town was putting on wrestling shows and Randolph travelled all round. You join the wrestling business as a stooge – paid to lose, mostly. It's part of how they build it up to let established wrestlers look like the hardmen. Randolph could have taken them apart anytime he wanted to but, instead, he had to let hisself get thrown all round the shop.

It's a charade, innit? A mime. I mean, you couldn't really do all them things – there'd be busted legs and arms all over the place. Not that you don't get hurt. Randolph reckoned he picked up more injuries wrestling than he ever did in boxing – mostly from bad falls. Occasionally it was from spectators having a go at you – some of them are idiot enough to think it's all for real.

I understand why Randolph done it. Retired boxers don't have many ways of getting a living and the name Randy Turpin attracted an audience, so why not? I actually think he enjoyed it

but I really don't like talking about it or hearing about it. People
who knew Randolph only as a wrestler liked his wrestling. It's
people as knew him as a world-class boxer who take offence by it.
I have another reason for not liking talking about it an' all, cuz it
was a bloke who got Randolph into wrestling who give him some
guns. One of them was a .22 revolver.

29

This Music is For Him

Bet come home unusually early that day: 17 May 1966. I took one
look at her and says, 'What's the matter? Somebody been on to
yer?' She put her arms round me and started crying her eyes out.

We was living in Leamington then and she worked in the office
of the taxi rank. That morning a nurse she knew finished her shift
at the hospital and come in for a cab. 'I'm surprised to see you here,
Betty,' she said, 'after what's happened to your brother-in-law.'

'What do you mean?'

'Oh, God, don't you know?'

When the Inland Revenue made Randolph bankrupt in 1962, he
sold the Summit Complex to Llandudno Urban Council and went
back to Leamington with Gwen. He'd bought a café, 'Gwen's
Transport Café', in Russell Street with money he'd scraped
together. It wasn't a very wise move, cuz the café already had a
demolition order on it.

Him and Gwen had got four lovely girls by this time: Gwyneth,
aged eleven; Annette, aged nine; Charmaine, aged four; and
Carmen, aged seventeen months. At the same time as the café,
Randolph was driving a truck and working in the scrapyard cutting
up cars for George.

Randolph had a bankruptcy examination in Warwick and they
made a Receiving Order on him. He'd already paid £40,000 but
they reckoned he still owed £15,000. He'd suffered a loss of

£10,500 on the Orme and he'd lost money on all the houses he'd bought. Him and Mosh went to see people as owed him money.

The fella that borrowed £6,000 said, unfortunately, the money had been stolen before he'd had a chance to buy the pub. There was a bloke up north who'd borrowed off Randolph for a taxi business but it'd gone bump and Randolph never got his money back. And so it went on. Some as owed him fearfully agreed to pay him back at so much a week but never kept it up. There was nothing really Randolph could do about it. One or two of them got a slap but Moshy held Randolph from going too far, cuz he didn't want things made worse by Randolph going to gaol.

If only Randolph had listened to George. Another great fella was Randolph's accountant, Max Mitchell. He fought for Lick with the tax people and got his bill terrifically reduced but it was still more money than he had.

Our families had drifted apart. Randolph had fallen out with most of us through Gwen – never anything big. He knew she didn't like us, so he turned his back on us. Occasionally one of us would pop in the café but we was never made to feel very welcome. P'raps, on his side, he'd got the idea we'd more or less abandoned him. When we did see him, he seemed happy enough. He had his daughters he doted on. He missed Randolph Junior but he dealt with that like he always did with anything that hurt him – he just shut it out.

Bet was holding me really tight: 'I came straight home to you,' she said. 'Randolph's dead. Somebody's shot him.'

It was like everything had gone cold. Me brain stopped moving and I just . . . Well, if you'd pushed me, I would have very likely fell over . . . I just stood there. I thought, 'I've got to shake myself out of this.'

'Look,' I told Bet. 'Don't cry no more. It's only what somebody's saying. I'll go up the café and find out.'

Randolph's café was right up the top of the town by the old police station. I cut through Jephson's Gardens, over the bridge and out into Russell Street. The usual oglers you get with these things were hanging around gawping. I shoved past them and walked up to the door. This copper put his hand out to stop me. 'You can't come in,' he said. I nearly slugged him.

'That's my brother in there,' I told him. 'I wanna go and see what's up.'

'Oh,' he said, 'I'm sorry.' But he still stood there. So I said, 'Well, get out of the fucking way, then!' and knocked his hand down.

'All right, now,' the copper says. 'Tak' it easy.' But he still wouldn't let me in.

'Tell me what's happened, then,' I said.

'We're not sure yet.'

'What d'yer mean you're not sure? My wife's told me Randolph's been shot.'

'Well, yes, I'm afraid he has.'

Bertie Harris, who always claimed he was Randolph's best mate, had got to the café first and when Gwen asked him to go upstairs to see what'd happened, he said, 'Oooh no.' I'd have gone up the stairs two at a time. And if Randolph had, like I s'pose what Bertie must have thought, gone raving mad and started shooting everybody, I would have risked that to see what had happened. Harris is dead now but that's the fella that took Randolph's Lonsdale Belt off of Gwen and sold it for her. When he come to give her the money, he took a chunk out of it he reckoned Randolph owed him from the scrap-metal business they was supposed to have been partners in.

Little Carmen had been shot too. We went to the Accident Hospital in Birmingham to see her and brought Gwen and the other children to stay at our house. In the morning, Gina opened the front door to go out to telephone her work to let them know she wouldn't be attending and was besieged by reporters.

'We don't want to upset you . . . ' one of them started telling her. As soon as I heard that, I come to the door. 'If you don't want to upset us,' I said, 'what the fucking hell are you doing here?' It was like they hadn't heard me.

'Which one of the Turpin brothers is your dad?' one of them asked Gina.

'Jackie,' she told 'em. Once they'd got that out of her, they all started firing questions. I grabbed the nearest one, flung him backwards across a parked car and the others suddenly lost interest. It was only a temporary respite, cuz they hounded us for months. I had one or two set-tos with reporters. A lot of what I did and said at that time, you know, was just reactions. You go like a zombie, don't you, with the shock.

Sugar Ray Robinson had retired two or three times but he retired for real at the end of 1965 and Madison Square Garden put on a celebration for him. They invited the five people he'd taken the World middleweight title off. They sent Randolph aeroplane tickets and paid his hotel bills and over he went.

Carmen Basilio was there and Gene Fullmer, Olsen, Jake LaMotta and Randolph. Robinson was given a 'World's Greatest Fighter' trophy and a standing ovation. At the party afterwards, a young fighter come along: Cassius Clay, Olympic light-heavyweight champion and current heavyweight champion of the world. Randolph spent a couple of hours chatting to him and they got on great.

As soon as the news broke of Randolph's death, a sympathy telegram come, signed 'Muhammad Ali'. We wondered who the hell it was. Jackie Junior told us, 'It's Cassius Clay.'

Three weeks before your 38th birthday is no age to die, is it?

Bet took Gwen shopping to get black clothes for the funeral. There's a myth that nobody come to the service but there was quite a crowd. Mind you, there was a few hundred more who'd benefited from Randolph who should've been there but were too guilty or too bleeding callous to show up.

Gwen and the girls stayed with us until Carmen was well enough to come out of hospital. I drove them up to Wales to be with Gwen's sister till Gwen got herself sorted out. After she'd left here, Gwen told the press her husband had forbid her to have anything to do with the Turpin family. A lot of people think she went along with that but she didn't – not entirely.

People sometimes come to say goodbye, don't they? I don't mean people who know they're going to die. I've often wondered if Randolph was doing that the last time I saw him. It's strange, now, going over it. I hadn't seen him for a few months, then, one Saturday afternoon, me, Bet and Georgina was all sat there in the kitchen and, suddenly, I could feel somebody staring at me. I looked up. The outside door to the kitchen was slightly open and Randolph was staring through the crack. He always did things like that.

He was with his second youngest, Charmaine. When he see me look up, he said, 'Hello' and come in. Georgina says to him, 'Shall I take Charmaine to the shops to get some sweets?'

'Yeah, go on,' he says.

'Everything all right?' I asked him.

'Yep.'

Georgina told me afterwards she'd taken Charmaine to the shops cuz she'd got the impression Randolph wanted to talk to me and Bet on his own but he never really said anything. He just sat there and when I asked him if everything was all right, he says, 'Yep', and that was it. The funny thing is, he went to see George around that time an' all. Him and George had drifted apart, too, but Randolph called round there and George said Lick was laughing and joking just like he used to, and playing games with their dog.

Suicide or murder?

I get sick and tired of that question. Every time I'm interviewed, they work towards it. It annoys me, cuz Randolph wasn't just a famous boxer; he was my baby brother and I loved him. We'd drifted apart in later years because of Gwen but that didn't alter what I thought of him. How would you like it if you'd lost someone you loved like that and every time a complete stranger spoke to you they went on about it like it was a film they saw once and didn't quite understand the ending? I'm not getting at *you*, because this is one time I want to talk about it but complete strangers write things without even bothering to talk to us first, and they've been doing that for more than 30 years.

I'd dearly love to come up with an explanation of my brother's death that would end all the speculation and he could be allowed to rest in peace but, truth is, I can't. But, no, I don't believe Randolph committed suicide. And, no, I don't know who killed him. And, no, I don't know who was most likely to have killed him.

If you say suicide, then you could say everybody was part of it, including people like me and Bet, cuz, although we loved him, we didn't know the extent of what was going on in his life. We were shut out. There's the well-meaning people who wanted him to win when he couldn't; the yobs in the crowd who are never satisfied till they see blood on your gloves; the reporters and camera people who pried and published bad things about him; the businessmen who took advantage of his trust; the women who wouldn't leave him alone; the fair-weather friends who took advantage of his kindness then vanished as soon as his money had dwindled away; and the tax man who was always padding along two paces behind him. I mean, the day Randolph died a tax demand come through the post.

Randolph's doctor said, 'Mr Turpin wasn't the sort of person to worry about money or people letting him down.' He thought Randolph's mind had been upset by damage done with boxing. He wasn't called as a witness, though. He said that to the papers. The coroner only seemed interested in the cause of Randolph's death and not reasons why. Like, he didn't call for the brain tests they usually do with boxers. They didn't find anything at the autopsy that said his mind was disturbed.

No man who ever walked this earth loved his kids more than Randolph. It's impossible to believe he'd shoot his little girl. If he did, then it must've been cuz he couldn't bear to leave her behind. Why Randolph should've tried to kill his own baby was never brought up. I believe a more careful job should've been made of the inquest and I'd still like to know why it wasn't.

If you say murder, people talk of a connection between his death and him coming out of a hall after wrestling down London way, finding the tyres on his car slashed so's he couldn't get away and being beaten up by four blokes. I asked Randolph, 'Do you know who it was?'

'Yep.'

'What about Stan Parkes, me and Mosh get a mob up and sort 'em out?'

'Don't talk bleeding stupid,' he said, and absolutely refused to say no more than that.

I tell you, if anybody knows more than I do about it, they didn't get it from Randolph. When he was interviewed, he said it must've been wrestling fans who'd taken it too serious. Some of them were stupid enough.

You know those guns I told you about from the wrestling bloke? One was faulty and that's the one that killed him and hurt his daughter, and that's why it had to be done twice.

The official entry on my brother's death certificate is:

Gunshot wound of the heart
Self-inflicted
(Suicide)

There were two shots: one in his head and one in his heart. The one in the skull evidently wasn't fatal. It was two similar shots with little Carmen but she pulled through, thank God. Two of Randolph's kiddies were at school and Charmaine was in bed with a cold. Gwen said Randolph went upstairs to check on Charmaine and Carmen and never come back. Four pistol shots rang out unnoticed. After a while, Gwen went up to see why Randolph was so long and found him slumped over dead and Carmen wounded beside him.

They said my brother shot himself using the gun in his left hand. Well, like I've told you, he was ambidextrous but he *predominantly* used his right hand – same as he could box southpaw but *predominantly* boxed orthodox. I can't see him reaching with his left hand automatically. I believe a more thorough job should have been made of the police investigation and I'd still like to know why it wasn't.

Gwen pushed us out of it. She had a close friend – someone who's not in a position to speak now – come up to the café to break into the safe, cuz she'd misplaced the key. A letter was found in it. I'd fallen out with this person at the time but when we were friends again, I asked him, 'What was in that letter? It's very important to me to know.' All he'd ever say was, 'Sorry, Jack. Can't tell you.' He swore it was addressed to him and him alone but I never saw it.

Remember when they showed some of a letter they claimed was found in Randolph's safe in that *64-Day Hero* documentary on Channel Four? I phoned Georgina and Cledwyn, and told them, 'Terry's pointed out Randolph's middle name is typed wrong in the letter that's supposed to be from the safe in the café: "A-D-O-L-P-H-**O**-U-S" – an extra O in Adolphus.'

We tried to get in touch with Gordon Williams, who wrote and presented the film, but we couldn't get hold of him. It might have been a studio prop, mightn't it, but Williams seems to be saying it's the actual one. If it was, I'd like to know who really bloody well typed it, because there's no way in this world that Randolph would spell Adolphus wrong.

The letter was dated Wednesday, 4 March 1964, and Randolph – if it was him – is saying how depressed he is over the government making him bankrupt over money he's never actually had and how he can't afford the two pounds a week they're making him pay it back at. It says Jack Solomons had been in touch with a 'certain body in London who do away with folks they don't wish to talk' and when Randolph told them he wasn't frightened of dying, they'd switched the threat to Gwen and the three girls – little Carmen hadn't been born then. The letter ends with him saying he's perfectly sane and three attempts had been made on his life already.

Jack Solomons, with the boxing lark, could make or break your career. He wasn't a vicious man but you mustn't cross him – he could blacklist you in London. I got on all right with him. He paid me for fights that boxers at the stage I was at would've virtually boxed for free. I've never heard him threaten anybody but, then again, p'raps he never had to, cuz he was always surrounded by very, very big fellas – gangsters are always hanging around the professional ring – and he had talked about Mafia involvement in boxing.

Randolph reckoned he was being made to carry the can for the people who'd actually had the money the Inland Revenue said *he'd* received – £20,000 was the figure mentioned. That's very possible, cuz sometimes boxers, well, not only boxers, arranged to have some cash on the side over the top of the official contract money to get out of paying tax on it. If the money was for film rights from the Robinson return, like's been suggested, it'd be that size of money. It's possible Randolph was talked into summat like that but was never actually given the cash.

Someone had grassed Licker up to the Inland Revenue. George Middleton thought he knew who it was but he wouldn't say in case he was wrong.

The inquest was in two parts cuz of further enquiries. Gwen asked for the letter to be read out at the resumed inquest but the coroner said no. All sorts of rumours went round. Some people warned me that mobsters were involved and were telling witnesses what to say. Other people told me the police were telling everybody what to say.

An old lady who lived opposite the café was wondering whether she should go to the police, cuz the café hadn't been open like they said but had been closed for three days before the shooting and she'd heard a terrible row coming from there. I don't know if she reported it. If she did, nothing come of it.

Mosh Mancini had been out with Randolph the night before Randolph died. Mosh said he hadn't noticed anything untoward apart from Randolph not asking him in for a coffee like he usually did.

In the evening of the day Randolph was shot, Mosh went into the front room of his house where he keeps his piano and sat there in the dark, playing, with tears rolling down his face. His wife, Maria, told me, 'All night long this beautiful music was pouring out of the room.' By the morning of the next day he'd composed a piece of music he called 'Sea of Tranquillity'. He told Maria, 'Randolph's at peace now and this music is for him.'

Years later, me and Mosh went to Weston-Super-Mare fundraising for the amateur boxing club down there. Mosh took dozens of copies of 'Sea of Tranquillity' hoping to sell a few and give the money to the boxing club. Inside the music there's a photo of Randolph wearing his Lonsdale Belt and underneath it's got:

> *Memories remain of 'Licker' in the last few weeks before he*
> *took his life and these memories are in my music.*
> *Bless you, 'Licker', there will never be another like you.*

> *Mosh.*

You can't keep Moshy away from a piano and on the way to Weston-Super-Mare we stayed overnight at a pub. They had a piano in the bar and Mosh started playing the music he'd composed for Randolph. It was a lively old pub full of people drinking and talking and laughing. One by one, they all went quiet and the whole room filled with sadness. Two old ladies by the piano started crying their eyes out and an old bloke in the corner was also crying. I thought, 'Christ, Moshy, I can see you ain't gonna sell many of these.' I anna kidding, in half an hour all the copies had gone at a pound each. Everybody loved my brother.

Randolph had been a multimillionaire by today's standards and when they say he died broke, it's a bloody lie. He died with a load of money. It's just that other people had it. I suppose whichever way you decide it, it was money that killed him.

If people want to think it was suicide like the coroner said, then Lick must've have been ill and the things he wrote in his suicide note would be what an ill man would write and not what he would've wrote if he'd been well. With so many questions left unanswered, I think the proper way of dealing with it would've been an open verdict pending more enquires.

I don't think we'll ever find out exactly what happened, now. I told Georgina and Cledwyn, 'Terry's had a letter saying some of Randolph's file at Her Majesty's Coroner's Office is missing.' I'd like to know what's missing and how it got lost.

Gwen had a headstone put up on Randolph's grave:

TO
THE DEAR MEMORY OF
RANDOLPH ADOLPHUS
TURPIN
DEVOTED HUSBAND OF
GWYNETH
AND FATHER OF
GWYNETH, ANNETTE,
CHARMAINE & CARMEN
WHO PASSED AWAY
17 MAY 1966. AGED 38
—

World middleweight
boxing champion 1951.

We thought it was such a shame she didn't put Randolph Junior's name on it, cuz we knew Randolph thought the world of him, but she didn't consult us about anything, so the first we knew about it was too late.

Randolph, we all miss him. He had something about him. If you'd have known him, you'd have really liked him. He was under pressure but he never ever walked away from trouble, never ever sidestepped anything, regardless of size or weight. As for money: 'Memories are worth more than money,' he used to say, and if there was one thing the Turpins knew it was how to get by without it. I will never ever believe Randolph took his own life.

30

You'd Have Fell About Laughing

Danny McAlinden, an Irish lad from Coventry. George had a half-share in him.

As well as looking after Jackie Junior, I'd train others I thought were good. George asked me to get McAlinden ready to fight Jack Bodell for the British heavyweight title. About 1972 this was.

I liked Danny. He'd got a smashing left hook and he could box. The Irish, especially, revered him for his bravery. I told George 'yes' and our Dick agreed to help me.

Oooh, McAlinden was an ungrateful sod to train. I'd say, 'Do this,' and he'd say, 'I don't want to,' and do summat else. Dick wasn't much more of a help either. While I'd got Danny working away doing all the groundwork – over there punching the bag; over here on the speedball; in the ring sparring three rounds – Dick'd be sitting in a chair with a newspaper and a pencil doing the crossword. I'd shout, 'Dick, for Christ's sake, give us a bleeding hand, will yer!'

He'd call back, 'An island with four letters?'

McAlinden moaned a lot an' all. I had him sparring with my lad one night and he hit Jackie Junior that hard he sent him about four foot in the air. I says, 'Hey, Dan, you should go easy!' Danny says, 'Well, he hurts me' – a heavyweight complaining about a bleeding light-welter! This was when he was training. It was different when he was contesting.

The other half of Danny McAlinden was owned by Jack

Solomons. All boxing managers still done the Highland fling any time Solomons squeezed his bagpipes, so, when George got a call from him saying for 'publicity reasons' George should take McAlinden off us and send him up to Merthyr Tydfil to be trained by British ex-champion welterweight Eddie Thomas, George immediately did it.

A fortnight later, I got a call from Thomas saying he was sending Danny back to the Nelson. I was OK about having Danny back but Thomas had said something I didn't like the sound of, 'Watch his leg, Jack. His ankle keeps slipping out.' When Danny turned up here, he was limping.

I pulled at his foot a couple of times and the bleeding thing was flopping about just by pulling it. The cup that the bone sits in was damaged and the bone kept slipping out. It hurts just describing it. It must have been bloody agonising. Apparently, Thomas's gym had a raised seam across the floor canvas of the ring and Danny had caught his heel on it and done his ankle in. Thomas must've phoned Solomons to tell him what'd happened and Solomons said send him back to us.

'What we're gonna do, Dan,' I said, 'is strap you up really tight and train you for three minutes, slack the bandages off, rest you for three minutes, an' so on. You'll have to work twice as hard as you normally would, and if there's any arguments I'm gonna piss off home, cuz I don't want to be the scapegoat for what's happened up at Wales.'

It was a nightmare. He shouldn't have been boxing at all, really, but he was dead keen on having a shot at the championship. If you're a boxer, all you can do is box, and the only way to improve your career is by winning titles. Besides, there was Jack Solomons to please.

The day of the fight come. When we got to Villa Park in Brum, I told Dick, 'We've got to hold Danny back from the ring until the last possible moment so's he won't have to stand on that ankle too long', and while we were going down to the ring, I stressed to Danny, 'Circle away from his left hook. His right hand's no danger. You've got three rounds to get this over in then I'm throwing in the towel. No arguments, cuz if I don't, you'll have a leg missing by the time you get out of the ring.'

You've got to give it to McAlinden, 99 out of 100 boxers wouldn't have had the bottle to fight carrying an injury like that. George and me wouldn't have put him on if it'd been up to us but

Solomons didn't want his top-of-the-bill to go missing. On the surface, it give Danny no chance but, like I say, he could box and he had that left hook.

It was a fight no one who was there would forget in a long time. Danny was a real good-looking fella – 6 ft 1 in. tall, with light brown hair and blue eyes. He'd got his trademark emerald green knicks on with 'Danny Boy' picked out in white letters on the leg. Bodell, another big fella, was a coalminer from south Derbyshire. He'd done some sparring for Muhammad Ali sometime when Ali needed practice with a southpaw. Anyhow, he was British, European and Commonwealth heavyweight champion. He'd took his titles by beating Joe Bugner. He'd got a big, big heart, Bodell but, unfortunately for him, he'd also got a big, big Desperate Dan jaw and a tendency to lead with it.

I tell you, you'd have fell about laughing. The British heavyweight championship? It was more like two farmer's boys having a scrap in the hen shed over a new-laid egg.

The bell went and they both rushed forwards, crashed into each other and fell arse-over-tip on the floor. McAlinden went to get up and Bodell thumped him on the back of the head while he was still on his hands and knees. Danny swipes him with a back-hander; they both jump up; they crash together again and fall through the ropes, almost out of the ring. They get up on their feet and wrestle each other to the floor again. The bell goes and Bodell chins Danny with a big left-hander after the bell.

I'm almost peeing meself. Danny comes back to the corner. 'How am I doing?'

I kep' my face turned away from him. 'Bleeding lovely,' I says. 'But try not to fall on the floor with him. Let him go on his own.'

The second round's another tear-up. Bodell goes down from a right to the temple 20 seconds into the round. He gets up; they're both on the floor again – I think they was pulling each other's hair this time. McAlinden's going frantic. He tagged Bodell with a cracking punch and Bodell went down. His pride forced him back on his feet but he fell back over and went along the canvas on his nose. He struggled up, staggered into the ropes, fell halfway through, and Danny's raining punches on him. Bodell plunges forwards, hits the deck and rolls over on his back.

The referee, George Smith, hadn't finished counting him out before every Paddy in bleeding Birmingham jumped in the ring to congratulate their new champion. If it'd been a competition to see how many people could get in a boxing ring at one time, it would have made the *Guinness Book of Records*. It was bloody MAYHEM!

I've got to get Danny out of the ring, fast, to get that bandage off his leg before it stops his circulation and does some serious damage. But he's disappeared. He's floating in the air, held up by his fans. I get him down and I'm heaving him out of the ring when my leg gets wrapped round the bottom rope and a big Irishman falls across it and locks me in. I got holt of his head and shook it. 'FOR CHRIST'S SAKE, LET ME GO!' I screamed. He rolls over and releases me leg. 'Help me get Danny out,' I said. 'I've got to get him to the dressing-room quick.' He gets us through and I bundle Danny onto a chair.

I grabbed me scissors: SCWEEETCH – shot them through his laces and up the bandage, nearly slicing his leg in the process, and his boot and the bandage fell away. From his big toe, all round his ankle and right up his leg was absolutely black. 'Come on, Jack,' I says to meself. 'You've got to work like bleeding hell now!' I told Danny, 'Be prepared for pain.'

I got a hot towel soaked it in water and whacked it down on his leg to try and get the blood circulating.

'Fucking hell!' Danny screamed. 'That's hurting!'

'Not as much as it will do if I don't get the blood going,' I warned him. I rubbed hard and whacked the towel down again, working like a maniac. At last, his leg started changing colour from black to purple. I was beating on his foot and calling out to Dick, 'COME AND MASSAGE THE TOP OF HIS LEG, FOR GOD'S SAKE!'

'What for?'

'If we don't get his blood moving, he'll lose his leg.'

Dick ambled over and had a look. 'You've got it going now,' he said, and strolls away again.

'Roll over,' I told Danny. I got him laid on his stomach and I was slapping away at his leg with a towel when, joy of joys, it started turning from purple to a nice rosy red. 'Wiggle yer foot,' I told him.

'Like that?'

'Yes. Now try to stand up.' He stands up.

'Oh,' he says, walking carefully around. 'It aches like buggery but I can walk on it all right. Thank you.'

'Am I hearing things?' I asked him. 'Did you say thank you?'

'Yeah. I realise now, Jack, when you look after me you're interested in *me*. When Solomons told Eddie Thomas, "Get him in that ring," all he was interested in was the outcome of the fight.'

'Why did they send you back for me to look after?'

'Eddie didn't want the blame for me foot. You've done a great job. I'm British champion. Thanks again.'

Jack Bodell announced his retirement after that fight.

I lost touch with Danny for ages. I heard he was bouncing for a Glasgow bloke up in London and he'd been stabbed about four times. He come round here a few years ago and said he had a job for Jackie Junior. 'You bleeding well ain't,' I said, 'and don't you even mention it to him.'

31

The Queen of Boxing

My Bet, it was her who trained him more or less, our lad, Jackie Junior. She done the road work with him on her push bike and worked on the pads with him. I anna kidding, he could box like his uncle Dick and punch like his uncle Randy. I used to go down the gym and supervise his work there but Bet worked as hard as I did.

Jackie Junior loved boxing that much when he was little, the only way we had of punishing him was grounding him from coming to the gym. He started when he was about six, had a great amateur career and went professional with George in 1967. He won his first nine fights, with seven inside the distance, and in 1971 he didn't lose a single fight and got voted 'Boxer Of The Year'. Later on he had a run of twelve wins with eleven of those inside the distance.

One day, he went to Birmingham for a television interview with Gary Newbon and they went out on the town afterwards, nightclubbing. Newbon got Jackie playing football with a team of actors and pop singers. Trouble was, Jackie started enjoying the socialising that comes with being famous. I used to think, 'If only he could be as dedicated as I used to be.' He used to be out till two or three o'clock in the morning and only come down the gym when he felt like it, and train his way instead of doing what I wanted him to. Bet used to tell me, 'You shouldn't get on at him all the time, duck.'

'I just want to know where I stand,' I'd tell her. 'Am I supervising him or is he supervising hisself?'

He did have some bad luck as well. The insole was faulty on a new pair of boxing boots he had and tore the skin off his foot, and he ended up with a boot full of blood. It was treated but the wound wasn't cleaned properly and he got blood poisoning. He was due to box a Spanish fella, Antonio Torres, at Wolverhampton. We tried to stop him fighting but Solomons said, 'You can't let your fans down,' and rode roughshod over me and George.

Torres knocked our Jackie down at least a dozen times in that fight. That, and cuz he'd lost his previous fight on a second-round KO, was enough to make the Board of Control withdraw his licence as unfit to box.

His mum took up the cudgel there. She got solicitors and went to court, and Jackie got vindicated. But it'd took three years to sort out and he lost his spark in the lay-off. He packed in after a couple of fights and went wrestling like his Uncle Randy.

Jackie Junior's one of those people who's talented at sport in general. He could have been a top tennis player; with his golf, he got down to a handicap of eight; with his football, he played for the Showbiz Eleven. But he used to get to a certain peak and that was it. He'd give it up.

His professional boxing record come out at 32 fights, with 24 wins – 23 inside the distance – 7 losses, 1 draw and no disqualifications. He done all right with his wrestling, too, and made challenges for the British welterweight and light-heavyweight titles. He was in a tag team as Big Daddy's partner but that was as far as he went with that.

It all could've been my fault, really. George used to say to me, 'You haven't got enough ambition, Jack,' and I think Jackie Junior was the same – no killer instinct. He could have been another World champion, though. He broke my heart with his boxing.

When I was professional, you'd see two blokes practically trying to kill each other. Nowadays, you see two blokes having a cuddle. I haven't got much time for it. I'd been scornful of amateur boxing when I was younger but later I got right into it.

Running an amateur boxing club is hard work and no money but the whole thing is it gets local kids off the streets and helps them do things they couldn't do before. Bet got right in on it, too, and we'd started our own club in Leamington at the request of Inspector Gibbs. One kid who was doing well said, 'Thank you Betty and Jack for showing me the world is for me as well.' That's what makes it worthwhile.

After we got the club up and running, a priest, Father Penny, come to see me to ask if I'd teach boxing in the gym of a local school. We was doing all right there until Father Penny moved away. The school was suddenly sold and I lost all my gym equipment and a lot of my memorabilia.

Bet and me went round Warwick and Leamington begging people to let us have premises – people as I'd done favours for. They all thought it was a great idea but nobody was willing to help. Then Dave Bradshaw, who was on the committee of the Warwick Racing Club, took me down to Warwick Racing to meet Moshy's nephew, Martin Mancini. 'How would you like to run a boxing club here?' he asked me.

Warwick Racing were brilliant. They allocated some space for us and we put up a portakabin and kitted it out with punch bags, a speed ball, a sparring ring, skipping ropes – all what we needed. And we've gone on like that with Warwick Racing Club supporting us all the way.

Bet was an absolutely marvellous secretary and great with the lads – like a mum to them. They'd bring her all their troubles. Our house used to be full of kids all the time.

Georgina presented us with a granddaughter, Lydia, named after Granny Whitehouse. I'd always been away somewhere boxing when Gina and Jackie Junior were growing up, so Lydia coming along give me the chance to be the part of her childhood I'd missed with my own kids. And, I suppose, a chance to be a kid again meself.

Mum died in 1974. I was brokenhearted. I mourned and mourned for her. She'd had a tough ol' life. I don't think she'd have lasted as long as she did if she hadn't been as hard as she was. We all thought the world of her and would've done anything to get her eyesight back for her. Through boxing, we were able to give her a better life than she would have had. After she'd died I give her a kiss. All her wrinkles had gone.

In 1986, I had a slight heart attack and was granted early retirement from Lockheed. We moved from our second-floor flat in Leamington to a ground-floor flat in Warwick, where I'd have no stairs to climb.

It was like coming back home for Bet, like starting all over again. We did everything together. I used to think, 'If it could have been like this all the while, what a fantastic time we could have had,' but it never is, is it?

Bet got even more into the boxing. She knew an amazing amount even for someone married to an ex-professional. People all over the country used to phone her to get advice on matchmaking for the amateurs. She got so well known and respected, people never used to bother with me. I worshipped Bet but I don't think she believed it. I don't think she believed it right up to the end.

I wish I'd known how ill she was cuz she must have known for at least two years. She'd look really poorly but swear she was all right. We'd be in bed and she'd start coughing and I'd say, 'Oh, no, not that again,' and she'd say, 'I'm sorry, duck, I'll get a drink of water.' After a while, I used to automatically get her a jug of water to put by the bed but it didn't occur to me it was anything serious. Then some tests were done and it was found out Bet had cancer of the throat. We were given the impression it could be dealt with.

People was always asking us why wasn't there something on display in Leamington or Warwick recognising Randolph's achievements. They couldn't believe the towns were ignoring him. Adrian Bush – his grandmother was my mother's sister – run an amateur boxing club in Leamington and he come to us one day and said we should do summat about it. Bet popped up and said, 'What say we start a collection and build up some money?' and that was it, 'The Randolph Turpin Memorial Fund'.

The Navy Club in Leamington let Bet have their premises for nothing to put on a dance. Tickets were two pounds each and, I'm not akidding, it was a sell-out. Halfway through the dance, she goes on stage and says to the drummer, 'Give us a drum roll.' Bet announces, 'You all know this dance is being run to raise a fund to make a tribute to Randy Turpin' – and she had to put this little bit in – 'my brother-in-law. What I'd like to do now is give you all a chance of owning a bit of it. I'll be taking donations until the end of the dance.' She raised hundreds of pounds that night and it carried on from there.

We were at this fundraising do and Charlie Kray arrived. He give me a big hug and a kiss on the cheek. 'Good to see you again, Jack,' he says. We sat and chatted while me and Bet were playing bingo. 'Ooh,' Charlie says, 'you only want one number there.'

'Right,' I said. 'Put yourself about and make sure no one else gets it.' Hell of a laugh Charlie is. Bet was uncomfortable around a bloke who'd got the reputation of being a gangster but they're a great crowd, the Krays. People go on about them but if you look it all up, they never harmed anybody ordinary.

When Bet become too ill, she handed the memorial fund books over to Ady Bush and his wife took over as treasurer. I used to say to Bet, 'I hope people realise how much you've done for this,' because, in the beginning, she was the main one and there were times when she should have been in hospital but she'd say, 'No. We've got to get money for Randolph.'

Me and Gina were sitting by Bet's bed in the hospital and this young nurse come across and puts her arm around my neck to tell me summat. Georgina told me, 'If looks could kill, that nurse would have dropped dead from the look in my mum's eyes.' Bet pulled Gina down to her and whispered summat – she could only talk in whispers by then. Gina said, 'Mum said tell that silly old bugger I love him.'

When her time come, Bet slipped away peacefully. I was heartbroken. Devastated. But, I was glad that she didn't suffer like I've seen some people suffer. Even so, she must have gone through hell at times and never said a word. When I was sorting her things out I come across about a dozen train tickets for Coventry to see the cancer specialist. I also found painkillers hidden under the mattress. She'd thought I'd go to pieces if I knew how ill she really was and swore all the doctors and nurses to secrecy. I felt ever so cheated when I found that out, cuz if I'd have known, I could've p'raps helped her more. I miss Bet so much, you know . . . Fifty-two years we'd been married . . . She . . . Can we leave this a minute?

At Warwick Racing Amateur Boxing Club they've put up an engraved brass plaque:

IN MEMORY OF
'THE QUEEN OF BOXING'
MRS BETTY TURPIN
WHO SADLY PASSED AWAY
1ST NOVEMBER 1999

My Bet. She was a fantastic girl, I tell you. I was a lucky bloke to have a girl like that.

32

Well, Daddy, Just Look What You've Done!

The money collected for the Randolph Turpin Memorial Fund was going to be for summat small to start with – a plaque or a bronze head. But Randolph was that well remembered the money come piling in and we found we could go for summat bigger.

Me and Ady Bush went on TV saying as we wanted to commission a statue. A young fella phoned up, Carl Payne, a student, saying he'd do it for nothing.

'If he's a student, he can't afford to do it for nothing,' I said. 'Somebody's got to supply him with all the stuff he needs.' So that was the arrangement.

When the statue was put on show at the Castle foundry in Wales, me and Ady shot over there. It was marvellous. I stood gazing up at it and I don't know whether it was a trick of the sunlight, or a tear in my eye, or what, but I could've swore it winked at me. I said to Ady, 'It needs a piece of writing attached to it. We'll get Terry to do it.'

Having a statue's one thing but the other thing is where do you put it? The local councils were approached and one councillor said, 'Randolph Turpin was born in Leamington and died in Leamington, and Leamington is where they had his big victory celebration. His statue should be in Leamington.' Another one piped up, 'Randolph Turpin was educated in Warwick and he trained in Warwick. His statue should be in Warwick.' Another one calls out, 'Do we want a statue of Randolph Turpin in the first place, considering the manner of his death?' Luckily, the people I was with held me back or I'd be in prison.

'On the contrary,' this other one says. 'It's an absolute disgrace the council didn't put one up 50 years ago instead of leaving it to the Turpin family and the people of Warwickshire to do it.' It was going backwards and forwards, backwards and forwards, and time was quickly running out for the special date we'd got in mind for the unveiling.

At the eleventh hour Warwick council come up with a terrific site: Warwick Market Place. And, what's more, the unveiling could be staged on the day we wanted: 10 July 2001.

When the long-awaited day finally come, I was that excited I was up at four o'clock in the morning pacing up and down in the flat. I had an interview to do with the BBC radio in Warwick Market Place and I went up early for it. It was still only ten to seven. Randolph's statue was on its plinth, covered with a bright red sheet and lashed round with ropes. I could feel rain in the air and I was worried that bad weather was gonna spoil everything.

The radio people arrived, pulled the red cover to one side on the statue and sneaked a photo of me with it. After they'd finished interviewing, I walked back home and tried to relax by watching the telly but the phone never stopped ringing: people wishing me well; newspapers, radio and TV asking for interviews, or trying to do them over the phone; friends, casual acquaintances and complete bloody strangers trying to beg tickets off of me for the evening buffet do.

At quarter to twelve, I went back up the square to be filmed for a *Midland Reports* documentary. I was glad to get out of the flat again. The interviewer asked me, 'What does this day mean to you, Jack?'

'I think it's great,' I told them. 'My baby brother being officially recognised at last. It's a proud day for the whole family. My Bet would've been dancing all round this square today.'

'What would it have meant to Randolph?'

'It would've embarrassed him. He'd have most probably jumped in his car and cleared off.'

As I'd feared, it started raining and coming down hard enough to stop the filming. It seemed set in for the day. Georgina had taken time off work to be with me. She looked up at the sky and said, 'You know who's doing this, don't you?'

The rain eased off just long enough for me to get back to the flat, then it come down in stair rods. I tried to rest but it was no use. I got changed early for the pre-ceremony do for the guests of honour.

At five o'clock in the evening, it was umbrella out and up to the Judge's House in Northgate Street. As I was climbing the big staircase to the upper room, I stopped to read some of the names on the paintings and plaques – magistrates, and all that. It was funny to think those people want to be friendly with us now but, when we was kids, they'd have seen us as enemies.

In the VIP room, there was a long table with half a dozen waitresses fluttering round it pouring out glasses of fruit juice and glasses of champagne. I took an orange juice and waited for everyone to arrive. One of the first was Earnie Shavers and his wife.

Earnie was a top-class heavyweight with a ferocious punch. If Earnie hit you on Monday, you'd wake up the following Sunday asking what'd happened. He knocked out Ken Norton in the first round and Jimmy Ellis. He fought Jerry Quarry, Joe Bugner, Ron Lyle, Jimmy Young, James Tillis, Larry Holmes and, of course, the all-shouting, all-dancing, Muhammad Ali. Like Licker was, Earnie's a quiet-spoken real gentleman.

People started arriving in droves: Randolph Junior; Carl Payne with his wife and kids; Ady Bush and his family; Hamilton Bland of Sporting Memorabilia, Warwick, who was Master of Ceremonies; Richie Woodhall, former WBC super middleweight champion; Neil Simpson, who'd reclaimed the British and Commonwealth light-heavyweight title for the Midlands that Randolph had once taken from Don Cockell; the representative of the Lord Lieutenant of Warwickshire; Bob Mee the Sky Sports and *Daily Telegraph* boxing correspondent who'd done a brilliant job writing the biogs and publicity for the memorial fund fundraising events; Colin Hart, boxing columnist with *The Sun*; TV crews; photographers; journalists – it was getting so's you could hardly move.

World champion cruiserweight Johnny Nelson was to be coming down from Sheffield to be with us but sadly couldn't make it. One of my favourite photos of Bet is of her with me and Johnny. He trains at Brendan Ingle's gym. Remember, Randolph fought Brendan's brother, Jimmy, in 1946? They talk about Randolph's punching power in that gym today. That's quite a punch, innit, when it still hurts more than 50 years later?

Sir Henry Cooper, who was doing the unveiling with me, come through the door flashing his big 'Our 'Enery' grin, and shook hands all round. There's only five boxers in the world who've knocked Muhammad Ali down in the ring and two of them, Henry Cooper and Earnie Shavers, were standing side by side in that room to honour Randolph.

The talking and laughing got louder and louder; flashbulbs were going like a tropical storm; video and TV cameras were being aimed at us from all angles; reporters were standing in front of little groups of boxers and nodding their heads and squiggling in their notebooks; old friends and total strangers were grabbing me from this side and that side for a few words, and I shook hands that many times I felt like I'd done ten rounds in the ring.

When it was time for us all to move up to the square, I took a look through the window. The rain was falling softer. Then, as we stepped on to the pavement outside, the rain suddenly stopped and the sun come out bright and warm and clear. It was a beautiful summer evening.

Southpaw Allan Minter, who'd took the World middleweight championship from Vito Antuofermo, joined us outside and we started the walk up to town.

It was quite a sight, I tell you, flyweights to heavyweights, young and old, wearing the bashed noses, scars and cauliflower ears of our trade, processing through Warwick in our best suits to pay tribute to my baby brother – champion of the world when there was only one title for each weight, on the exact 50th anniversary of his victory over Ray Robinson. Randolph Adolphus Turpin, the Leamington Licker, the man who give the Sugar Man a caning; the man Robinson admitted was 'one of the best fighters I have ever met'.

Jackie Junior and Randolph's girls, Charmaine and Annette, chose to stay with the crowd outside the VIP enclosure. I felt sorry we couldn't all be together but it was their choice, innit? At least they were there.

The Cubbington Silver Band was playing a show tune as we mounted the podium to the right of the veiled statue. Danny McAlinden tugged at my sleeve, 'We had some great crack, didn't we, Jack?' he said. Nowadays that sounds like drug talk but the Irish mean it for having a great time.

Hamilton Bland got on the microphone:

Welcome to the Market Square. As you will see on the stage alongside me here, a host of guests. Would you please welcome, first of all, the Mayor of Warwick District Council, Councillor Marion Heywood [*applause*]; the chairman of the Warwickshire County Council, Councillor Dot Webster; the chairman of Warwick District Council, Councillor Hayden Thomas; and, representing Her Majesty the Queen this afternoon, the Lord Lieutenant of Warwickshire, Martin Dunn, who would like to say a few words. [*applause*]

He handed over to Martin Dunn:

Ladies and gentlemen, today Mr Bush received the following letter from Her Majesty the Queen, which I will read out to you:

'The Queen thanks you and all those involved with the Randolph Turpin Memorial Fund for your kind and loyal message of greeting sent on the occasion of the unveiling of the statue of this famous boxer at Warwick town centre today. Her Majesty much appreciated your thoughtfulness in writing and sends her best wishes to all those who have taken part in this worthy project.'

It is dated the 10th of July, and has been received from Buckingham Palace this morning. [*applause*]

Hamilton Bland got back on the mic:

Our principal guest this afternoon, however, without any question whatsoever, is the one-and-only Jackie Turpin [*applause and cheering*], middle brother of the Fighting Turpins: Dick, Randy and Jackie. Mum and dad, Beatrice and Lionel, met at Hill House – the Hill House hospital just a few hundred metres from here in Warwick. Jackie Turpin, easily the best-looking of the three [*pause for laughter*] – he told me to say that! Jackie, who began boxing in 1946, his career ended in 1954, fought 130 contests [*sic*] – won 87 [*sic*] of them. More than Randolph and Dick added together – the little guy behind me here! Ladies and gentlemen: Jackie Turpin. [*cheers and applause*]

He went on to thank Adrian Bush for three years' hard work and to list all the people Ady wanted to thank in connection with the fund. I was keeping my ears open for this: *'I'd also like to thank Betty Turpin.'* I thought, 'If only she could have been here to see all this.'

After a bit more speech making, the moment arrived and me and Sir Henry loosened the ropes and slid off the red cover, and Randolph, cast in bronze, was standing there against the blue and gold sky of a perfect summer evening. Randolph Turpin, Britain's first middleweight World champion since Bob Fitzsimmons took the title from Jack Dempsey way back in 1891 and Britain's first ever black World champion. Cameras whirred and flashed and clicked, and, I tell you, a lot of handkerchiefs come out of pockets and handbags. I never felt tearful, though, I just felt proud.

There was me brother, middleweight champion of the world, the man who'd brought about the twentieth century's biggest upset in boxing, in his moment of triumph, standing 8 ft 6 in. tall, on a 5-ft stone plinth. On the bronze plaque below his feet:

In Palace, Pub, And Parlour,
The Whole Of Britain Held Its Breath

I thought to meself, 'You've done a marvellous job there, Terry. That's just right.'

Underneath that it's got:

Celer Et Audax.

Latin for 'Swift and Bold' – the motto of the King's Royal Rifle Corps who me dad fought with for the freedom of all British people, and perfect for Randolph. I thought, 'Thank you, Terry. That's a real nice touch. Randolph would have loved that.'

Up on the platform, I remembered the time, such a long time ago now, when I asked Randolph what he wanted to do in life. 'I don't know yet, kid,' he said, 'but whatever it is, I want to find the man who's best in the world at it, and beat him.'

I thought of me mum, and Bet, and Dick, and Joan, and Kath, and Ernie Manley, and George Middleton, and Mick Gavin, and all my other friends and relatives who've passed on. I thought especially of my dad, from British Guiana. Lionel Fitzherbert

Turpin, the first African man Leamington Spa and Warwick had ever seen.

I looked out over the crowd at the beautiful brown faces of my extended family, with Randolph Adolphus Turpin, champion of the world, towering up against the sky behind me, and I thought, 'Well, Daddy, just look what you've done!'

33

The Last of the Fighting Turpins

It's 50 years since I left the professional ring. The last of the Fighting Turpins. Some people think we're all dead and try to talk to me as if I was a friend of theirs. When I say, 'No, I'm Randolph's older brother,' their mouths drop open and they bleeding near pass out. They've gotta think then what they've been saying to me.

Me and my brothers brought credit back to British boxing and we fought and broke the colour bar, but it should have been me mum that was the most famous one, cuz she fought her whole life against hardship, against prejudice and against her blindness. Most of all, she fought for us, each one of us, and she never give up. She'd use her fists against absolutely anybody as crossed us. Later on, we was able to make up a little bit for what she'd done for us. But you can't really repay it, can you?

Do I have any regrets? Well, a big one is I was always away somewhere when my kids were growing up. Those years you can never recapture but I done my very best to provide for Bet and them, and I done a better job of it with boxing than I ever could've just in a factory job. There was absolutely thousands of featherweights around England at that time. I was average size, sort of thing. That's why I could keep so busy. You knock one down and ten more spring up.

I'm not sure this is a regret – and this is ABSOLUTELY no disrespect to George Middleton, cuz George always did his level best for all of us – but I honestly think I would have been better

268

off with a different manager. I was glad George was doing so well and had a big stable but p'raps he had too many horses in it, cuz there was a downside for me with him being so busy.

Big stars outshine little stars and most glamour and public interest in boxing is attached to the heavyweights – the giants. Then, a lot of people find the middleweights exciting, cuz they still pack a punch, they're faster and the competition's more-so because a few more of the population is at that weight. The little blokes, flyweights, bantamweights and featherweights, like me, get the least attention. Dick and Randolph, both top middleweights, inevitably got most of George's time.

George made sure I was being looked after all right but it didn't give him time where he could plan my career properly. I realised what was happening and I never got shirty about it. It's just the way it was and I wouldn't have changed George for anybody. I suppose, on my side, I never took boxing serious enough.

I would have loved to have fought for the British featherweight title. I like to think I would have won it. I mean, I out-pointed the reigning champion Ronnie Clayton in a non-title fight. Georgina met Al Phillips a few years ago. He turned out to be a real nice fella. 'Your old man was a bloody good fighter,' he told her. 'I didn't want to meet him for fear of losing my title.' Having a good reputation sometimes works against you.

You might think it strange but I still don't like violence. I hated fighting, I hated getting hit, but I had that many fights it become an everyday thing for me. Some people find it hard to believe that getting in the ring and trying to knock a fella out who's trying to knock you out at the same time becomes routine, because if they'd done it just once, they'd talk about for the rest of their lives; but that's how it gets: routine. I'd still rather have a laugh than a ruck, though.

Josie Middleton says I was always the peacemaker – keeping me brothers away from each other's throats. Looking back, yes, I was always doing my best to joke them out of it but I didn't particularly notice I was doing it at the time.

I used to read reports of my fights occasionally and think, 'Good God! Did I do all that? I must be pretty good!' About another fight I'd think, 'Why did I do a stupid thing like that? I must be useless!' We was more for the sport than they are today.

If I'm proud of anything it's the part I played in making Dick and Randolph's careers successful, especially Randolph's. It was worth every mile of road I ran with him – and we sometimes ran so fast I thought me boots would catch fire – and, although I didn't always think so when I was somersaulting over the top rope or picking meself up off the canvas, it was worth every bruised rib and dislocated jaw he gave me to help him prove he was the best middleweight in the world and to give British boxing its best ever night in the ring.

Randolph proved he was the best not once but twice, although the Americans only allowed once to be officially recognised. But now they've done something they only do for boxers who've displayed exceptional talent, skill and courage: they've enshrined him in the International Boxing Hall of Fame.

The name Randy Turpin stands alongside other modern all-time greats like Joe Louis, Rocky Marciano, Max Schmeling, Willie Pep, Sandy Saddler, Muhammad Ali, Sugar Ray Robinson and Marvin Hagler, and alongside old-time fighters like Jack Johnson, Bob Fitzsimmons, Harry Greb, James Figg, John L. Sullivan, Tom Sayers and Tom Molineaux. With the statue here and the Hall of Fame there, Randolph has been recognised properly at last. In 2000, he was listed with Britain's Millennium Sporting Legends.

Dick's bit of history, being the first British black man to win a Lonsdale Belt, will stand for ever. When he died, Nigel Benn sent a wreath in the colours Dick used to box in, with a message thanking him for what he'd done for black British fighters.

As for Battling Jack, I was what you'd call a club fighter, a high-ranking contender – number one or two in most listings. I was the main event on most of the shows round here; I topped the bill at Liverpool Stadium three or four times; I fought twice in America – there's not many British boxers who could say that, even British champions – and I won both times. I started out my career with six-rounders – straight in at the deep end and I fought the best and always held my own and most often beat them.

Reg Gutteridge, who's commentated on all the big fights, describes me as a 'top featherweight'. Not bad, I suppose, for someone who, like I've told you, just sort of drifted into the fight game.

The Rotary Club of Warwick recently awarded me a certificate for what I've been doing in amateur boxing:

The Last of the Fightng Turpins

An Award in Recognition of Outstanding Service by
Individual Members of The Community; Such Service
Performed in Accordance With The Ideal of
'SERVICE ABOVE SELF'

Inspector Gibbs would have been proud of me. They also gave me £150 to donate to my favourite charity, which I give to the blind.

I've become president of our Warwick Racing Amateur Boxing Club. Steve Myrie, our trainer there, has put me on to reggae. I've gone back to me roots. Steve's kid, Peliko, he's a smashing kid – not four years old and he's showing a real natural talent for boxing. He's not training, of course. It's just with him being around fighters. If he sticks to it, he's gonna be World champion. I was telling Steve how great me and Peliko get on. 'I should think so,' he said. 'You're both the same bleeding age.'

So many people have gone now: me baby brother Randolph in 1966; our wonderful mum in 1974, she was nearly 70, God bless her; my lovely Bet in 1999; our Joan in 1985; our Kath in 1992; our Dick in 1989; dear old George Middleton in 1991. When Joan died, it affected me like Dougie Kensit. I hardly moved for three days. Our stepdad Ernie died back in 1962. We loved him a lot, too. He wasn't our dad and he never could be, but he looked after us as kids and, more important, he looked after our mum. He always wanted us to call him Dad but we couldn't out of respect for our real dad. Actually, I did once. We was having a drink in a pub in Leamington and it just slipped out and we was both embarrassed about it.

I've got a picture of my Bet holding up some boxing gloves. There's a little bit of contempt in her smile as if she's thinking, 'Yeah, you just try an' take these gloves off me.' When I'm going to bed, I say to that photo, 'You can keep your bloody gloves. I'm off to bed. Goodnight!' and I sometimes I swear her face changes slightly. She was a girl and a half, she was, I tell you. Cancer – I hate that bloody word.

I could never stand being on my own, you know. When Bet wasn't speaking to me, that really used to hurt. I'd have much rather she'd hit me on the head with a saucepan or summat. I think that had a lot to do with me wanting to box. I used to think, 'If I don't do it I'll be left out.'

After Bet had gone, one bloke says, 'What are you going to do about a secretary now, Jack?'

'There won't be another one like Bet,' I said. 'But I've got one as is close like her. My granddaughter, Lydia.' Lydia's a replica for Bet, the way she goes on. Her and Georgina have been marvellous. If they hadn't have come round so often after Bet died, I'd have been climbing up the walls or summat. Gina's a lovely girl. She's my daughter, so I shouldn't brag about her but I do because she really is great.

Me and Moshy are still going strong. Banjo's still around and Arthur Fairy, my old shipmate from HMS *Myngs*, still keeps in touch. When there was any trouble, I always knew Arthur would mind my back. He's a great friend. I think the world of him.

Dick was always saying he could've been World champion if it wasn't for the war. But George give him the chance of staying at home, so it was his own fault. Though I suppose it was only what we all did and what our dad had done. Our dad didn't have to fight in the First World War but he travelled 4,000 miles to sign up for it. That's why it makes me so mad when racist scumbags spread crap, as the only reason they're free to do it is cuz enough African people and enough Asian people give their lives in two world wars to help keep the right of saying what you want to over here. 'Free speech', they call it but it cost people like my dad their lives.

I never bothered claiming my medals after the war – Burma Star, Atlantic Star, Russian Peoples Medal, '39–'45 Campaign Medal, an' all that, till Cledwyn persuaded me. He said I should be proud of them. To be honest, just getting through it all alive was enough for me. When I look at them now, it's hard to believe I done what I did. I was only a kid, really.

It's an odd feeling being the last surviving member of your generation of a family and I dearly wish Dick and Randolph, Joan and Kath was here to hear all about what I've learnt about our dad.

We lived our childhood in a special time – between the wars, in the last days of the British Empire; in the days of ocean liners, when we was still a seafaring nation; in the days when there was more horses than motor cars; before television; before the Welfare State; before the atomic bomb. We lived in places where they'd never seen a black person before. We had a great ol' life.

We all left school at 14 year old and done the best we could. We made mistakes, of course. Who hasn't? You shouldn't judge us, though, cuz you don't know what you would've done in the same position. You might think you do but you never really know till it happens.

Whatever I've done, good or bad, I've always been me and I always will be me. I'd rather be me than say, 'My brother was champion of the world' and go swanning about like that. He's Randolph Turpin, not me. It upsets people cuz if they come and ask me silly questions, I give 'em silly answers. And, sometimes, if they've got no right to ask the question, I tell them 'fuck off' or summat. I'm me. John Matthew Turpin, senior. Battling Jack.

*

I had a dream the other night. I was waiting at the end of Willes Road for my father to come home from work. I got out of bed, still half asleep, and went wandering around the flat looking for him. I'm well into my 70s now and you'd think I'd know better. It's funny how these things never leave you, innit?

Appendices

(a)

The Turpin Brothers' Professional Records

LIONEL CECIL 'DICK' TURPIN: ACTIVE 1937–50
(Former: Midland Area middleweight champion; British Empire middleweight champion; British middleweight champion – first black man allowed to contest the British domestic title)

Middleweight
1937

27	September	Eric Lloyd	Rugby	W rsf 4
4	October	Trevor Burt	Coventry	L ko 3
16	October	Eddie Harris	Evesham	W rsf 6
1	November	Frank Guest	Birmingham	W pts 4
15	November	Trevor Burt	Coventry	W pts 6
20	November	Phil Proctor	Evesham	W rsf 2
13	December	Frank Guest	Birmingham	W ko 6
18	December	Ray Chadwick	Evesham	W ko 4

1938

19	February	Bill Blything	Evesham	W rtd 4
28	February	Wally Rankin	Nuneaton	W pts 8
7	March	Bob Hartley	Rugby	Draw 8
19	March	Frankie Smith	Evesham	W rsf 4
28	March	Trevor Burt	Coventry	W pts 8
23	May	Sid Fitzhugh	Northampton	W pts 8
11	June	Rex Whitney	West Haddon	L pts 10
15	August	Johnny Clarke	Gloucester	W pts 10
3	October	Alf Bishop	Gloucester	Draw 10
10	October	Mick Miller	Leamington	W ko 2

7	November	Trevor Burt	Bristol	W ko 4
14	November	Charlie Parkin	Coventry	L pts 10
21	November	Jack McKnight	Leamington	W pts 10
10	December	Charlie Parkin	Evesham	L pts 10
26	December	Alf Bishop	Leamington	W pts 10

1939

19	January	Wally Rankin	Kidderminster	W pts 10
28	January	Butcher Gascoigne	Coventry	L pts 10
24	February	Mick Miller	Banbury	W pts 10
6	March	Johnny Thornton	Cirencester	W rtd 5
13	March	Jack Hammer	Northampton	W pts 12

(Won right to contest Midland Area middleweight title)

17	March	George Robey	Banbury	W pts 10
30	March	Jimmy Griffiths	Coventry	L pts 10
17	April	Jimmy Griffiths	Leamington	W pts 10
21	April	George Robey	Banbury	Draw 10
7	May	Wally Pack	London	W pts 8
22	May	Jack Millburn	Northampton	W pts 15

(Won Midland Area middleweight title)

4	June	Nat Franks	London	W pts 10
7	August	George Robey	Shipton	W rsf 11
18	August	Harry Ainsworth	Coventry	W pts 12
30	October	Charlie Parkin	Northampton	W pts 10
26	November	George Howard	Coventry	L pts 10
11	December	Ben Valentine	Coventry	W pts 10
24	December	Ben Valentine	Coventry	W pts 10

1940

21	January	Maurice Dennis	Coventry	W rsf 8
25	February	Ginger Sadd	Coventry	W pts 10
4	March	Dave McCleave	Birmingham	W ko 5
15	March	Syd Williams	Oxford	W pts 10
1	April	Eddie Maguire	Birmingham	Draw 10
14	April	Tommy Smith	Coventry	W rtd 10
20	May	Eddie Maguire	Birmingham	L pts 10
27	May	Jim Berry	Manchester	W pts 10
3	June	Tommy Davies	Swansea	W pts 10
10	June	Paddy Roche	Nuneaton	W pts 10
13	July	Albert O'Brien	Northampton	W ko 2
24	August	Pat O'Connor	Coventry	W pts 10
16	December	Ginger Sadd	Nottingham	L rtd 7

1941–3
INACTIVE – WAR SERVICE

The Turpin Brothers' Professional Records

1944

18 March	Dave McCleave	Coventry	L pts 8

1945

INACTIVE – WAR SERVICE

1946

26 February	Jack McKnight	Rugby	W ko 1
24 September	Johnny Boyd	Birmingham	L pts 8
30 September	Paddy Roche	Stroud	W pts 10
14 October	Johnny Blake	Oxford	W rsf 4
16 October	Jack Lord	Birmingham	W ko 3
28 October	Art Owen	Leicester	W rsf 6
11 November	Trevor Burt	Malvern	W ko 3
19 November	Johnny Best	London	L rtd 4
9 December	Johnny Boyd	Oxford	W ko 4
16 December	Billy Mayne	Birmingham	W rsf 7

1947

14 January	George Howard	London	L ko 7
10 February	Bert Sanders	Oxford	Draw 8
17 March	Ron Cooper	Malvern	W pts 8
24 March	Frank Hayes	Birmingham	W ko 4
3 April	Tommy Braddock	Leamington	W rtd 4
14 April	Gordon Griffiths	Oxford	W rsf 4
6 May	Jim Wellard	London	W pts 8
23 May	Norman Rees	Trealaw	W rtd 2
29 May	Billy Stevens	Liverpool	W rsf 3
23 June	Jim Hockley	Coventry	W pts 8
5 July	Des Jones	Bedford	W pts 8
12 July	Bert Sanders	Stratford	W pts 8
24 July	Tommy Davies	Liverpool	W rtd 5
9 September	Vince Hawkins	Coventry	W rsf 6
18 September	Art Owen	Tunbridge Wells	W rtd 2
22 September	Johnny Boyd	Wolverhampton	W pts 8
23 October	Billy Stevens	Newcastle	W pts 10
7 November	Freddie Price	Manchester	W pts 10
20 November	Ron Cooper	Smethick	W pts 8
1 December	Bert Sanders	Leeds	W pts 8

1948

2 February	Mark Hart	Nottingham	W pts 12

(Won right to contest British middleweight title)

18 May	Bos Murphy	Coventry	W ko 1

(Won British Empire middleweight title)

28	June	Vince Hawkins	Birmingham	W pts 15

(Won British middleweight title – first black man to be allowed to contest a British domestic title; first black man to win a Lonsdale Belt. Retained British Empire middleweight title)

27	September	Bert Sanders	Birmingham	W pts 8
18	October	Duggie Miller	London	W rtd 7
29	November	Tiberio Mitri	`London	Draw 12

(Draw – for right to contest European middleweight title. Contest to be re-fought)

1949

12	March	Tiberio Mitri	Trieste	L pts 12

(Unsuccessful bid for right to contest European middleweight title)

29	March	Marcel Cerdan	London	L ko 7
30	May	Robert Charron	London	W disq 5
30	June	Albert Finch	Birmingham	W pts 15

(Retained British and Empire middleweight titles)

6	September	Dave Sands	London	L ko 1

(Lost British Empire middleweight title)

1	November	George Ross	Birmingham	W rsf 7
12	December	Ron Cooper	Nottingham	W pts 8

1950

16	January	Vince Hawkins	Coventry	W pts 8
6	March	Ron Pudney	Croydon	W pts 8
14	March	Baby Day	London	L pts 10
24	April	Albert Finch	Nottingham	L pts 15

(Lost British middleweight title)

13	May	Cyrille Delannoit	Brussels	L rtd 6
3	July	Albert Finch	Nottingham	L rtd 8

Reord complied by Vic Hardwicke, Jackie Turpin and W. Terry Fox

JOHN MATTHEW 'BATTLING JACK' TURPIN: ACTIVE 1941–54
(Former: Midland Area featherweight champion)

Featherweight
1941

9 A ugust	Sammy Stopps	Leamington	W rtd 3
Date Unknown	An Irishman	Coventry	W pts 6

1942

9	February	Eddie Giddings	Northampton	L pts 6

The Turpin Brothers' Professional Records

1943–5

INACTIVE – WAR SERVICE

1946

21	May	Percy Pateman	Birmingham	W ko 2
24	June	Wilf Stacey	Birmingham	W pts 8
8	July	Billy Peach	Birmingham	W ko 1
2	September	Hal Bagwell	Cirencester	L ko 9
14	October	Eric Millward	Leicester	W ko 4
28	October	Arthur Wright	Leicester	L pts 8
11	November	Al Smith	Malvern	W rtd 3
18	November	Tom Cummings	Leicester	L ko 5
26	November	Ivor Roberts	Birmingham	L ko 3
9	December	Les Turner	Oxford	W pts 8

1947

13	January	Arthur Marriott	Leicester	W pts 6
24	January	Bert Donaldson	Birmingham	W ko 5
10	February	Tommy Kelly	Oxford	W pts 8
18	March	Sammy Ervin	London	W ko 5
3	April	Moe Walker	Leamington	W pts 8
8	April	Sammy Ervin	London	W pts 6
14	April	Johnny Catlin	Oxford	W ko 1
28	April	Ivor Simpson	Birmingham	L ko 4
6	May	Dave Sharkey	London	W pts 6
12	May	George Simmons	Oxford	W pts 8
19	May	George Green	Cirencester	W pts 10
23	May	Len Jones	Trealaw	W pts 8
29	May	Billy Kendrick	Liverpool	L rtd 4
3	June	Johnny Molloy	London	L rsf 2
6	June	Arthur Benton	West Bromwich	W pts 8
23	June	Tommy Cummings	Coventry	W pts 6
5	July	Tommy Griffiths	Bedford	W rsf 2
12	July	Les Turner	Stratford	W rsf 4
24	July	Terry Riley	Liverpool	L disq 4
30	August	Mias Johnson	Nuneaton	W rsf 1
9	September	Tony Brazil	Coventry	W disq 3
18	September	Ron Kitchen	Tunbridge Wells	W ko 6
27	September	Tom Bailey	Hanley	W pts 10
29	October	Hecky Houldsworth	Croydon	W pts 10
6	November	Billy Marlow	Rochester	W pts 8
17	November	Johnny Collins	Northampton	W ko 4
20	November	Stan Mace	Smethick	W ko 4
1	December	Jackie Robertson	Leeds	W rsf 3
8	December	Johnny Morgan	Oxford	W disq 4
17	December	Ray Fitton	Willenhall	Draw 8

1948

5	January	Tommy Plowright	Derby	W ko 2
9	January	Jimmy McIntyre	Canterbury	W rsf 7
23	January	Ray Fitton	Blackpool	W pts 10
26	January	Tommy Madine	Coventry	W pts 8
2	February	Jackie Horseman	Nottingham	W disq 6
9	February	Teddy Peckham	Bridgewater	W pts 8
5	March	Terry Riley	Leamington	W rtd 5
15	March	George Albrow	Derby	W ko 2
29	March	Ron Gladwell	Northampton	W pts 8
12	April	Albert Bessell	Cheltenham	L pts 12

(Unsuccessful bid for Southern Central Area featherweight title. Albert Bessell, holder)

10	May	Hecky Houldsworth	Nottingham	W rtd 5
18	May	Ben Duffy	Coventry	L rsf 5
28	June	Ben Duffy	Birmingham	W pts 8
12	July	Jock Bonas	Aylesbury	Draw 8
27	July	George Simmons	Ramsgate	W rtd 6
10	August	Johnny Morgan	Portsmouth	W pts 8
21	September	Ronnie Taylor	London	W pts 6
14	October	Tom Bailey	Liverpool	W pts 8
1	November	Harry Croker	Chesterfield	W rtd 4
22	November	Jackie Lucraft	London	L pts 8
9	December	Bert Jackson	Liverpool	L ko 6

1949

3	January	Danny Nagle	London	W pts 8
17	January	Eddie Dumazel	Sheffield	W pts 8
31	January	Jackie Lucraft	London	W pts 8
17	February	Jackie Lucraft	London	Draw 8
24	February	Ronnie Clayton	Hanley	L pts 8
28	March	Chris Kelly	Preston	W disq 5
16	April	Teddy Peckham	Chard	L ko 4
25	April	Joe Carter	Bedford	W rtd 4
5	May	Sammy Shaw	Norwich	W pts 8
17	May	Sammy Shaw	Hanley	W rtd 5
8	June	Peter Guichan	Dundee	L pts 8
20	June	Selwyn Evans	Birmingham	W pts 8
11	July	Denny Dawson	Carlisle	Draw 8
4	August	Bernard Pugh	Liverpool	L pts 8

1950

9	January	Ivor Simpson	Cheltenham	L ko 7

(Lost right to contest Southern Central Area featherweight title)

7	February	Tommy Blears	Blackburn	L ko 5
6	March	Johnny Rawlings	Croydon	L pts 8
27	September	Peter Guichan	Dundee	W pts 8

27 October	Jimmy Dwyer	Blackpool	W ko 7
13 November	Eddie Dumazel	Abergavenny	W ko 2
30 November	Tom Bailey	Liverpool	L pts 10
6 December	Harry Croker	Birmingham	W ko 1
18 December	Terry Riley	London	W pts 8

1951

5 January	Tony Lombard	London	L pts 8
19 January	Joe King	Blackpool	W rsf 8
20 February	Jackie Lucraft	Watford	W pts 8
27 February	Tommy Miller	London	W pts 6
19 March	Eddie Moran	Leicester	W rsf 3
16 April	Gene Caffrey	Weston SM	W pts 8
23 April	Gene Caffrey	Reading	W rtd 5
15 May	Billy Daniels	Brighton	W rsf 8
29 May	Dai Davies	London	L rtd 4
18 June	Jackie Summerville	Weston SM	Draw 8
28 June	Gus Foran	Liverpool	W pts 10
12 July	Denny Dawson	Bristol	W rtd 7
25 July	Teddy Peckham	Portsmouth	W rtd 4
11 August	Denny Dawson	Sheffield	W pts 10
12 September	Joe Wamsley	New York	W pts 6
2 October	Benny Chocolate	Kendal	L pts 8
12 November	Gene Caffrey	Epsom	L pts 8

1952

22 February	Jim McCann	Blackpool	W rsf 7
6 March	Stan Skinkiss	Liverpool	Draw 10
17 March	Jimmy Bird	London	W ko 1
24 March	Jackie Summerville	London	W rsf 3
31 March	Gene Caffrey	London	W ko 1
7 April	Sammy Bonnici	London	L pts 8
22 April	Dan McTaggart	London	Draw 8
30 April	Denny Dawson	London	W pts 8
19 May	Jim McCann	Belfast	L rtd 6
10 June	Sammy McCarthy	London	L rsf 4
8 July	Tommy Higgins	Ipswich	W pts 8
25 July	Billy Daniels	Ramsgate	W rsf 4
16 October	Alby Tissong	Liverpool	L rtd 6
17 November	Charlie Tucker	London	L pts 8

1953

17 January	Tommy Higgins	Birmingham	W pts 12

(Won vacant Midland Area featherweight title)

16 February	Gene Caffrey	Leicester	W pts 8
13 March	Alby Tissong	Blackpool	L ko 2
20 April	Freddie Hicks	London	W pts 8

283

7 May	Irvin Newton	Cleethorpes	W ko 1
18 May	Harry Ramsden	London	L disq 7
20 June	Glyn Evans	Chester	W rsf 5
10 August	Harry Ramsden	Sneiton	L pts 12

(Lost Midland Area featherweight title)

21 October	Jose Paniagua	New York	W pts 6

1954

26 January	Neville Tetlow	Hanley	W ko 1
23 February	Charlie Simpkins	Willenhall	Draw 8
9 March	Tommy Higgins	Hanley	L ko 6

Lightweight

15 June	Frank Parkes	Hanley	L rsf 6

Record compiled by Vic Hardwicke, Jackie Turpin and W. Terry Fox

RANDOLPH ADOLPHUS 'THE LEAMINGTON LICKER' TURPIN: ACTIVE 1946–64

(Former: British middleweight champion; European middleweight champion; World middleweight champion; undefeated British and Empire light-heavyweight champion)

Middleweight
1946

17 September	Gordon Griffiths	London	W rsf 1
19 November	Des Jones	London	W pts 6
26 December	Billy Blything	Birmingham	W ko 1

1947

14 January	Jimmy Davis	London	W ko 4
24 January	Dai James	Birmingham	W ko 3
18 February	Johnny Best	London	W rsf 1
18 March	Bert Hyland	London	W ko 1
1 April	Frank Dolan	London	W rsf 2
15 April	Tommy Davies	London	W ko 2
28 April	Bert Sanders	London	W pts 6
12 May	Ron Cooper	Oxford	W rsf 4
27 May	Jury VII	London	W pts 6
3 June	Mark Hart	London	W pts 6
23 June	Leon Fouquet	Coventry	W ko 1
9 September	Jimmy Ingle	Coventry	W rsf 3
20 October	Mark Hart	London	Draw 6

The Turpin Brothers' Professional Records

1948

26 January	Freddie Price	Coventry	W ko 1
17 February	Gerry McCready	London	W rsf 1
16 March	Vince Hawkins	London	W pts 8
26 April	Albert Finch	London	L pts 8
28 June	Alby Hollister	Birmingham	W pts 8
21 September	Jean Stock	London	L rtd 5

1949

7 February	Jackie Jones	Coventry	W rtd 5
21 February	Doug Miller	London	W pts 8
25 March	Mickey Laurent	Manchester	W rtd 3
3 May	Bill Poli	London	W disq 4
20 June	Cyrille Delannoit	Birmingham	W rsf 8
22 August	Jean Wanes	Manchester	W rtd 3
19 September	Roy Wouters	Coventry	W rsf 5
15 November	Pete Meade	London	W rtd 4

1950

31 January	Gilbert Stock	London	W pts 8
6 March	Richard Armah	Croydon	W rtd 6
24 April	Gustave Degouve	Nottingham	W pts 8
5 September	Eli Elandon	Watford	W ko 2
17 October	Albert Finch	London	W ko 5

(Won British middleweight title)

13 November	Jose Alamo	Abergavenny	W ko 2
12 December	Tommy Yarosz	London	W disq 8

1951

22 January	Eduardo Lopez	Birmingham	W ko 1

(Won right to contest European middleweight title)

27 February	Luc Van Dam	London	W ko 1

(Won European middleweight title)

19 March	Jean Stock	Leiceseter	W rsf 5
16 April	Billy Brown	Birmingham	W ko 2
7 May	Jan DeBruin	Coventry	W ko 6
5 June	Jackie Keough	London	W rsf 7
10 July	Ray Robinson	London	W pts 15

(Won World middleweight title)

12 September	Ray Robinson	New York	L rsf 10

(Lost World middleweight title)

Battling Jack

1952
Light-Heavyweight

12 February	Alex Buxton	London	W rtd 7
22 April	Jacques Hairabedian	London	W ko 3
10 June	Don Cockell	London	W rsf 11

(Won British and Empire light-heavyweight titles)

Middleweight
(Relinquished British light-heavyweight title to pursue World middleweight title)

21 October	George Angelo	London	W pts 15

(Won British Empire middleweight title)

1953

19 January	Victor D'Haes	Birmingham	W ko 6
16 February	Duggie Miller	Leicester	W pts 10
17 March	Walter Cartier	London	W disq 2
9 June	Charles Humez	London	W pts 15

(Won vacant World middleweight title but American authorities downgrade this to European middleweight title)

21 October	Carl 'Bobo' Olsen	New York	L pts 15

(Unsuccessful bid for vacant World middleweight title)

1954

30 March	Olle Bengtsson	London	W pts 10
2 May	Tiberio Mitri	Rome	L rsf 1

(Lost European middleweight title)

1955
Light-Heavyweight

15 February	Ray Schmit	Birmingham	W disq 8
8 March	Jose Gonzalez	London	W ko 7
26 April	Alex Buxton	London	W ko 2

(Regained British and Empire light-heavyweight titles)

19 September	Eddie Smith	Birmingham	W pts 10
18 October	Gordon Wallace	London	L ko 4

1956

17 April	Alessandro D'Ottavio	Birmingham	W rsf 6
18 June	Jacques Bro	Birmingham	W ko 5
21 September	Hans Stretz	Hamburg	L pts 10
26 November	Alex Buxton	Leicester	W rsf 5

(Retained British light-heavyweight title and won Lonsdale Belt outright)

The Turpin Brothers' Professional Records

1957

11 June	Arthur Howard	Leicester	W pts 15

(Retained British light-heavyweight title)

17 September	Ahmed Boulgroune	London	W rsf 9
28 October	Sergio Burchi	Birmingham	W rsf 2
25 November	Uwe Janssen	Leicester	W rsf 8

1958

11 February	Wim Snoek	Birmingham	W pts 10
21 April	Eddie Wright	Leicester	W rsf 7
22 July	Redvers Sangoe	Oswestry	W rsf 4
9 September	Yolande Pompey	Birmingham	L rsf 2

1959–62

INACTIVE	Semi-retirement

1963

Heavyweight

18 March	Eddie Marcano	Wisbech	W ko 6

1964

22 August	Charles Seguna	Malta	W ko 2

Record compiled by Harold Alderman, Jackie Turpin and W. Terry Fox

KEY

W	Win
L	Loss
ko	Knockout. Fighter fails to be in a position to continue after a ten-second count
pts	Points. Fighter judged to have won the greater number of rounds after contest has gone the scheduled distance
rsf	Referee stops fight to save loser from unnecessary punishment
rtd	Retired. The boxer or the boxer's seconds decide boxer is unfit to continue
disq	Disqualification. Fighter disqualified from contest for persistent fouling or rule breaking
Draw	Contest goes the scheduled distance and the contestants are found to be equal when the points are totalled

(b)

Of the Research

Battling Jack: You Gotta Fight Back is the result of hundreds of hours of taped interviews, correspondence, record searches and cross-referencing. The nature of memory is such that, occasionally, facts had to be uncovered first to further fuel Jackie Turpin's admirable power of recall. I am grateful to the following people who offered advice – not always taken but much appreciated; or whose work or anecdotes provided memory prompts or contributed to the validation of my own findings; or whose wisdom, specialist knowledge, donated equipment, selfless help and loyal support made the completion of this book possible:

Georgina Turpin; Lydia Turpin; Cledwyn Randolph O'Connell; Josie Ellis (nee Middleton); Mosh and Maria Mancini; Eddie Mo Phillips; Joanna King; boxing historian Harold Alderman; the late Vic Hardwicke; author and Turpin family friend, the late Jack Birtley; Jackie Turpin's shipmates Len Bruce and Harold Burndred; June and Phil Colclough MA; Ken Incley; Ron and Jill Milne; Grahame Shrubsole; John and Jean Rivers; John Pinnock; Chris Golby, whose MA dissertation 'A History of the Colour Bar In British Professional Boxing 1929-1948 (1998)' deserves the widest possible readership; Eric Newton; Geoff Walton MA; Jessica Rose Cole; Manoubi Ben Lamri; Karl Bromage; Jim Burns; Dr. Heather Leach; Owen Bailey MA; Dave Wright; Amy Fox, and Lynda Fox.

My apologies are extended to all those friends and acquaintances who, during the realisation of this manuscript, made the mistake of asking me, 'How's the book going?', only to leave, several hours later, dead-eyed and stooped, having learned more about boxing than they ever wished to know.

I sincerely hope the work I have done is a worthy reflection of the admiration, respect and affection I have for John Matthew Turpin, senior – Battling Jack.

W. Terry Fox